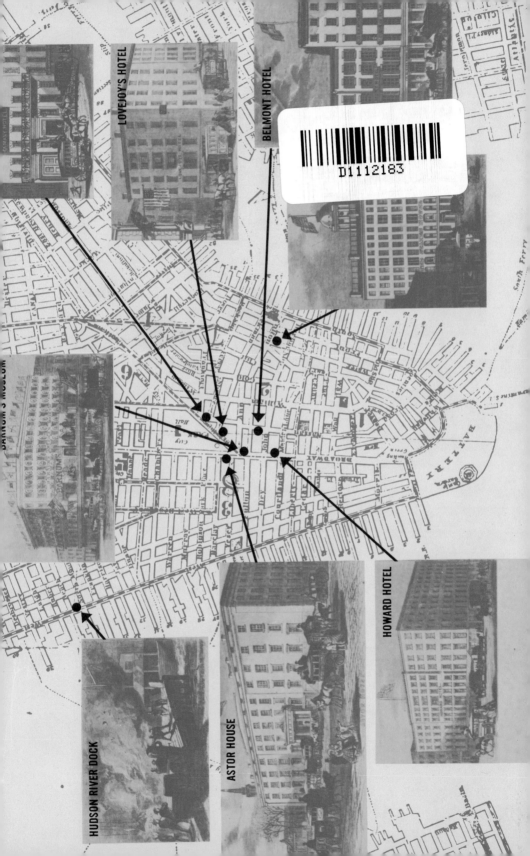

LOVEJOY'S HOTEL

BELMONT HOTEL

BARNUM'S MUSEUM

HUDSON RIVER DOCK

ASTOR HOUSE

HOWARD HOTEL

D1112183

Lewiston City Library
428 Thain
Lewiston, Idaho   83501

(208) 743-6519

Robert Cobb Kennedy three days before his execution at Fort Lafayette in New York Harbor. He sent copies of this photograph to his family in Louisiana. Courtesy of Mr. and Mrs. W. A. LaFleur.

The Man
Who Tried To
BURN
NEW YORK

Nat Brandt

SYRACUSE UNIVERSITY PRESS 1986

Copyright © 1986 by Nat Brandt

All Rights Reserved

First Edition
Second Printing 1986

The paper used in this publication meets the minimum requirements of American National Standard for Information Sciences—Permanence of Paper for Printed Library Materials, ANSI Z39.48-1984.00 ∞™

Library of Congress Cataloging-in-Publication Data

Brandt, Nat.
    The man who tried to burn New York.

    (A York State book)
    Bibliography: p.
    Includes index.
    1. New York (N.Y.)—History—Civil War, 1861-1865.
2. Kennedy, Robert Cobb. 3. Spies—New York (N.Y.)—
Biography. I. Title.
F128.44.B73 1986   973.7'85   86-5833
ISBN 0-8156-0207-3 (alk. paper)

Manufactured in the United States of America

To my wife Yanna, without whose encouragement, support, and faith
this book would never have been written or published

contents

ILLUSTRATIONS

TRUST TO LUCK

Trust to luck, trust to luck, stare fate in the face,
Sure the heart must be aisy* when it's in the right place;
Let the world way away, let your friends turns to foes,
Let your pockets run dry, and thread-bare your clothes,
Should woman deceive when you trust to her heart,
Never sigh, 'twont relieve it, but add to the smart.

Trust to luck, trust to luck, stare fate in the face,
Sure the heart must be aisy when it's in the right place;
Trust to luck, trust to luck, stare fate in the face,
Sure the heart must be aisy when it's in the right place.

Be a man, be a man, wheresoever you go,
Through the sunshine of wealth, or the tear drop of woe;
Should the wealthy look grand, the proud pass you by,
With the back of their hand, and scorn in their eye,
Snap your fingers and smile, as they pass on their way,
And remember the while, every dog has his day.

Trust to luck, trust to luck, stare fate in the face,
Sure the heart must be aisy when it's in the right place;
Trust to luck, trust to luck, stare fate in the face,
Sure the heart must be aisy when it's in the right place.

In love or in war, sure it's Irish delight
He's good humored with both, the sweet girl and a fight;
He coaxes, he bothers, he blarneys the dear,
To resist him she can't, and she's off when he's near;
And when valor calls him, from his darling he'd fly
And for liberty fight, for Ould Ireland he'd die.

*Easy.

acknowledgments

The genesis of this book occurred on a fall afternoon in 1964 while I was leafing through I. N. Phelps Stokes's *The Iconography of Manhattan Island.* I was looking for feature stories for the newspaper I worked for and, as usual, was searching for one that might have a 100th, 200th, or 300th anniversary as a reason for printing it. The entry under November 25, 1864, was very brief, a few short lines to the effect that a number of hotels had been set on fire by Confederates and that one of the latter, R. C. Kennedy, had been subsequently caught and hanged. Although a native New Yorker and a Civil War buff, I had never heard of the incident. I checked contemporary newspapers to verify it. The result was "New York's Great Fire That Wasn't," which appeared in *The New York Times Sunday Magazine* on November 22, 1964. Even after the story appeared, however, it continued to fascinate me. I also became aware that the article, brief as it was, contained inaccuracies. I wrote an expanded version—" 'New York is worth Twenty Richmonds' "— while on the staff of *American Heritage* magazine; it appeared in its October 1971 issue. Both my articles dealt only with the plot. However, I felt there were larger issues involved, and that they could best be handled by making "R. C. Kennedy" the central character of a book, around whom a number of themes could revolve. Moreover, the research, if it were to be done correctly, had to extend beyond the record of contemporary newspapers and magazines, or the brief accounts in old and sometimes untrustworthy books. There were dozens of riddles, some of which I have been fortunately able to solve. As the mystery—or so it seemed to me—unfolded, I revised and revised, until I felt that I could properly tell the story against the background of prewar Louisiana and West Point as well as the Civil War itself.

The book, however, could not have been written without the cooperation of a legion of individuals—friends, librarians, archivists, descendants of the Kennedy family—all of whom, over many years, responded to my needs and queries without reluctance. There are two persons, however, who deserve special mention. The first is my wife, Yanna, to whom this book is dedicated. The other is Sara D. Jackson, now archivist, National Historical Publications and Records Commission, who initiated me into the treasures at the National Archives. If I showed signs of tiring, she persevered; if I ran out of ideas to track down, she came up with a gem; if I got too cocky, she reminded me of what else still had to be done. I will be most satisfied if Mrs. Jackson reads this book and says, "Not bad."

Many essential parts of the book could not have been written without the aid given to me by members of the Kennedy family, especially Mr. and Mrs. W.A. LaFleur, Mrs. LaFleur's mother, the late Mrs. John A. Anders, and J. J. Davidson, Jr., of Lafayette, Louisiana, who provided material covering Robert Cobb Kennedy's early life as well as photographs of him and his family.

A number of friends merit thanks, too: Murray Belsky and Bernard A. Weisberger are two who generously provided help when it was sorely needed. Another, Dr. Magda Denes, a psychologist-psychoanalyst, gave precious time to go over with me the details of Kennedy's life, his letters, and what others said about him in order to give me a better grasp of his personality and emotional makeup. If there are any misunderstandings, they are mine.

Then, too, Wendell Tripp, Director of Publications of the New York State Historical Association, took a special interest in my manuscript. I am indebted for his calling it to the attention of Syracuse University Press.

I also wish to thank Mrs. Pope McAdams and The Filson Club of Louisville, Kentucky, for permission to use the diary of John D. Allison; Vallie Tinsley White of Greenville, Mississippi, a former resident of Homer, Louisiana, for permission to use the black field songs, hymns, and prayers that appear before each section of the book, all of which were taken from Mrs. White's "Some Negro Songs Heard on the Hills of North Louisiana," which appeared in *Historic Claiborne* in 1962; Russell V. Bleecker of Cleveland, a fire buff and collector of fire-company memorabilia, for a photocopy of Chief Engineer John Decker's journal covering the events of November 25-26, 1864; Mrs.

William N. Hansen of Sandusky, Ohio, who found the fair copy of
the letter written by Kennedy to his former prison friends on Johnson's Island; Clyde A. Kennedy of Bernice, Louisiana, who—although
not related to Robert Cobb Kennedy—provided an interesting insight
into farming in northwest Louisiana that was based on his own experiences and those of his family, one of the first to settle in the area; and
to the staffs of a number of institutions for their unstinting assistance:
the American Antiquarian Society (which provided a photocopy of
the only known surviving copy of Dion Haco's *Rob. Cobb Kennedy,
The Incendiary Spy*, written in 1866), The New York Historical Soci-
ety, the New York Public Library, the Library of Congress, the Shreve
Memorial Library in Shreveport, Louisiana, the Archives and History
Section of the United States Military Academy, the Ottawa County
(Ohio) Historical Museum in Port Clinton, the Public Archives of
Canada, the Cleveland Public Library, the Louisiana State Archives
& Records Commission, the Brooklyn Historical Society, the Virginia
Historical Society in Richmond, the University of Virginia Library in
Charlottesville, the University of Kentucky Library in Lexington, the
Ray D. Smith Civil War Collection at Knox College in Galesburg,
Illinois, and both the Historical Service Division of the Department
of the Army and Cemetery Branch memorial, Office of Support Services, for their efforts in locating Kennedy's final resting place. There
was only one sore spot in researching the events surrounding November 25, 1864: the lack of records, police and fire, in New York City
because of the departments' routine of periodically destroying their
files. It made for frustrating moments and for some unresolved questions, particularly regarding the work of Sergeant John S. Young, head
of the city's detective force.

Many other Louisianians deserve my gratitude as well—too many,
unfortunately, to mention, but for one important exception: the late
Mrs. Mabel Moore Vail of New Orleans, a former resident of Homer,
Louisiana, who—I discovered—had been compiling notes about Kennedy for well over half a century. As a young girl, Mrs. Vail had had
the chance to interview the black slave who had accompanied Robert
Cobb Kennedy when he went off to war. She continued to pursue the
research on Kennedy sporadically during her many years as a teacher,
with the aim of someday writing a book about him. Unfortunately,
her eyes were badly injured during the onslaught of Hurricane Betsy
in the fall of 1965 and most of her papers were swept away. She

nonetheless gave me complete access to what remained of her notes (and to what she could remember), realizing that she could no longer proceed with her project. Her book, I should mention, would have been titled *The Death of Chivalry*—and I am sorry she never got to write it.

New York City   Nat Brandt
December 1985

INTRODUCTORY NOTE

Although others were involved in the plot to burn New York City, this book focuses on Robert Cobb Kennedy for a number of reasons. For one thing, he was the only conspirator who was captured and tried. Then, too, his life touched upon so many facets of the society and history of his time—in Louisiana, at West Point, during the Civil War (to mention the most obvious)—that he seemed a natural subject. But beyond that, he also represented to me a very personal, human story—a tragic one, symbolic of the type of inane behavior that war can engender. He died ignobly, and the question persists whether he should have been executed at all for what he did. Was it justice, or was it—as Francis Bacon put it—"Revenge . . . a kind of wild justice"?

THE MAN WHO TRIED TO BURN NEW YORK

part 1

THE FIRES

Hawk an' turkle dove
Went to war;
Hawk came back with a broken jaw.

Shoo, my Love
Shoo, my Love
Shoo, my pretty little turkle dove.[2]

prologue

Autumn, 1864

Civil war did not, as many had conjectured when it began three and a half years earlier, stunt New York City's prosperity. Nor did it change its personality, one that was to endure ever afterward: private sanctuary for the well-to-do, playground for the get-rich-quick, hellhole for the poor and newly immigrated.

The streets ran neatly north to south and east to west until the awkward angles below 14th Street. There, in the jumble, as the rivers on either side pressed around the tip of the island, was the heart of the city—Fulton and Nassau streets—building after building after building. In recent years merchants had begun moving uptown on Broadway beyond Chambers Street, and that section had become almost as densely crowded with stores, theatres, and homes. To the west of Broadway, along Greene Street, were row upon row of brothels. To the east, north of City Hall, was the Bowery, hundreds of saloons and gambling dens, gangs of hoodlums—an area unsafe even for a policeman to patrol alone, day or night. Anyone with enough money was moving up Fifth Avenue to live, or to the suburbs closer to Central Park.

In the beginning there had been talk of New York's seceding from the Union, to become a free port of trade. By 1864 none, however, questioned that the city had grown fatter and richer, more sophisticated and fun-loving. High rentals, rising property values, inflation— all attested to the devotion paid the dollar sign. Cynics scorned the war contractors and profiteers—their lavish parties, their fancy carriages and fast trotters, the silks and laces their wives and daughters strutted about in, the opulence of their homes: "The Age of Shoddy," they called it.

5

Looking south from Union Square—the dense area of buildings, most of
wood, in which the fires were set. From an 1851 lithograph by Bachman.
Courtesy of the New-York Historical Society.

While the wealthy cavorted, the slums they never saw festered in
disease and violence. New York was a Copperhead city, its politics
feeding on the downtrodden and the corrupt, its philosophy a mixture
of states' rights, appeasement, and outright support for the South.
"Did you see my black antelope?" ran one joke. "No, I didn't. Whom
did your black aunt elope with?"[1] More than 700,000 persons in all—
and twice they rejected Lincoln by a two-to-one vote margin.

Because of what it was—gateway, trade center, coffer for the nation, anti-Administration hotbed—New York had become a refuge for
those with Southern accents. Its hotels and boarding houses were
filled with businessmen and planters driven from New Orleans,
Charleston, and Savannah to the financial source of their former
riches; with families fleeing from ruin; with women turned prostitutes
while they waited for the war to end; with ex-soldiers on parole looking for a way to return home.[2]

By November of 1864 the war was moving into its final stages. Grant was besieging Petersburg, Sheridan was destroying Confederate harvests in the Shenandoah Valley, Sherman was pressing from Atlanta to the sea. Rebel leaders had lost all hope of upsetting the inevitable on the battlefield. Desperate, some were concocting wild schemes to force the North to accept Southern independence in return for peace.

chapter 1

NEW YORK CITY
Friday, November 25, 1864
6 P.M.

T he sixty-one-year-old police superintendent still bore the scars of the nearly seventy knife wounds and bludgeonings he had suffered sixteen months ago on the first day of the Draft Riots. More than 100 persons had been killed in that outburst of class and race hatred.

Rumors—indeed, strong reports—had reached both New York and Washington that another rebel-incited uprising had been planned for Election Day, November 8. Federal troops had been rushed from the trenches outside Richmond to bolster Superintendent John Alexander Kennedy's meager 1,400-man police force. The day had passed quietly, however, and the troops had returned to the front. But rumors were again circulating.

Of Kennedy's two top aides on this chilly autumn evening, Inspector George Dilks would be on duty at police headquarters on Mulberry Street. The other, Inspector James Leonard, planned to attend the Winter Garden Theatre.

Kennedy himself left his office to go home for Thanksgiving dinner. The superintendent had stayed at police headquarters the entire holiday on Thursday because he had had "a premonition" that there might be trouble.[1]

The doorkeeper in front of Barnum's Museum was worried about the four young toughs leaning against the railing that girded St. Paul's Chapel across the street. Were they members of the Dead Rabbits gang from Five Points? The doorkeeper had asked them to leave when they started heckling the giantess, but the toughs seemed anxious to make trouble.

Above the doorkeeper's head the wind flapped the banners: "EX-TRA PERFORMANCE FOR EVACUATION DAY—THE LONDON DRAMA 'WAITING FOR THE VERDICT'." "THREE MAM-MOTH FAT GIRLS WEIGHING ONE TON!" "THREE GIANTS 24 FEET HIGH!" "TWO DWARFS WEIGHING 17 POUNDS EACH!" "KANGEROOS, LEARNED SEAL, AND A MENAGERIE OF 50 OTHER LIVING ANIMALS."

Two blocks away at the Tammany Hotel the occupant of room 106, a Mrs. Dawson, was nursing her sick daughter. Although there was a warm glow from the fireplace, the young girl lay wrapped in blankets on the large bed, her face flushed with fever.

The porter at French's, across Frankfort Street from the Tammany, had already invited the hotel's bookkeeper to join him in his upstairs room later that night to share a bottle. He also had a new revolver the hotel proprietor had given him that he wanted to show to the book-keeper.

Police Court Judge John M. McCunn was due at the Winter Gar-den Theatre. Although the show was not scheduled to start until eight o'clock and his home on West 21st Street was only a mile from the theatre, there was certain to be some difficulty getting near there tonight. The three Booth brothers—Edwin, Junius Brutus, and John Wilkes—were appearing together for the first time. The occasion was a benefit performance of "Julius Caesar" to raise more money for the statue of Shakespeare planned for the Mall in Central Park. The turn-out was expected to be so large that chairs and benches were being set up in the aisles, the makeshift seats selling for five dollars apiece.[2]

William Wheatley was expecting just as large an audience at Niblo's Garden, next door to the Metropolitan Hotel. "The Corsican Brothers" had received rave notices, but Wheatley—who portrayed both brothers in the melodrama, and also managed the theatre—had only scheduled the show for another eight days. With extra seats, the theatre could handle 3,000 persons every night.

Frank Mahedy was the foreman of Peterson Engine Company No. 31. He worked for the municipal board that supervised the volunteer outfits and, in his free time, was a volunteer fireman himself. The firehouse at 49 Chrystie was, as Fire Marshal Alfred E. Baker complained, "in bad condition." Approval to build a new one, however, had been delayed by the debate over reorganizing the department into a paid, uniformed force, with horses to draw the heavy equipment. Insurance companies were pressing for the reform; they were fed up, as most citizens were, with the volunteers' constant shenanigans. The red-shirted volunteers were more interested in the sport of racing the gaudily ornamented "masheens" to a fire than in saving lives and property. They abjured the use of horses, preferring to pull the pump engines, hose carts, and ladder wagons themselves, as tests of strength. Drinking and fighting had become routine at every fire, particularly between companies that were traditional rivals.

The pride of No. 31, "The White Ghost," was, like the volunteer fire department itself, antiquated: a hand-pump engine, it took fourteen men to build up pressure. It had belonged to Fulton Engine Company No. 21 before so many of its members had joined the First Zouaves to go off to Bull Run that the company had to be disbanded. Peterson No. 31 was using the old derelict because its own engine, a modern steamer, had been requisitioned by the Government for service at Fort Monroe.

The war, John D. Allison could readily believe, was over for him. Allison, who sported "mutton chops" and, typically, a moustache and goatee, had served the Confederacy through the battle of Murfreesboro, been captured, escaped to Canada, wooed and wed a Canadian miss, and—while on a blockade runner trying to get around Union lines in order to return home to Kentucky—been recaptured and imprisoned. He had convinced Federal authorities that he was now a British citizen and eleven days earlier been released from the prison at Fort Lafayette in New York Harbor. Allison was hoping to borrow enough money from Southern friends in the city to continue his journey home. He entered the St. Nicholas Hotel to play billiards with a group of them as the clock on the marble wall of the spacious lobby struck six.

At about the same time, Oliver D. Ward also entered the St. Nicholas. The owner of a prosperous shirt store on nearby Broadway,

Ward made his home on Staten Island, but week nights he stayed at the hotel. He had just closed his store and, as was his custom, was on his way to his room to wash up, read the evening papers, and then have dinner.

Meanwhile, an attractive guest from Baltimore had rushed from the hotel. She was trying to find somebody.

The clerk at the Everett House on the north side of Union Square was suspicious of strangers. His attention was riveted on a black canvas bag behind the hotel desk. A few hours ago a man in his late twenties had stopped by, saying he would like a room for the night, and asking if he could leave his valise until he returned. When told that there was nothing available, the man said he would come back anyway, in case some guest checked out—and could he leave his valise until then? The clerk had accepted the carpetbag, and put it on the floor. It was too small to carry anything more than a change of linen, although it seemed unusually heavy. . . . (The clerk later recalled that he thought at the time it might have contained a bottle of liquor.)

Several miles away, in a small cottage bordering on Central Park, six men huddled over a table, packing vials of colorless liquid into small black bags. One was a man in the black-braided overcoat of a Federal officer—although his hat, strangely, lacked the customary silver leaf ornamentation. The other men were dressed in civilian clothes. Another, a bearded man who, by coincidence, was named, like the police superintendent, Kennedy—Robert Cobb Kennedy— shuffled when he walked. He had been wounded at Shiloh, fighting for the Confederacy.

chapter 2

The first alarm sounded from the St. James Hotel, at Broadway and 26th Street, at 8:43 P.M. A guest in room 85, on the topmost floor, smelled a peculiar odor, opened his door into the hallway, and found it full of smoke. He immediately ran down the stairs, calling for help.[1]

Within minutes, the second alarm sounded at the St. Nicholas Hotel at Broadway and Spring, after Ward the merchant had heard two men furtively speaking in the lobby on their way out of the hotel. "It's all right," he would remember one as saying. As Ward reached the sixth floor he saw smoke billowing from room 174. At almost the same time, a waiter on the fourth floor smelled smoke and traced it to two rooms, numbers 139 and 140. Upon opening number 139, a burst of flame shot up.

Instead of the customary nine o'clock all-clear gong, the watchman at the City Hall fire tower was repeatedly plunging the lever that rang the enormous 23,000-pound bell. One ring for the First District; a pause; four rings for the Fourth District; a pause; then the cycle repeated, over and over again. The tolling was picked up by watchmen at the other fire towers throughout the city. Soon they had interspersed eight rings for the Eighth District. The continuous cacophony of bells filled the night.

Aided by the cashier, the doorkeeper at Barnum's was slugging it out with four toughs on the street outside the museum when an usher ran out, flinging the doors onto Ann Street wide open. "Fire—there's a fire upstairs!"

In the Lecture-Room on the fifth floor, panic seized both the actors and the audience. Cries of "Fire! Fire!" came from every side. Several persons slid down the pillars from the gallery to the parquet. Women and children shrieked with fear. As men fought to get by them to the exits, several women fainted.

The alarm spread to the floors below, too. The seven-foot giantess, her hair flying wildly behind her, lurched down the stairs and out the exit past the fist fight. Turning the corner, she ran down the street and straight into a saloon.

Windows on the second and third floors, meanwhile, were thrown open by people desperate for a way out. Bleecker, the manager, called frantically for help with the animals. Those that were able to reach the street burst out of the museum in a virtual stampede.

Uptown, at the luxurious Lafarge House on Broadway facing Bond Street, the servant girl stationed on the third floor passed by room 104 and noticed, through the transom above the door, a light in the room—even though, the girl knew, the room's occupant had left a few minutes earlier. Believing he had left the gas light on by mistake—he had made such a fuss searching for matches to light it—she paused by the door. As she did, a burst of flame lit up the hallway. The girl ran to the speaking tube at the side staircase to shout down to the office below that the hotel was on fire.

Next door to the Lafarge, a man in evening clothes—apparently a late arrival—paused outside the entrance to the dress circle at the Winter Garden Theatre.[2] He watched the firemen as they arrived at the hotel, then went inside the theatre and up the stairs to his box. There, he leaned toward the persons he was seated with and whispered that the Lafarge was on fire. Others nearby seemed to have heard only the last word: "Fire." Soon it was being repeated throughout the theatre, a steady murmur that grew in intensity, breaking the silence that had enveloped the audience while the second act of "Julius Caesar" was in progress.

Several women in the dress circle stood up. When they did, almost the entire audience, from parquet to dome, followed their example. Judge McCunn leaned over the railing of the dress circle, trying to restore order. *Don't panic!* he cried out. *There are plenty of exits!*

In the parquet below, Police Inspector James Leonard was standing on a seat, calling in a loud voice, "It's only a drunken man—keep your seat!"[3]

On stage, meanwhile, the play had stopped. Edwin Booth had broken off his lines as Brutus to race to the wings. He returned to the stage, stood in the center by the footlights, his arms outstretched, calling for order. Many were already at the doors, however, pushing and shoving to get out.

At police headquarters, Inspector George Dilks was relaying what information he had to Superintendent Kennedy. The chief of detectives, Sergeant John S. Young, was on his way to the Metropolitan Hotel to alert its proprietor. All reserves were assembled at precinct houses, all on duty told to be vigilant. The Fire Department had taken similar action.

The next message was from the Metropolitan: another fire. The superintendent immediately took further steps to meet the crisis. All other hotels—and the Army, too—were to be alerted, telegrams going to those with telegraph offices, roundsmen dispatched to the others. The superintendent also ordered double watches everywhere and extra fire buckets in every hotel hall.

It was shortly after ten o'clock when the cry of "Fire!" ran through the Metropolitan Hotel at Broadway and Prince Street. Heavy smoke was coming from room 302, on the top floor. The chambermaid who sounded the alarm said she had seen a woman coming down the stairs at the same time that the fire broke out. It was the woman from Baltimore, the one who had rushed away earlier from the St. Nicholas Hotel.

Next door to the Metropolitan, William Wheatley, as Fabien dei Franchi, and his co-star, Charles Pope, as the villainous Chateau Rexaud, were dueling back and forth across the stage as the dramatic last act of "The Corsican Brothers" reached its climax. Someone in the gallery suddenly shouted, "Fire!" The audience rose as one to its feet as the cry passed through the theatre.

Wheatley and Pope stood with swords dangling from their hands, stunned. Women were hoisting their skirts and leaping from chair to chair toward the doors. Up in the balcony, men tried to hold back others from throwing themselves down to the parquet. Those who were nearest the exits were already rushing through them.

The pattern was clear as midnight approached and the alarms continued. Hotels, theatres, and the docks—uptown and downtown, from the Hudson to the East River—were being set afire en masse.

Fear fanned the excitement in the streets. Wild stories passed by word of mouth. Looters in droves from the grim sections that girded the business district swarmed around the scenes of the fires, so many appearing so suddenly that at first the fires were blamed on them. Then, another rumor began to spread from block to block: a Confederate attack. The mood of the mobs gathered in front of the hotels and theatres grew angry and ugly.

As detachments of police struggled to keep order, new alarms rang through the chill night. A roundsman from the Second Precinct spotted flames in an upper-story window of the United States Hotel at Fulton and Water streets. The hotel, one of the oldest in the city, was a tinderbox.

Ten blocks north, near the heart of the Bowery, the staff of the New England Hotel, alerted to the possibility of trouble, was checking each room when the night watchman stopped in front of number 58. He had seen the occupant leave earlier. The door was unlocked. As the watchman opened it, a sheet of flame sent him hurtling backward.

A half-mile away on Park Row, overlooking City Hall, a guest going up to his room on the fourth floor of Lovejoy's Hotel saw smoke billowing from under the door of room 121. The blaze was no sooner put out than a second was discovered in another wing of the same floor.

At the same time, along the Hudson, a police officer and a dozen sailors were pouring water on the flaming bales of hay stacked on a bulkhead opposite North Moore and Beach streets.

The next alarm came from across town: at Fulton Street again, but this time just off Broadway, at the Belmont Hotel next door to the Herald Building. The source of the acrid smoke was room 28 on the second floor—a room, the clerk later recalled, that had been taken earlier that evening by an Army officer.

An artist's rendition of one of the arsonists setting fire to Room 108 at the Tammany Hotel. Although the evilly leering face does not fit, it was Robert Cobb Kennedy who torched the room. From *Harper's Weekly*, December 17, 1864.

A few short blocks away, the porter and bookkeeper at French's Hotel stood transfixed. Directly across narrow Frankfort Street, which separated French's from the Tammany Hotel, a man seemed to be having trouble starting up the fire in the hearth in a third-floor room. A burning piece of paper in his hand disclosed his bearded features.

The man limped to the door and left the room. The fire went out.

Suddenly, the man reappeared. He stooped down and struck several matches. Then, the entire room seemed bathed in light. Incredibly, he was setting fire to it!

The porter, forgetting the new revolver that lay on his table, made for the door, the bookkeeper close behind him. The latter was frightened. Just before midnight, he had given a room to a soldier—an officer whose hat, he remembered now, did not have the usual silver leaf on it. And the officer had spoken with a Southern drawl.

Frank Mahedy's firemen were operating outside their district. He had led them to the Belmont Hotel to the continual tolling of the watch-tower bells, but Fire Marshal Baker had ordered "The White Ghost" back to its post in case of an emergency in its own densely populated neighborhood. The volunteer firemen were hauling the engine along Park Row when the porter of French's Hotel ran into the street. He was gesturing toward the Tammany Hotel across the street.

Mahedy's men immediately began to lay hose to a hydrant. The foreman himself went into the Tammany with the porter. Behind them, a policeman materialized. He had been sent to notify hotels in the vicinity of Printing House Square to be on their guard, and had just noticed the smoke pouring from an upper-floor window.

Mahedy made for the stairway. The third floor was so thick with smoke he could hardly see. Someone had broken into room 108 and water was being poured on the flames inside. A Negro waiter was pounding on the door of the room next to it, where Mrs. Dawson and her daughter were asleep.

Mahedy heaved his body at the door, again and again, until it banged open. His eyes were smarting and he was choking as he groped his way inside. Lying in the bed, asleep, were a woman and a child, the child's head resting in the crook of her mother's arm. Mahedy lifted the child and stumbled back out of the door, as the child awoke and began to scream. He returned inside and tried to waken the woman. When he couldn't, he hoisted her into his arms, too, and headed again for the hallway.

There was still no letup in the tolling of the firebells.

It was 2:30 A.M. when Michael Perry, the house detective, opened the door of a room in the Fifth Avenue Hotel, an elegant white-marble edifice that overlooked Madison Square and occupied the entire front between 23rd and 24th streets. Perry was greeted by a rush of smoke.

Several miles south, at the Howard Hotel on Broadway at Maiden Lane, the guest in the room next to number 44 was hastily pulling on his trousers. Smoke had begun to fill his room.

The sailors had gone back to their ships along the Hudson River after putting out the hay fire when another alarm sent them scurrying back ashore. A block away from the earlier fire, on West Street between Franklin and North Moore, the barge *Merchant* was ablaze.

Almost directly crosstown, along the East River, two members of the staff of Handfield's Hotel were battling to put out the flames in a fifth-floor room. Neither had had time to send for help, although behind the hotel, as they knew, were a huge mill and lumber yard.

And, as dawn came up, two workmen at Horton & Lewis, lumber merchants at West and Clarkson streets on the Hudson River, found the stacks of wood beams and the hay in adjacent stables smoldering when they came to work.

Almost twelve hours after the first alarm, the last was sounded. It was close to nine in the morning when Charles A. Stetson, Jr., the manager of the Astor House, on Broadway across from Barnum's, was talking to some guests outside the breakfast room. The hotel was very lucky, he is reported to have boasted, but then he was sure that nobody would think of trying anything at the Astor: it didn't harbor incendiaries.

Stetson had set up a double watch and placed extra buckets of water at the foot of each stairway the night before, but he had waited until daylight to inspect the Astor's 1,000 rooms, certain that the inconvenience to his boarders that an earlier search would entail would prove unnecessary. He was telling the guests this when an employee rushed up and blurted out his report: A fire had broken out in a top-floor room.

Sergeant Young sank into the banquette in the parlor of the Exchange Hotel on Greenwich Street. The burly veteran detective—everyone called him "Old" Young behind his back—had been up all night on the wildest chase of his life.

Young had just checked with the manager of the Exchange to warn him to put on additional watchmen until the police believed the danger was over. He had seated himself next to an Army officer who was reading the first accounts of the fires in the newspaper. His eye did not catch the fact that the officer's hat was missing its silver leaf.

"I'm looking for who did it," Young said, "and I'll be damned if I don't get them."[4]

Just then a patrolman approached: the superintendent wanted Young back at headquarters as soon as he was finished. The officer watched intently as Young left the hotel, then glanced toward a man sitting in the corner of the parlor. The man had been watching Young, too. He now rose and limped toward the officer.

chapter 3

Superintendent Kennedy spent the entire night at police headquarters. Fire Marshal Baker arrived early in the morning to confer with him, and Sergeant Young was on the way, too.

So far, the police had three persons under arrest. All had already been questioned at the nearby Army headquarters by Major General John A. Dix. Kennedy believed that John D. Allison, the former Confederate recently released from Fort Lafayette, was his best lead. Allison had been picked up at the Lafarge after midnight and had been seen earlier at the St. Nicholas, both sites of fires. Allison was now in a cell at police headquarters.

The second suspect—the woman from Baltimore who had been apprehended at the Metropolitan—was in custody, too, but insisted that her appearances at both the Lafarge and the Metropolitan were coincidental. She was just searching, she contended, for a clerk from Stewart's department store who'd sold her some fabrics. She'd made a mistake in the purchase and was trying to return the material before catching a steamer home early the next day. The clerk, she said, had told her he roomed at one of the hotels—she'd forgotten which. Stewart's was being checked to verify her story.

A Lieutenant James M. Kellogg, attached to a colored regiment at Rock Island, Illinois, was the third person under arrest. He'd registered at the Belmont, he conceded, but never went to his room because the hotel clerk told him the chambermaid hadn't had time to fix it up. Kellogg was adamant about having then left the Belmont to have dinner without ever going up to his room. The clerk bore out his story, and Kellogg's papers seemed genuine enough, but Kennedy wanted him in custody pending a further check: a porter had seen an officer leaving Kellogg's room shortly before the fire broke out.

The superintendent's chief clue was a note found at the Astor. It was a summons to a meeting held Thanksgiving night at the Metropolitan. The note was on stationery from McDonald's piano store, which was now under surveillance. Gus McDonald was a well-known Southern sympathizer. The superintendent was evidently using him as bait, hoping to catch any incendiaries that tried to contact him. He had put off pulling McDonald himself in for questioning for at least several hours. Commenting on the several arrests already made, Kennedy told newspaper reporters that he was certain that fifteen persons or more had been involved in the attempt to set fire to the city.

Fire Marshal Baker, on the other hand, was just as certain that more than 100 persons had taken part in the scheme. He was convinced that it was a well-planned conspiracy. He'd been appalled at the scenes uncovered by his men at each of the thirteen hotels: furniture piled on top of beds, bedclothes bundled up, even the draperies added to the pile, all saturated with phosphorus and sometimes with turpentine and rosin as well.

Baker brought to police headquarters a variety of the items found at the hotels. There were, among other things, vials from a carpetbag discovered at the St. James. There was no doubt that they contained some mixture of phosphorus. The bag itself was charred. It had burst into flame when Baker's men were examining it—probably the result of one of the vials having leaked. (The rest of the vials were now being analyzed.) The fire marshal had also assembled a number of other carpetbags—all of them black except for a russet portmanteau found at the Metropolitan, and all inexpensive, easily purchased at any of a hundred shops in the city. Besides the vials of phosphorus, they contained an odd assortment of objects—an old cavalry boot was in one of them, for example. Baker also had in his possession scattered cartridges discovered in a room at the Fifth-Avenue, the matches flung about at another, a sperm candle found at yet another.

Young provided further information. The chief of detectives had compiled the names of all those who had registered for the rooms set on fire at the hotels—and he had descriptions, too. True enough, whoever had set the fires could have been in disguise: beards and moustaches were easy enough to apply. But one or two of them seemed to fit the descriptions of men shadowed several weeks earlier by Young's squad, following up on a tip. There was, in any case, one description that stood out from all the others: that of a man with florid complexion and whiskers who walked with a limp.

The detective also had a hunch. He was sure that the incendiaries, if they were indeed rebels, were tied in with McDonald and were probably already headed back to Canada. If General Dix agreed, he'd like to send some of his men up there right away.

Kennedy, however, vetoed Young's idea for the moment. The hunt would have to be confined to the city. The superintendent needed all his "shadows" to cover the slips and depots, in case the conspirators hadn't bolted yet, and an additional detail for a raid on McDonald's sometime that afternoon.[1] In the meantime, Kennedy wanted Young to take a crack at questioning Allison: his alibi was the weakest.

Almost concurrently, two orders were being drawn up at Army headquarters nearby. General Dix, one order read, was renewing his order that all Southerners in the city register with the Army. In the second order, Dix took the prosecution of the incendiaries out of civilian hands:

> A nefarious attempt was made last night to set fire to the principal hotels and other places of public resort in this city. If this attempt had succeeded, it would have resulted in a frightful sacrifice of property and life. The evidence of extensive combination, and other facts disclosed today, show it to have been the work of Rebel emissaries and agents. All such persons engaged in secret acts of hostility here can only be regarded as spies, subject to martial law, and to the penalty of death. If they are detected, they will be immediately brought before a court-martial or military commission, and, if convicted, they will be executed without the delay of a single day.[2]

Detectives hovered about the ticket window of the Hudson River Railroad at 30th Street and 10th Avenue as six men slipped aboard a sleeping car on a spur outside. At 10 P.M., a locomotive with coaches backed up to the sleeper. Forty minutes later a whistle blew and steam hissed from under the engine's wheels. The train left.

part 2

THE MAN WITH A LIMP

Long summer day,
Old massa an old missis a-settin' in the shade,
Drink their coffee and their tea,
Give po' nigger de black-eyed pea.
Long summer day,
Long summer day.

chapter 4

Mr. Franklin Pierce,
President of the United States

Your petitioner John B. Kennedy respectfully solicits that
you will appoint to the vacancy from the Fourth Congressional
District of Louisiana, in the Military Academy at West Point, his
son Robert Cobb Kennedy as Cadet. My son has resided in said
district for the term of five years—was eighteen years of age the
25th of Oct. last, is a good arithmetician, has no classical knowledge, but is a good English scholar. For further particulars, I
would refer you respectfully to the Hon. Roland Jones, Representative in Congress from this district.

His petition granted will ever be gratefully remembered by

Very Respectfully,
Your Obdt Servent,
J. B. Kennedy[1]

A good arithmetician. . . ." Rob's father, Dr. John Bailey Kennedy, was so intent on gaining the appointment for his
son that he overstated Rob's qualifications. The father's
anxiety is easily understood: graduates of the academy had entrée into
virtually every social circle in the nation. The cadet corps itself was
nearer to being an aristocracy than any other group in government or
civilian life. Its members were chosen from the best families, the
appointments coveted and secured for their sons by business, political,
and social leaders. At "the Point" itself, however, democracy prevailed: no flaunting of wealth or birth, no sectional or social cliques
were allowed—"a great character-builder, perhaps the greatest among

27

our institutions of learning," one graduate would declare. "The habit of truth-telling, the virtue of absolute honesty, the ready and loyal obedience to authority, the display of courage—that virtue called regal—to establish these elements of character, she labors without ceasing."[2]

West Point, moreover, demanded an "inexorableness of standards" in all departments, especially in mathematics, where "the ground was strewn, so to speak, with the bones of victims."[3] Algebra, descriptive geometry, analytical geometry, trigonometry, mensuration, differential and integral calculus—the course of instruction was clearly spelled out in the manual. Secretary of War Jefferson Davis was so concerned about the difficulty cadets encountered in mathematics that he was to publish a pamphlet warning that only an average of one-third of those who entered the academy graduated, and that unless an appointee had an aptitude in mathematics it might be wisest not to accept appointment. Davis's pamphlet, however, was as yet unwritten in February of 1854 when Dr. Kennedy wrote President Pierce. On March 7, Representative Roland Jones endorsed the back of the letter and the next day the president approved the appointment.[4]

Two months later Rob arrived at West Point. He carried with him a small leather trunk, with the underclothes and toilet articles required by regulations, and $200 in cash. The sum, an impressive one for a young man to have, was twice what was permitted. (The academy sent Dr. Kennedy a check for $100.)[5] Rob would earn forty-eight dollars a month as a cadet. Against that (and his $100 balance) would be drawn the costs of food, haircuts, baths, uniforms, bootblacking, classroom equipment, firewood.

On June 21, Rob passed the perfunctory physical and academic tests—there were as yet no competitive examinations—and on July 1, at the age of eighteen years and eight months, he became officially a member of the class of 1858, pledged to serve in the Army for eight years "unless sooner discharged" and to "bear true faith and allegiance to the United States of America."

It was at this time that Rob first met a New Yorker from nearby Tarrytown who was to play an influential role in the next two years. Stephen De Witt Clinton Beekman was the great-grandson of New York's first Governor, George Clinton, and related to its sixth, De Witt Clinton. Rob also befriended two other plebes—Joseph Wheeler, Jr., of Alabama and Edwin H. Stoughton of Vermont[6]—who would play a part in his life a decade later.

The superintendent of West Point at that time was, by a stroke of fate, Robert E. Lee. A graduate of West Point himself and "sup" of the academy for the last two years, Lee, a brevet colonel, had reason to be especially proud that summer of 1854: his son, George Washington Custis Lee, was being graduated at the top of his class. Young Lee and forty-five classmates had weathered four years of rigid discipline and courses that ranged from military engineering, infantry, and cavalry tactics to geology, philosophy, swordsmanship, and dancing. The prize: the insignia of a second lieutenant. For many, the future meant four years of fighting Indians on the frontier; for others, duty at isolated Army posts. Many of the names—J. E. B. Stuart, Oliver Otis Howard, John Pegram, Thomas H. Ruger, William Dorsey Pender, John B. Villepigue—would appear on the battle reports of a war still seven years away.

In contrast with young Lee's class, Rob's—the class of 1858— would produce no officer of lasting fame. For that matter, twenty-seven would graduate; fifty-eight would flunk out. Wheeler and Stoughton became members of the class of '59, for the Army decided to break up the newcomers that summer into two classes: those under eighteen would attend five years instead of four, a decision based on the academy's high percentage of failures. Of the members of the class of '59 only two would achieve national notice in the years ahead— Wheeler, because of his generalship; and Stoughton, because of the embarrassing circumstances of his capture.

Like most plebes during those first warm days of the annual summer encampment, Rob eagerly embraced the Point's traditions. There was, oddly, nothing severe or military in the academy's appearance. The library was the first building to come into view as one ascended the slope where the Hudson River steamboat docked. The artillery and cavalry drilled on the Plain, and the old brass guns of the little battery were parked there, too. Parade drills were held under the horse chestnuts on the east side of Academic Hall, a three-story building with a clock tower. To the north, on the very brink of the bluff, 160 feet above the river, stood a stone-and-brick hotel. Built by the Government to accommodate guests of the cadets and the distinguished members of the official Board of Visitors, it was known as Cozzens' Hotel, after the man who operated it. It was off limits to cadets except by written pass during certain hours on Saturdays.

Following summer bivouac, schooling began in September. The regimen was inflexible, except that reveille varied between 5 A.M. and 6 A.M. depending on the season. Roll-call was held after reveille, followed by the policing of rooms and cleaning of arms and accouterments until breakfast at seven. At eight, the class parade took place. The next three hours were for instruction in mathematics, after which two more hours were given to grammar, recitation in French, sword exercises, and study. Dinner was at 1 P.M., and after a short recreation period another class parade was held at two. The next two hours were devoted to grammar and more French. From four until sunset, a period that varied with the seasons, military exercises were held, and—after another short recreation period—a parade. Supper followed the parade, and after supper there was still another brief recreational period, until the Call to Quarters—the signal for studying. Tattoo was at 9:30 P.M., and lights were extinguished a half-hour later. This schedule was followed for eleven months of the year, with only upperclassmen allowed to go home on Christmas holiday or summer furlough.

The strain was broken by periodic dances, which attracted fashionable young girls from as far away as Albany and New York City. Moustaches and beards were banned, but a dandy could sport about (when it could be done without an officer noting it) with a blue riding cap set at a rakish angle, an ivory-handled cane in one hand and the other hand thrust inside the coat à la Napoleon. Fast friendships were made—friendships unmarred as yet by the political climate that was moving the nation toward war.

As exacting in detail as the uniforms the cadets wore were the rules they had to abide by. Two hundred demerits in any year meant dismissal, and after plebe year an additional proportion of demerits was automatically added every time a cadet was "skinned," or disciplined. A cartridge belt out of place cost one demerit; talking in the ranks, two; a light after taps, three; profanity, eight; gross insubordination, ten. Taboos ranged from drinking, using tobacco, card playing, and duels to visiting another cadet's room without permission and neglect of one's weapons. Irreverence in chapel on Sunday—attendance at which was "earnestly recommended"—meant immediate dismissal. In short, "All immoralities, disorders, neglects, or misbehavior, of which Cadets may be guilty, to the prejudice of good order and military discipline . . . are to be punished according to the nature and degree of the offence."[7]

From the start, Cadet Beekman bridled at the restrictions. Within six months he accumulated 100 demerits, missing dismissal by only one point at the end of his first year. Juvenile and arrogant, he was continually late for parades, was caught smoking, talked during classes, visited other cadets' rooms after hours—even chewed tobacco in front of an officer!

It was a bad example for his friend Rob, and—as his studies faltered—Rob fell more and more under Beekman's rebellious influence. For the first twelve months, however, Rob had only thirty-three demerits lodged against him, all for minor infractions. He had, in fact, been cited for good deportment in both November and December, when he had gone without a demerit. Rob was to be cited for deportment only once again, in May of 1855, when his general standing was 20th in a class of 35. By July, following some dropouts, he ranked 21st in a class of 31 and was cited for punishment for the first time because of "highly unsoldierlike conduct" in front of a sentinel. (The punishment was two extra hours of guard duty.)

As his marks grew worse, so did his conduct. In all, Rob committed eight infractions that resulted in punishment, including smoking, neglecting his equipment, communicating at the board during mathematics class, insulting an officer, and spitting in French class. He was twice stripped of the chevrons of lace he wore as a corporal. By the time of the annual exams in the second week of June, 1856, Rob ranked 157th out of 208 cadets on the Academy's conduct roll, with 152 demerits. (Beekman, with 233 demerits, ranked 207th.)

The academic tests that month were all-important: Rob's chances of continuing into his third year were good, provided he could pull up his marks. Even the lowly Beekman, if he were able to earn exceptionally good marks, could appeal to the Academic Board for another chance. The Board made exceptions if a cadet's general merit seemed to warrant consideration.

The results were posted on Tuesday, June 24. Out of a possible score of 100, Rob had received 69 in drawing, 54.7 in French, and 49.3 in conduct. He was found "deficient" in mathematics and general merit. Beekman also flunked mathematics, and was found deficient in conduct and general merit.

That night, the two cadets, facing certain dismissal, slipped out of their quarters and headed toward Cozzens' Hotel. Beekman had got hold of a bottle of whiskey, and by the time they got by the sentries

and reached the hotel both were drunk. Cozzens refused them admit-
tance. After he slammed the front door in their faces, they started to
curse loudly and throw stones at the windows, mocking a fusillade:
Ready! Aim! Fire! They were still shouting abuses and hurling rocks
when two officers rode up.

Cadets Kennedy and Beekman, the official report of the incident
read, had committed "outrages discreditable to the Academy." "The
reputation of good order & decency of the Corps is scarce ever thus
compromised in this way," wrote Captain John G. Barnard, who had
replaced Lee as superintendent. Barnard urged Secretary of War Davis
"to act at once" to discharge the young men. "It is always most
prejudicial to the discipline of the Academy," he declared, "when
serious offences of this nature are not promptly dealt with."[8]

The Academic Board sealed the judgment. On its annual report it
described Rob as of "very little" aptitude and, although "rather studi-
ous," generally "inattentive to regulations" and lacking military bearing. Beekman's aptitude, the board declared, was "fair," his habits
"variable," and although military in his bearing, he was "extremely
inattentive to regulations." The board ruled "that they ought not to
be permitted to return to the Military Academy."[9]

With the six-cents-a-mile traveling allowance stipulated in the
rulebook, Rob returned home to Louisiana after two years. He had
failed.

chapter 5

All spring and into the summer the talk had been of secession and of the possibility of war. It had infected everything. Even the slaves covertly talked about it, although few understood what it might mean to them. The hard-working, self-made farmers of northwest Louisiana were convinced that separatism would open direct markets to Europe, meaning not only higher profits on cotton but also independence from Northern mercantile interests. It was 1860—a Presidential election year—and the farmers believed, with their Governor, Thomas O. Moore, that "the success of Mr. Lincoln would justify the Southern States in withdrawing from the Union."[1]

"Secesh" talk had been the major topic also at the Kennedy place, on the road northeast of Homer that led to the Arkansas border. It was what Dr. John Bailey Kennedy had on his mind as he sat in his library. Like the threat of conflict hanging over the nation, a solar eclipse on that morning of July 18 had darkened the countryside, frightening the children, the blacks, and the animals.[2] The sun, however, had worked itself free, and Dr. Kennedy could hear through his open window the sounds of work and play.

War, the doctor believed, could not be averted. Even so, he meant to preserve some degree of sanity about it. Not that he was personally against secession: on the contrary, if the alternative was abolition (Dr. Kennedy would say), *We couldn't run this farm without our slaves; it's our way of life, we couldn't do otherwise, it wouldn't work, it wouldn't pay.* On the other hand, he was a religious man: brother should not kill brother . . . .

The evening before, there had been a dance at the house—an orchestra from St. Louis had been specially imported to play—in honor of his son Rob's guest, Stephen Beekman.[3] Beekman had detoured from a trip to New Orleans to answer an invitation to visit the Kennedys. Rob, the oldest child, was now overseer of the family's large farm—a withdrawn, moody, quick-tempered young man. As he spoke to the two young men, Dr. Kennedy was overheard by Rob's slave-companion, who sat outside the library window. As he later recalled the conversation: "You'll both be in it if it ever gets to war," the doctor said, "and someday there would have to be an end to that, too. I want you both to promise me that you will never fight against each other."[4]

Six miles away, J. W. Dorr flicked the thin whip at Crescent's back, sending the horse into a trot as his rig came in view of the Greek-columned courthouse under construction in Homer. Dorr, business agent for *The New Orleans Crescent*, was crisscrossing the state, seeking new subscribers and advertisers and sending back a series of portraits of the parishes he visited. *The Crescent* was printing them under the headline "Louisiana in Slices."

Dorr had started his meanderings in late April of 1860. He had followed the Mississippi's course, turning westward to Alexandria, traveling by steamboat up and down the Red, and finally pressing into the hinterlands in the northwest corner of the state. He had had his share of adventures: A cow chewed up his notes near Bayou Goula while he was napping by the roadside; the dog he bought in St. John the Baptist Parish ate clean through its halter and fled; and in Bossier, four days ago, he had to eat bacon and bread for breakfast, dinner, and supper at a hotel where pigs ran freely through the public rooms. "We have bacon on the table and bacon under the table," Dorr informed his readers, "the latter very much alive and uncured, the former very salty and rusty."[5]

Traveling eastward in mid-July, into Claiborne Parish where the Kennedys lived, however, had proved delightful, albeit slightly confusing. The road between Minden and Homer, the parish seat, was, he observed, either nineteen miles or twenty-one, depending on which way one was headed "on account of the crooked, hilly, and generally eccentric nature of the road. . . . Indeed," he wrote, "the mile-boards along the road set forth this somewhat extraordinary fact."[6]

The other extraordinary thing about Claiborne Parish was its hills—low, undulating bluffs that separated the streams that ran into the Red on the west and into the Ouachita on the east. The state's highest point—535 feet above sea level—was here. The countryside was utterly unlike what most Louisianians, Dorr included, thought of when they described their state. No marshy bayous, infested with mosquitoes; no heat, clinging day and night; and no vast plantations, either—although this was cotton country. Instead, farms with patches of clearings given over to cotton or feed corn; porous soil, easy to cultivate for potatoes, butter beans, pumpkins, goober peas, watermelons, cabbage, tomatoes, turnips, onions, beets, lettuce, and grains. The woods sheltered turkeys, deer, bear, and game fowl, and yielded blackberries, dewberries, huckleberries, haws, pawpaws, walnuts, chincapins, hickory nuts, acorns, and medicinal herbs. The climate was the healthiest in Louisiana, free of malaria, yellow fever, typhoid, and even on those rare days when the thermometer touched 100, the nights were cool. In winter, it hardly ever went below twenty-five. There were maybe three snowfalls a year, but the Gulf winds that originated 140 miles to the south always chased away the cold spells from the north after a few days.

Now, in midsummer, there were bowers of pink wild honeysuckle as well as dogwood. And the gum trees and sumac lit up like "burning bushes" at the edge of the dark green forests. Homer, concluded Dorr, "is one of the most picturesque and pleasant places I have yet seen in Louisiana."[7]

The virginal quality was even more pronounced when Dr. Kennedy had first settled in Homer a dozen years earlier. The land he chose was familiar—similar to the hills and valleys that he and his ancestors before him were accustomed to live in and to tend.[8] Dr. Kennedy traced his family to Antrim County in North Ireland and—so family legend held—to the sixth earl of Cassilas. His grandfather, James Kennedy, Sr., was eighteen years old and his grandmother, Margaret White, fourteen, when they immigrated to America in 1770. On the crossing, the doctor's father, James Jr., was born. The family lived on a plantation in colonial Chester District in South Carolina, and when the Revolution came James Sr. went off to fight the British as a lieutenant.

Shortly after the turn of the century, James Jr. wed Elizabeth Bailey, and on March 4, 1805—the day after her thirty-second birthday—John Bailey Kennedy, their second son, was born. James Jr. died in 1816, outlived by both his parents, but not before providing in his will the means to educate his two sons. John Bailey Kennedy decided on a medical career, and—in his twenties—to seek his fortune elsewhere. The young physician followed the path of the great wave of pioneers of English, Scotch, and North Irish stock that had pushed aside the Cherokee, Creek, Chickasaw, and Choctaw. He skirted the Appalachians, moving south among the foothills and then westward, until he came to Sumter County, Georgia. There he met and courted the daughter of one of the most famous of "upcountry" Georgia families, Eliza Lydia Cobb.

Eliza Lydia's heritage was part Welsh, part Scottish, and part English, with a trace of Dutch blood added when a Cobb of Aberdeen fought the Spanish and married a Hollander in the sixteenth century. Her forebears had also fought in the Revolutionary War. Eliza Lydia herself was born near Columbus, Georgia, on September 18, 1815, to Obedience Dutiful Bugg, who traced her family to a baronetcy in England, and her first husband, Henry Willis Cobb, a planter of substantial means. One of Eliza Lydia's uncles, Howell Lewis Cobb, had served in Congress. Another, John Addison Cobb, sired and named for his brother a son, Howell Cobb, who was destined to be Speaker of the U.S. House of Representatives, Governor of Georgia, Secretary of the Treasury in James Buchanan's cabinet, and a Confederate major general.

It was "Cousin" Howell, a great admirer of Eliza Lydia, who gave the Kennedy family the silver spoons it so treasured. Henry Willis Cobb, who died in 1824, left Eliza several hundred slaves, and these made up her dowry when she and Dr. Kennedy were wed in 1832. Eliza Lydia, however, never thought it fitting to own slaves, perhaps because of a childhood memory that rankled her all her life. Her father had taught his slave children to sing and dance, and when company came to his plantation home, he would invite them out on the porch, blow the horn he kept especially for the occasion, "and the little darkies would come from all directions, take their places around the door step, sing and dance, much to the amusement of his guests."[9]

Warm, gracious, devout, Eliza Lydia frowned on such sport. She tended the slaves when they were sick and she taught them her religion, despite the joshing of Dr. Kennedy, a Presbyterian, who made fun of her "ignorant" circuit-riding Methodist preachers.

The couple stayed three years in Georgia before moving to Cusseta, Alabama, just across the Georgia border. With them they took Eliza Lydia's teen-age stepbrother, John Burch, the offspring of widowed Obedience Dutiful's second marriage, as well as Obedience's brother, Charles Bugg, a friendly though "curious" bachelor whose devoutness amused Eliza Lydia. Uncle Charles, as he was known, a teacher by profession and future tutor of the Kennedy children, believed in keeping the Sabbath strictly holy. "Can't you cook what I eat on Saturday?" he would plead with Eliza Lydia, refusing to eat anything prepared on Sunday. The young woman, "full of fun," would rise early every Sunday morning to supervise the cooking of Uncle Charles's food, which was then put on the porch to cool before he awoke.

On October 25, 1835, shortly before leaving for Alabama, the first Kennedy child was born. He was named for the doctor's older brother, who had died at the time of their wedding three years earlier before reaching the age of thirty. For posterity's sake, Eliza Lydia's surname was added. They called the boy Robert Cobb Kennedy.

In the next eleven years, four more children were born in Alabama: Mary Willis, in 1837; Hyder Ali, named for a family friend, in 1840; John E. ("Little Johnny") in 1841; and Algernon Clifton in 1846.

The family's fortunes, in the meantime, ebbed. Dr. Kennedy was forced to divide his time between his medical practice and managing his lands, with no great success in either. The soil paid out (a common occurrence), and the doctor finally resolved to move again and to give up medicine, a profession that earned little beyond prestige in sparsely settled rural Alabama. Consequently, after Algernon Clifton's birth in 1846, Dr. Kennedy headed west alone. He traveled through Mississippi, and from Natchez—hub of the great "traces," or roads, from north and east that led south and west—he crossed into Louisiana. He intentionally avoided the swamplands of the delta, where yellow fever—"the black vomit"—periodically took thousands of lives. It was in northwest Louisiana, off the main pioneer route to Texas, that he tarried, drawn to the rust-red earth, hills, and forests. He returned to Alabama to sell his property and move his family and the score of slaves remaining to Louisiana. They went by carriage, ox-drawn wagon, and horseback, crossing the Mississippi on flatboats,

Dr. John Bailey Kennedy, father of Robert Cobb Kennedy. Courtesy of Mr. and Mrs. W. A. LaFleur.

Susan Ann Eliza Kennedy, sister of Robert Cobb Kennedy. Courtesy of Mr. and Mrs. W. A. LaFleur.

Catherine Cobb Kennedy, sister of Robert Cobb Kennedy. Courtesy of Mr. and Mrs. W. A. LaFleur.

Hyder Ali Kennedy, brother of Robert Cobb Kennedy. Courtesy of Mr. and Mrs. W. A. LaFleur.

Algernon Clifton Kennedy, brother of Robert Cobb Kennedy, and his family.
Courtesy of Mr. and Mrs. W. A. LaFleur.

Dr. Thomas Battle Hopkins, husband of Robert Cobb Kennedy's sister, Mary Willis Kennedy. Courtesy of Mr. and Mrs. W. A. LaFleur.

and then following old Indian trails into Claiborne Parish. It took nearly two months to reach the clearing Dr. Kennedy had decided would be the site of their new, and everlasting, home.

The Kennedys arrived in Homer shortly before it was incorporated and made the parish seat.[10] Claiborne, a huge parish from which five other parishes were eventually to be carved, was established in 1828, twenty-five years after the Louisiana Purchase. It was named for the state's first territorial governor general, William C. C. Claiborne. Before 1835, when the peaceful, agrarian Caddo Indians relinquished all their lands in northwest Louisiana for $80,000, there were about 1,800 settlers in the area. As the Caddo burial mounds disappeared into the underbrush, white settlements began to dot the hills. Oriented in the classics, the pioneers gave their towns such names as Antioch, Sparta, Arcadia, Athens, Homer.

The earliest settlers, unlike the "cajuns" of Creole Louisiana downstate, were Protestants. Most were of the same Scotch-Irish strain that had given the nation Andrew Jackson, James K. Polk, Sam Houston, Davy Crockett—grim, stern, strong, yet simple people, subject to stormy passions; lovers of freedom. Generous and courteous, they loved liberty but saw no evil in slavery, were literate but superstitious. They sang the songs of Scotland and north Ireland, spoke of the headless banshees and ominous fetch light, feared God and cherished the land they called their own. They represented each of the older states of the South—"Dixie in a nutshell."[11] "On the whole," one traveler wrote, "I could have selected an abler body of men from North Louisiana in 1860 than I have ever seen assembled in the capitol of any state, North or South."[12]

Following local custom, neighbors from miles about helped to build the newcomers' home. Dr. Kennedy found he had a choice: a narrow "shotgun" with a series of rooms, each opening into the next behind it—cool, economical, sufficient for small families; or a "dogtrot," two shotguns placed side by side with a covered, connecting breezeway down the middle, with the rooms opening onto it. The shotgun got its name from the sighting from front to back when all doors were opened to let in a breeze, while family pets that raced along the open center hall gave the dogtrot its name. Both types of houses could be easily added onto, and each had an overhanging roof to provide shelter for a porch.

Dr. Kennedy chose the one-story dogtrot for his growing family. The clearing was swept clean of grass, bushes, and shrubs, as a precaution against fire. Piles of rocks were then placed along the outlines of the building. The house would rest off the ground on the rocks, which bore traces of the iron ore that tinted the soil red. The walls were made of strips of rough pine, with the cracks between covered with smaller pieces of wood. Glass and screening—the Kennedys could at least afford them—protected the windows. For heat, a fireplace of twigs, pine straw, and mud was fashioned in the main room. Due to its tendency to "melt" in heavy rains, the fireplace was in a state of more or less constant repair.

Behind the house the kitchen shed and eating rooms were built, kept separate from the main house as another precaution against fire. Nearby, sunk a foot in the ground, was a large smokehouse. (Sorghum syrup and potatoes would be kept here also.) A root cellar was dug for the perishables. Some distance away, built up off the ground like the main house, were the one-room cabins of the slaves, the stables, the barn, and the corn crib.

Soon, vegetables poked above the ground in the small plots the slaves kept by their cabins. Beds of flowers ringed the main house itself, and vines wound along the paling fence that circled the main yard, and on the split-rail fences that separated the fields. Firearms hung on wall pegs along the breezeway of the dogtrot, and coats and hats on antlers. A fire burned continually in the kitchen shed.

Inside the main house, the extent of the Kennedys' wealth was displayed. A clock sat on the wooden mantel above the hearth, banked by huge bowls and vases of fresh-cut flowers. The parlor—"the inner sanctum," because it was opened only on Sundays, holidays, or other special occasions—was carpeted in red velvet and contained the best pieces of furniture: gilded mirrors in the French style of southern Louisiana; chairs of cherry, mahogany, and walnut, covered with velvet or horsehair; a rosewood breakfront; a square piano; and—on a marble-topped table—the family album and the dried flowers that contributed to the musty smell of this seldom-aired room.

There was no lack of goods to purchase in Homer's stores—port wine, cigars, plows, groceries of all kinds, even dental plates—but the Kennedy farm was, like most of its neighbors, virtually self-sustaining. Mops were made from corn shucks; mattresses, from cotton and the feathers of chickens and geese. The soap used on wash day (Monday) was made from oak-wood ashes. The men carefully nipped off the tips of cattle horns to make "spoons" they could use to frugally measure out the gunpowder for their muzzle-loaders—just so much for small game; a shoulder-bucking priming for deer or bear or long-range, 100-yard shots. It was a tricky, easily boggled chore that explains the saying, "I'll make a spoon or spoil a horn."[13] If successfully executed, the rest of the horn could be used to keep the powder dry or as a hunting horn.

At night, Eliza Lydia and her daughter worked on the quilts that so resembled the patchwork farms of the region. Pieced together from sewing scraps, each square recalled a dress or a shirtwaist, and the sad or happy times during which it had been worn. The quilts were given names—"Wedding Ring," "Goose Nest," "Road to California"—and, once completed, became the most important part of a girl's hope chest.

The making of the family clothes as well as those worn by the slaves was the province of a mulatto, Mary Jane, who lorded over the sewing shed. When the sewing machine was invented, Dr. Kennedy was the first man in Homer to buy one. He also put up a tannery where a young male slave (who had on occasion been apprenticed out) taught other slaves how to make shoes and boots.

In time, two more daughters were born to the Kennedys: Susan Ann Eliza, known as Susanna, in 1852; and Catherine Cobb, a happy, lovable child who was called Kate, in 1855. Uncle Charles took charge of the education of the four boys and three girls. He taught them to read, to write, to do some arithmetic—and each day he led them in prayer. Otherwise, though, there were no fences to hold in the youngsters. Like all young Southerners of their day and class, they were given horses and learned the tricks of guiding their mounts through dense undergrowth and across swollen streams. Each of the Kennedy children also had a slave of his or her own age and sex for a companion. They played together, filched biscuits from the kitchen for each other, fished side by side, and at night, after supper, stole down together to the cabin of The Story Teller. This huge black slave had an endless catalog of ghost stories. Invariably, when he got tired and wanted to shoo them away, he would say, "Well, children, you know I come from Africa and there they eat little children." With that, The Story Teller would grit his teeth and the children, white and black alike, would scamper away.

Although eight roads darted out from Homer, much like the spokes of a wheel, the town was nevertheless virtually isolated. The rivers were too shallow for boats six months of the year, the rutted dirt roads too frequently mired in mud. And the nearest railroad heading, just beginning to poke westward from Vicksburg toward Homer and Shreveport beyond, was still sixty miles away.

Once a year, when the waterways were high enough to navigate, Dr. Kennedy journeyed to Natchez to purchase cloth for the sewing and to settle his cotton accounts. Cotton—the money crop—was picked starting in the latter part of August. It was ginned locally for the seed, baled, and transported to Dauchite Bayou, the nearest landing place, twenty-two miles distant from Homer. The trip, slow and laborious over the primitive roads, was relieved by overnight stops at camping grounds. A knowledgeable farmer could get about a bale of cotton (roughly 500 pounds) to an acre, and the half-dozen large estates in the parish like the Kennedy place produced as many as 250 bales annually.[14] However, because of high freight costs and interest rates, cotton that should have brought ten cents a pound brought only eight. It was an expensive loss to farmers such as Dr. Kennedy. Instead of grossing $12,500 on his crop, he would make $10,000—a difference of $2,500 at a time when a strong thirty-year-old male slave to work his fields cost more than $500.

Claiborne Parish nevertheless prospered, and the doctor's success closely paralleled that prosperity. Land that once sold for $2.50 an acre rose to $7 an acre by 1860, reflecting the large influx of families during the 1850s. The population rose from 842 families to 1,510 in that decade, and by 1860 there were nearly 16,000 residents in the parish—one-third of them slaves.

Dr. Kennedy, meanwhile, had been steadily acquiring land. He picked up forty-acre pieces through the 1820 Homestead Act, in addition to bottom lands that the state didn't want. He also purchased the bonus grants of some veterans of the wars of 1812 and 1846. (Every so often he would sell some land, too, as he did to John Burch, Eliza Lydia's stepbrother, who took Uncle Charles with him to set up his own farm nearby.) Eventually, the Kennedy farm covered more than 3,000 acres—a sizeable tract for upstate Louisiana. When the census-taker came by toward the end of that July (1860), Dr. Kennedy—who in 1850 had $13,000 in real estate and twenty-three slaves—could lay claim to $55,000 in personal wealth, $20,000 in property, and forty-nine slaves.[15]

Fifty-five years of age in 1860, Dr. Kennedy looked every inch the successful farmer—as indeed he was. Clean-shaven, he liked to don a thin bow tie on formal occasions. Hyder was now at the University of North Carolina. Mary—dark-haired, dark-eyed, "of a commanding appearance"—had wed a young physician, Thomas Battle Hopkins, and was living at the Kennedy place with her husband. Little Johnny, Cliff, the two younger girls—Dr. Kennedy had cause to be proud. Only Rob, the eldest, remained a problem.

Brown-haired, brown-eyed, about five-foot-eight, Rob was handsome, courteous, gentlemanly, poised—but not given to intimate relationships. Although nearing his twenty-fifth birthday, he was still a bachelor. (In fact, there'd never been so much as a rumor of his getting married.) Neighbors instead gossiped that he smoked, drank, and, when drinking, swore blasphemously.

Father and son quarreled often. Rob resented any interference in the farm's management, treating any piece of advice as though it were a command and automatically rebelling against it. When the Mississippi flooded in 1858, he had gone off like a hero to help supervise the shoring up of levees (no doubt hoping also that his presence on the farm would be missed). Rob must have already been committed both to proving his manhood and to justifying a way of life he found it natural to defend. Honor, duty, freedom, the Southland—the litany of jingoism seemed to buttress his own need to succeed. Embittered and frustrated, Rob probably fantasized that war would offer the chance for him to make his mark in the world—the opportunity to erase his failure at West Point.

chapter 6

The sun that would shine so brilliantly that first Sunday morning of April, 1862, had not yet erased the stars from the sky. Rob and the ninety-five other men of Company G, First Louisiana Infantry, stood listlessly in the small clearing, stamping their feet, rubbing their hands together, chewing on cold rations, for no fires had been allowed the night before or on this morning.[1]

Two nights earlier, as a heavy storm swelled the streams in the area, Braxton Bragg informed Brigadier General A. H. Gladden that Gladden's brigade was being detached from Bragg's Second Corps and being placed under William Joseph Hardee. It would form the right wing of Hardee's Third Corps. At the moment, the brigade (which included the First Louisiana) was poised on a ridge above the encampments of Union recruits led by Benjamin Mayberry Prentiss. Just behind the Federal lines and to the left stood a small church that ordinarily on a Sunday like this would ring with hymns and prayers: Shiloh Meeting House.

Lincoln's election in November of 1860 had exploded into war at Fort Sumter on April 12, 1861. Rob, refusing to wait until the cotton was planted, had ridden to New Orleans with—typical of a Southern officer—a Negro slave as his valet.[2] On April 30, he was enrolled in the First Louisiana, Colonel Daniel W. Adams commanding.

Except for a brief furlough home after a fever caught in the lowland Gulf regions, Rob spent the next twelve months in Florida. Both North and South spent that time jockeying for position: calling up troops, forging weapons, building fleets, scaring each other at Bull Run. Company G, under Captain John T. Wheat, cut its fighting teeth in two devastating but futile bombardments as Bragg laid siege to Fort Pickens in Pensacola Bay. Wheat's battery, a little to the east of the Marine Hospital at the Warrenton Navy Yard, took the brunt of the return fire from the fort's huge, 10-inch columbiads and other guns. On the first day—November 22, 1861—fifty-nine Federal shells were directed at the battery; on the next day, a round was fired at it every fifteen minutes. Amazingly, although the position was often struck, no man in Company G was seriously injured. And luck held out during the second artillery duel on New Year's Day, 1862.

Then, hundreds of miles away, Fort Henry on the Tennessee River and Fort Donelson on the Cumberland fell to a then-unknown Union brigadier general named Ulysses S. Grant. Albert Sidney Johnston was forced to evacuate Nashville and retreat to Alabama with the main Confederate force in the West. Bragg moved north to link up with Johnston, taking with him by special request the First Louisiana—"finely equipped and instructed"[3]—to form the "nucleus" that "would set an example of discipline and would give me the support of excellent officers."[4]

Company G traced Bragg's move north: from Pensacola to Blakely, outside Mobile, Alabama; then by train to Corinth, Mississippi, and into Tennessee at Fort Pillow and Bethel. Rob, meanwhile, applied for a commission as a first lieutenant, observing in his appeal that he had served two years as a cadet at West Point (but offering no explanation as to why he had left the Academy).

His brothers Hyder and Little Johnny were headed toward Shiloh, too. They had supervised the harvesting of the cotton, after which Hyder had helped to organize the Claiborne Volunteers. (He eventually became a lieutenant colonel commanding the Nineteenth Louisiana Regiment.) Noted for their sharpshooting, the local troops marched off from Homer to the playing of a band and the applause of families gathered from miles around. They reached Camp Moore, Louisiana, on December 31, 1861, and became Company C of the 19th Louisiana Infantry. Johnny went along as a private. (Mary's husband, Dr. Hopkins, had at the same time joined the 19th Arkansas.)

The war was not quite a year old as the Confederate troops, reinforced, advanced back into Tennessee—Johnston intending to confront the Union Army that was assembling under Grant. As yet, the full horror of the conflict was not generally understood. Many observers, Grant among them, believed that the fall of Forts Henry and Donelson had been such decisive victories that the rebellion would soon collapse.

Company G was roused at four in the morning on April 6, 1862. All about them, 40,000 other Confederates were being awakened, too. To the north was an equal number of Federal troops—still asleep, unsuspecting. (Hadn't Grant said there would be no battle today?) The Union general, on crutches because of a fall from his horse, had left his army and crossed the Tennessee River to wait for Don Carlos Buell, who was coming with 20,000 more men. A Confederate offensive was so unlikely that only cautious Prentiss had pickets out: they guarded the way the First Louisiana would have to come.

As the sun came up, the First Louisiana spread out into a long, thin line and moved ahead as silently as possible—no drums to beat the cadence, no band to lead the way. The undergrowth was thick and soggy. The first shots of the skirmishers ahead sporadically broke the silence.

Rob was with Company G on the right flank.[5] Intermittent shooting could be heard from ahead and to his right. Scuttling figures could be seen as Prentiss's pickets fell back toward the thick woods and bushes between them and their own encampments. Almost every man of the First Louisiana was in position, with only a gap here and there to note the place where a sharpshooter's bullet had found its mark. Colonel Adams was on horseback, riding up and down the line, using his sword to emphasize his orders as he passed the officers in each company.

General Gladden, head of the brigade, appeared as Rob's company was only 200 yards from the enemy's lines. All about, the pock-pock of the skirmishers' rifles had now escalated into the crescendo of a full-scale battle. Men ducked instinctively as bullets whined into their advance. Cannon boomed in the distance, and smoke shot up into the now clear-blue sky. Peach blossoms rained from the trees every time a shell landed.

Gladden, wheeling in front of his troops, sword raised high, pointed forward with it: *Let's go, Louisiana!* Rob and his men moved forward, a shrill cry in their throat. Burnt powder and flames spewed from cannon mouths in the thickets ahead as Prentiss's men opened a withering fire. Men toppled and lay writhing—or dead still. Somewhere, Captain Wheat fell. Gladden, still in the lead, was halfway to the Union guns, when suddenly he fell back from his saddle as a cannon ball struck. Adams rushed to Gladden's side as his own men crouched, reloading, seeking out cover. A few began to edge back.

Suddenly, Adams rode to the color-bearer of the First Louisiana, seized the battle flag, and galloped to the head of the brigade, shouting over and over again for the Louisianians to resume the attack.

Rob and the men of Company G got to their feet and started to trot forward toward the woods, stopping every few paces to fire and reload. As they reached the first row of Federal tents and still-smoldering campfires, a barrage of round shot raked through the company.

Rob was stunned. His boot filled with blood that ran from a severe wound in his thigh.

General Johnston was dead; Captain Wheat, two sergeants, and two privates also. Colonel Adams had been shot in the head but was still alive. One man was missing, more than twenty wounded. The regiment as a whole was all shot up. As for Hyder and Johnny, the troops were scrambled, but apparently they were all right. The next morning would find Rob moving back in a hospital wagon, before the fighting started up again.

Before the next bloody day of battle the old folk saying was being repeated in both camps: "Nobody ever wins who starts a battle on Sunday."[6] Grant took the initiative that next day, April 7, and the Confederates fell back. Grant—his army nearly 63,000 strong once Buell's force arrived—lost 13,047 killed, wounded, and missing; the Confederates, 10,694.

In New Orleans, as the first trains carrying the wounded (and Gladden's body) arrived on April 8, the *Picayune* had received news only of the first day's triumph. "The night of our disaster has passed," it trumpeted, "and the sun of victory has begun to dawn on the armies of freedom."[7] Both armies by then, of course, knew better. To Grant, it was a case of "Southern dash against Northern pluck and endurance" and the "severest" battle ever fought in the West. Grant, the victor, abandoned any idea of saving the Union "except by complete conquest." He also decided, as a result, that all supplies within reach of Confederate armies were to be regarded as contraband subject to destruction—a policy, the general believed, that "exercised a material influence in hastening the end."[8]

chapter 7

Before Rob returned to his post, New Orleans fell—and shortly after it, Corinth. The First Louisiana, shattered by what had happened at Shiloh, its strength sapped by a casualty rate of 25 percent, was reduced to reserve status.[1] The regiment plodded after Bragg again, advancing into Kentucky, retreating back to Tennessee, marching from Chattanooga to Tupelo, Bardstown, Harrodsburg, Knoxville. As the year closed, Bragg—because the entire brigade "had not been engaged in any heavy battle since that of Shiloh"[2]—placed it in the front line at Murfreesboro. It never recovered from the shock of that battle. Desertions became chronic. There were not enough men to form a line of battle, and the regiment was merged with a battered Arkansas regiment.

Rob, meanwhile, had been given command of Company D, but was apparently too weak to lead his men into battle. He turned down transfer and a promotion to commissary duties to stay with the regiment, but Bragg used him only for foraging duties or to round up deserters:

> Lt. Robt. C. Kennedy 1st La. Infantry will proceed immediately to such points as may be indicated by the Colonel of his Regiment to secure and bring forward all able bodied men absent without leave or on any detached service . . .[3]

After the disaster at Murfreesboro, Rob became adjutant to Colonel James T. Strawbridge, now commander of the First Louisiana, based in Tullahoma; however, the need for combat grew as the regiment shrank into impotence. He was shifted to Company K as captain in May 1863—but the command was a hollow one. Seeking action, Rob finally sought out an old West Point friend, Joe Wheeler, who at the age of twenty-six was already a major general and one of the South's leading cavalry officers. The transfer was arranged, and Rob joined Wheeler as Assistant Inspector General—in effect, another desk job. However, he persuaded the dashing cavalryman to take him along on a rampaging nine-day raid into Tennessee. The attack crippled an entire Federal army's supply train, although Wheeler's men were so vigorously pursued that he was forced to withdraw.[4]

On October 12, Wheeler was outside Courtland, Alabama, writing to Bragg in Chattanooga for orders as to his next move. The dispatch, along with reports of his raid and the regimental flag his men captured at McMinnville, was slipped into a large leather case. Wheeler gave it to Rob to deliver to Bragg.

Four days later, Rob was heading out of Trenton, Georgia, on horseback when a scouting party of 150 Union infantrymen appeared suddenly from behind the trees on both sides of the road. There was no chance to escape.[5] He was brought the next day to Stevenson, Alabama, where Brigadier General Joseph Hooker made his headquarters. The Union general quickly distributed the details of Wheeler's reports to the appropriate Federal commanders in the area.

Rob was taken to Nashville, for transfer to Louisville and then to Camp Chase, Illinois. He spent his twenty-eighth birthday on October 25 moving between prisons at Louisville and Camp Chase. Finally, on November 14, 1863, guards escorted him aboard a small steam tug at Sandusky, Ohio, for the twenty-minute ride to an island that lay in the harbor.

A line of tents was strung in front of the eighteen buildings that girded the prison yard. The ground was gutted with mudholes, the smell oppressive, the men unshaven and unkempt. Behind the barracks buildings were the latrines: long, open trenches, spanned lengthwise by logs. Near the picket fence on the bay side, long lines of men waited their turn at the two water pumps. A hospital flag flew from a building dead center across the yard from the main gate.

A tall picket fence and a blockhouse guarded the bay side of the prison; a twelve-foot wooden wall surrounded the other three sides. In front of it was a deep ditch staked out by tiny white flags: the "dead zone." A sentry was on duty inside the blockhouse that rose above the main gate. Behind it, outside the prison, were the pesthouse for small-pox cases, the bakery, the arsenal, and the guards' quarters and other buildings belonging to the prison command. This was Johnson's Island Military Prison—in all, forty acres of misery on the southern tip of 300 acres of unyielding limestone.

It was here that Rob first met General William N. R. Beall, a West Point graduate and veteran Indian fighter who had been cap-tured when Port Hudson, in Louisiana, surrendered. Here also Rob met Meriwether Jeff Thompson. The ex-mayor of St. Joseph, Mis-souri, had already established a better mail system at the prison, insti-tuted an accurate directory of inmates, organized a graveyard improvement committee, and written some original songs for the Thespian Society.

Thompson—one of six generals among the nearly 3,000 Confed-erate officers held on the island—had also turned his attention to escape plans. With four other brigadiers—John B. Jones, James Jay Archer, John W. Frazer, and Beall—Thompson had at one point en-listed 500 men to rush the gates and overwhelm the 200-man guard force. Each brigadier had selected ten colonels who could be trusted, and each colonel had in turn picked ten junior officers. The rest of the prisoners would rise up (so the plan went) once the vanguard had attacked the gates. Only the reluctance of the senior Confederate officer at the prison, Major General Isaac Ridgeway Trimble, delayed the attempted breakout. Trimble, minus a leg after being wounded (and captured) at Gettysburg, hesitated to order the attempt because he could not participate in it himself. Delay after delay followed as a result, until one morning in mid-October of 1863 Thompson's Mis-sourians gathered in the barracks nearest the main gate, waiting for it to be opened when the rations wagon arrived. One of the attack parties, however, sent word that it was not ready, and so the plan was put off for a day—and then for another, and another, until the Un-ion's only man-of-war on Lake Erie, the U.S.S. *Michigan*, appeared off the island. (A "razorback," as it turned out, had given the plan away.)

Most of the 500 men who were in on the plan laughed the miscar-ried project away; Thompson, however, was not one of them. He was "grievously [sic] distressed, and swore not a little, for we had evidently been betrayed by some man of the select 500."[6] The plan was aban-doned, although it would be resurrected before another year passed.

Rob joined Company 14, Mess 2, in Block 7, a barracks. It was considered preferable to living in a tent, although the officers, accustomed to having valets or orderlies, still had to do their own cooking and cleaning. Nevertheless, there were sentiments of encouragement:

> But comrades while we're here let's
> Try to help each other along
> For each can cheer another by
> Some story, joke or song
> And thus we'll laugh the hours away
> That would so tedious be
> We'll call on all that's bright and gay
> To cheer captivity.
>
> For here I'll stay and here I'll rot
> Through many weary years
> Before the South shall yield
> One jot or bow from craven fears
> I'll stay until the boys are men
> And learn to pull the trigger
> Before I'll be swamped for any man
> Who's an officer of niggers.

Except for a few grumblers in Block 7, the words of the song were symbolic of the camaraderie felt by the men Rob befriended: Lieutenant Amos C. ("Turk") Smith, Lieutenant T. E. Fell, and others. They sat around telling stories, embellishing on various feats of heroism and playing cards or baseball, or fashioned pins and brooches from buttons and gutta percha that they could trade to the sutler for jam, cake, clothing, or stationery. There was a laundry run by enterprising prisoners in another block, and a tailor shop, a barber, and a cobbler in others.

As the months passed, however, the prison population swelled past 3,000, the result of new Confederate surrenders and the fact that Grant—now in unchallenged command of all Union armies—refused to continue the policy of prisoner exchange that had fed back into the Southern armies some of their most valuable veterans. Morale grew as thin as the daily fare: a half-loaf of bread, eight ounces of beef (or six of bacon or salt fish), with perhaps a potato or an onion. Rats disappeared from the island as the starving men hunted them down, and quarrels over scraps of food became commonplace. "Dear Col.," wrote one inmate after the prison commandant's black Newfoundland disappeared, "For want of bread/Your dog is dead/For want of meat/Your dog is eat."[7]

Half a day was spent waiting to get water to drink or to wash with, and there was no water at all when the wells froze. Nor was there enough clothing, bedding, or wood to stave off the cold that so many of the men from the Gulf regions were not used to. In addition, restrictions were tightened even further in retaliation for conditions in such Confederate prisons as Andersonville. Orders from Union Secretary of War Edwin M. Stanton curtailed purchases from the sutler, and finally mail from home was forbidden: no packages, no money, no letters from loved ones. The prison commandant proved to be a disciplinarian first, a humanitarian second. And security was tightened when contingents of Ohio troops arrived to bolster the small guard force.

Johnson's Island was not the living cemetery that so many other prison camps, North and South, were: only 211 Confederates were to die there, chiefly of diarrhea and pneumonia. However, for its prisoners, death—once faced bravely in battle—seemed always perilously close. To fight it off, they joked, staged minstrel shows, wrote poetry, got into fist fights—and some turned informer.

Outside of a mass breakout through the main gate, escape seemed to be virtually impossible. The island was two and a half miles from Sandusky, and a mile from the nearest land. Therefore, a boat was essential to any escape, unless one waited until Lake Erie iced over and then chanced the freezing winds. As for the walls, they could not be tunnelled under: the same hard limestone that blocked the digging of deep, hygienic wells and sinks prevented this. No, one would have to scale the wall with a ladder or sneak through the main gate undetected. The aim, of course, was to get to Canada, where, as everyone knew, Confederates were being afforded asylum, and where they could readily find not only sympathizers but also many of their countrymen, fled before them.

Attempts were made to escape, though, and those who did succeed earned the begrudging admiration of their captors. Shortly before Rob arrived, a tunnelling attempt failed. However, on "Cold New Year's," January 1, 1864, when the temperature fell to twenty-seven degrees below zero, six men scaled the wall, and three made it across the ice into neutral Canada.[8] Others tried to make their way out by masquerading as Union soldiers, replacing their own tattered clothing with uniforms pieced together from Federal jackets and trousers captured in battle. One inveterate would-be escaper, Lieutenant Charles Pierce of the Seventh Louisiana, whittled wood and shaped tin cans into a rifle to complete his deception. Pierce was walking out with a squad of sentries when an officer stopped him to chastise him for failing to carry a cartridge box.

During the time Rob spent at Johnson's Island, only about a dozen prisoners escaped. But the entire camp bestirred itself in the fall of 1864, for another mass breakout was afoot—this time, with aid from the outside. Richmond was behind the move; officials in the Confederate capital were eager to tap the huge source of manpower represented by Johnson's Island and other prison camps in the Midwest.

Word of the attempted breakout reached Johnson's Island in the form of the innocuous personal newspaper advertisements that both sides used to transmit messages. The plan was a daring one: Confederates coming out of Canada would seize a lake steamer, and then, through trickery, board the *Michigan*. Once the latter was in Southern hands, a cannon would be fired—the signal for the prisoners inside Johnson's Island's camp to rise up. The *Michigan*, finally, would be used to transport the prisoners to safety.

The hope of freedom raised the spirits of the prisoners, and the old escape plan was revived. Groups of officers met after taps at nine o'clock to whisper and plot. Beds and chairs were pulled apart to make clubs. Spoons became knives. The date in everyone's mind was September 20.

On the nineteenth, a young and spirited Virginian named James Yates Beall led a score of Confederates aboard the *Philo Parsons*, a steamer that plied between the ports of Lake Erie and the islands on both sides of the international boundary. Once the steamer was under way, Beall and his aide—a Scottish adventurer named Bennet G. Burley—seized control of her at gunpoint and headed the *Philo Parsons* from Canada toward the Ohio shore. On the way, they captured and took in tow still another lake steamer, the *Island Queen*. They then headed toward Sandusky Bay, where a Southern spy, Captain Charles H. Cole, was supposed to be getting the captain and officers of the *Michigan* drunk at a dinner party aboard the warship. But Cole's signal that the *Michigan* was ripe for boarding never came.

On the twentieth, with the prisoners on Johnson's Island anxiously waiting, the *Michigan* steamed across the lake, hunting for the *Philo Parsons*. Troops, meanwhile, hastily positioned cannon along the island's rim, and extra details of sentries walked the walls of the prison camp. The *Philo Parsons* was finally found, beached. Again, informers had divulged the escape plan.

Rob Kennedy determined to escape on his own. The attempted mass breakout prompted the Union commandant to begin building two small forts as protection against outside attack. Prisoners were used to build them—and that meant wood would be on hand. In addition, a tornado struck the island on September 23, ripping off the roofs of several barracks and toppling a portion of the fence. The guards were so afraid that a break would occur during the storm that they fired cannon regularly as a deterrent. Rebuilding the roofs and fence also meant more lumber would be available.

The opportunity soon presented itself when Union Sergeant Edwin Hewitt, in charge of Block 7 at roll-calls, left Johnson's Island on furlough on October 1. A young, inexperienced private, Orlando Clark, was assigned to call the roll in his absence. Some sick prisoners were subsequently exchanged—too sick to cause Grant concern that they would fight again for the South. As a result, Private Clark inadvertently struck "Turk" Smith's name from the roll-call list.

Rob asked Smith for a favor: He had pieced together a ladder from scraps of lumber. If Turk could help him carry it to the prison wall . . . if Turk could drag the ladder back from the wall afterward and hide it . . . if Turk could answer to his name at roll-call. . . .

On Tuesday, October 4, 1864, a moonless night, Rob—bearded and gaunt after eleven months of imprisonment—waited until the camp fell asleep. Sometime around midnight, he and Smith crept out of Block 7, lugging the ladder through the shadows. Rob had chosen a spot near the blockhouse of the main gate where there was no ditch to prevent their getting a footing for the ladder. He scampered up the ladder, hoisted himself over the top, and dropped to the ground below outside the wall. He sneaked past the guards' quarters and found a small ducking skiff bobbing idly at the shore. By the time Rob was missed, ten days later, Turk Smith was facing close confinement and reduced rations—and Rob was safe in Canada.[8]

part 3

THE PLOT

You tol' me to preach,
You tol' me to preach,
I done done,
I done done,
You tol' me to preach
An' I done done what you tol' me to do.

You tol' me to shout,
I done done,
You tol' me to shout,
I done done,
You tol' me to shout,
An' I done done what you tol' me to do.

You tol' me to moan,
I done done,
You tol' me to moan,
I done done,
You tol' me to moan,
An' I done done what you tol' me to do.

chapter 8

The Confederate defeat at Gettysburg on the eastern front and the fall of Vicksburg in the west during the first week of July, 1863, dramatically altered the war. Within a few months, what Southern hopes remained in the west were dashed at Chattanooga. Finally, in March of 1864, Grant's appointment as commander of all Union armies doomed Lee in the east.

The Richmond government, plagued by growing shortages of men, arms, and food and unable to win on the battlefield, reacted by trying to terrorize the North into peace and by fostering revolution. Its most important effort was a conspiracy to tear the Union apart by teaming up with Northern Copperheads—the so-called Peace Democrats, who despised Lincoln and sought peace at any price. They had organized chapters in almost every state in the North, identifying themselves at various times as Knights of the Golden Circle, the Order of American Knights, and the Sons of Liberty. Many of the members in Ohio, Indiana, Illinois, and Kentucky were of Southern background. The most prominent Copperhead, Clement L. Vallandigham, even ran for Governor of Ohio in absentia while in exile in Canada—backed by Southern funds.

In the spring of 1864, several weeks after Grant's appointment, Jefferson Davis commissioned three men to carry out Confederate designs across the Union's weakest frontier: the more than 1,000-mile border with Canada. Canadian neutrality was to be respected and every diplomatic means of gaining peace exhausted, but—Davis said— military operations were to be carried out from Canada as a last resort.

Heading the mission to Canada was Colonel Jacob Thompson, a former aide to General P. G. T. Beauregard who before the war had been a congressman from Mississippi and secretary of the interior in Buchanan's cabinet. Thompson was obstinate, unimaginative, easily influenced.

The second commissioner was an Alabamian who was as gullible as Thompson, Clement C. Clay. Clay, a one-time United States Senator, was chronically ill, virtually an invalid.

Thompson and Clay met the third commissioner on their arrival in Canada. Scholarly, detached, James P. Holcombe, a former professor of law at the University of Virginia, always carried a book of poems. He was already busy helping escaped prisoners of war find their way back to the Confederacy. The favorite route was by neutral mail ship from Halifax, Nova Scotia, to Bermuda, then by blockade runner into Wilmington, North Carolina.

Assigned to handle the military side of their operations was a cavalryman whose effeminate appearance belied his audacity. Captain Thomas H. Hines, a Kentuckian who had served with the famed raider John Hunt Morgan, was helping Holcombe round up Morgan's men and other escaped prisoners. However, Hines intended to enlist them for raids against the North from Canada.

In addition, a number of other individuals of doubtful talents and loyalties gathered about the commissioners. Clay, the second commissioner, put his trust in debonair George N. Sanders. Sanders, who had been American consul in England in the 1850s, was an opportunist and influence peddler. He was constantly prodding Clay to underwrite raids on Northern banks and trains.

Thompson's "intimate counselor" was a former Union sutler who had fled to Canada after turning informer, William L. (Larry) Mc-Donald.[1] McDonald, who was from New York City, was a notorious schemer. In his spare time, he manufactured torpedoes, grenades, and other weapons.

Thompson also had great faith in a shadowy figure named Godfrey J. Hyams, who was privy to all the group's clandestine operations and often served as a courier. A former Little Rock, Arkansas, politician, Hyams managed to keep secret his own hostility toward officials in Richmond because he had been passed over for promotion while in the Confederate army.

Discord broke out as soon as Thompson and Clay reached Canada, and the two men soon went their separate ways. Clay, with Sanders at his side, stayed in Montreal with the nearly $100,000 in funds that Thompson had given him. Thompson set up his headquarters in Toronto, appointing a Kentuckian, William C. Cleary, as the commission's secretary. Holcombe left Canada altogether within a few months.

The commissioners remained in contact with Richmond by means of techniques that ranged from the sophisticated to the juvenile. Messages were often encoded or written in "imperceptible" ink between the lines of innocent-looking letters. Microphotography was sometimes employed to enable couriers to carry messages inside metal suit buttons. Cryptic advertisements were run in certain Northern newspapers that were available in Richmond. Confederate officials there, in turn, ran personals in the Richmond papers with the addendum, "New York papers please copy." The personals were invariably reprinted by such anti-Administration papers as *The New York Daily News*.

The couriers sent to Richmond used forged papers to enter the United States, then passed through Baltimore and Washington before slipping across the Potomac at night to enter into the Confederate lines.[2] Clay and Thompson used a variety of such couriers: Hyams, a prostitute named Annie Davis, a man named Douglass among others. At least one of them was in the pay of the War Department in Washington, where the letters were steamed open, copied, carefully resealed, and then given back to the courier for delivery in Richmond. The same procedure was being followed with messages coming from Richmond.

Canada was decidedly pro-Southern, albeit officially neutral, when Thompson and Clay first arrived there. Toronto itself was full of Southern refugees—Kentuckians, Missourians, Marylanders, and Virginians especially. The city was also, like other Confederate outposts-in-exile at Niagara Falls, Windsor, London, St. Catharines, and Hamilton, a roost of spies and informers. "The bane and curse of carrying out anything in this country is the surveillance under which we act," Thompson complained to Confederate Secretary of State Judah P. Benjamin. "Detectives or those ready to give information stand at every street corner. Two or three can not interchange ideas without a reporter."[3] He warned a countryman "against any stranger who might claim an acquaintance, etc., as a swarm of detectives from the United States, male and female, were quartered in Toronto."[4]

Commissioner Thompson nevertheless plotted on, traveling under the name of "Colonel Carson" to avoid surveillance, convinced finally that "nothing but violence can terminate the war."[5] The result was a series of ill-conceived exploits, all divulged in advance by either the informers at his elbow or the spies behind his back. An elaborate scheme to promote a Northwest Confederacy was attempted with Vallandigham's assistance—and fizzled. Raids on Maine, the seizure of ships on the Great Lakes, the freeing of the thousands of Confederates imprisoned at Johnson's Island and other camps in the Midwest, an uprising in Chicago coordinated with the Democratic National Convention, a financial crisis brought on by pushing up the price of gold—not one such stratagem succeeded. Worse still, a minor raid on St. Albans, Vermont, on October 19, 1864, which Clay sanctioned without informing Thompson, was to cause such an international ruckus that Canada would thenceforth become a questionable port of refuge.

Something approaching madness permeated the schemes—and the schemers. Surprisingly, Thompson seemed undaunted by the timidity of the Copperheads in the Midwest, and continued to be incautious regarding his confidants despite the disclosures that stymied every operation. If anything, he was more determined than ever to succeed—desperate, in fact, by the fall of 1864, since the war across the border was going badly: Sheridan was wreaking havoc in the Shenandoah Valley, and Atlanta had fallen to Sherman. Then, on October 15, an editorial appeared in *The Richmond Whig* and was reprinted in its entirety by *The New-York Times:*

> Sheridan reports to Grant that, in moving down the Valley to Woodstock, he has burned over two thousand barns filled with wheat, hay and farming implements, and over seventy mills filled with flour and wheat. This was done by order of Grant, himself, commander of all the Yankee armies. It is only the execution in part of the order to destroy everything in the Valley that will sustain life. The fell work is still going on. Now, it is an idle waste of words to denounce this sort of war. We have simply to regard it as a practical matter, and ask ourselves how it is to be met. There is one effectual way, and only one that we know of, to arrest and prevent this and every other sort of atrocity—and that is to burn one of the chief cities of the enemy, say Boston, Philadelphia or Cincinnati, and let its fate hang over the others as a warning of what may be done to them, if the present system of war on the part of the enemy is continued. If we are asked how such a thing can be done—we answer, nothing would be easier. A million dollars would lay the proudest city of the enemy in ashes. The

men to execute the work are already there. There would be no difficulty in finding there, here or in Canada, suitable persons to take charge of the enterprise and arrange its details. Twenty men with plans all preconcerted, and means provided, selecting some dry, windy night, might fire Boston in a hundred places and wrap it in flames from centre to suburb. They might retaliate on Richmond, Charleston, &c? Let them do so if they dare. It is a game at which we can beat them. New York is worth twenty Richmonds. They have a dozen towns to our one, and in their towns is centered nearly all their wealth. It would be immoral and barbarous? It is not immoral or barbarous to defend yourself by any means, or with any weapon the enemy may employ for your destruction. They chose to substitute the torch for the sword. We may so use their own weapon as to make them repent, literally in sackcloth and ashes, that they ever adopted it. . . .⁶

It was in this atmosphere of intrigue and adventure that Rob found himself when he reached Toronto in the second week of October 1864, shortly before the editorial above appeared. According to Lieutenant Fell, his messmate at Johnson's Island, Rob walked from Sandusky to Buffalo and thence into Canada, a distance of nearly 250 miles.⁷ It seems more likely, however, that he took the shorter route to Windsor, Canada, via Detroit, a distance of only 110 miles and an established escape route, and that he was given assistance and money by sympathetic Copperheads along the way.

What is certain is that once in Canada Rob made straight for Thompson's headquarters at the Queen's Hotel in Toronto. There, in a suite of rooms adorned with Confederate flags and emblems, he was confronted with a choice: to run the blockade and try to return home, or to remain in Canada and join in the harassing of the North across the border.

The decision must have been a difficult one. The farm in Homer was still in Confederate territory, but cut off and continually threatened. A Union army under Nathaniel P. Banks had advanced up the Red River that spring in an attempt to seize Shreveport. Federal troops, followed by bushwhackers, fanned out throughout the area. "Banks's marauders," as the residents of Homer would forever afterward call them, pillaged for food and destroyed some farms. The Kennedy place escaped destruction, but the family was hard-pressed.⁸ Rob's father, now fifty-nine years old, had only Cliff, eighteen, to help him both to run the farm and to maintain a vital road in the parish that local authorities had charged him with overseeing. His daughters did their share: Susanna, twelve, and Kate, nine, helped with the kitchen chores, while Mary, who at twenty-six was pregnant with her first child, did what she could to manage the household. Eliza Lydia, ten years younger than her husband, was in an almost continual state of worry about her sons. The family had no idea where Rob was. Hyder, twenty-four, was in a hospital somewhere in Georgia after having been wounded on July 28 at the battle of Ezra Church while fighting Sherman's army outside Atlanta. Johnny, twenty-three, wounded in the same battle, was missing and presumed captured.

Mary's husband returned home periodically to lend a hand. Dr. Hopkins, nearing his thirty-second birthday, had been captured but paroled and was now attached to the Trans-Mississippi Department, which covered Confederate territory west of the river. He received furloughs twice yearly, and tried to time them to the planting and harvesting seasons. Cotton, however, although it commanded a high price, was virtually worthless because there was no place to sell or ship it; thousands upon thousands of bales belonging to Homer farmers had been burned when New Orleans fell in 1862, and again when Shreveport was threatened two years later.

The need and desire to return home were strong. But Rob undoubtedly wanted to make amends for his capture and his long period of inactivity while in prison. Edward A. Jackson of Yazoo City, Mississippi, who roomed with Bob at a boarding house in Toronto, recalled that there were "some fifty of us" who had escaped from Union prison camps:

> It seemed to us that if our fifty could retain some fifteen or twenty thousand Federal troops on the Northern frontier—troops that otherwise would have helped in crushing our comrades down South—we were doing as much for the cause as any fifty men in the ranks. We ran, besides, risks greater and more fearful than those faced by the regular service.[9]

Asked to render "a service" to his country, Rob agreed. He thus became a party to the latest of Thompson's ideas: a bold scheme to seize control of major Northern cities—New York, Chicago, and Boston in particular—on Election Day, November 8, in a show of strength and solidarity with Copperhead factions.

Long after the event it would be said that Rob had actually led the expedition to New York. It would also be charged that he had met with John Wilkes Booth in Canada and conspired to assassinate Lincoln, that he had even traveled to Washington to confer with others in the plot, and that he had been a vociferous and leading exponent of rebellion and hatred in the social circle surrounding the Confederates in exile in Canada.[10]

None of this is true, however. Rob undoubtedly voiced his hatred of "Ape" Lincoln and "black" Republicanism, but no reliable evidence was ever found to connect him to the attack on Lincoln or on members of his cabinet. The leader of the small band being sent to New York was actually Colonel Robert M. Martin of Kentucky. He and a fellow Kentuckian, Lieutenant John W. Headley, were, like Hines, former officers who had served with Morgan. They had been sent to Canada by Richmond in September to aid in military operations against the North. Martin, in his mid-twenties, had steel-blue eyes and wore a moustache and goatee. He was six feet tall, but walked with a slight stoop because of a bullet wound in his right lung. Martin, unlike Rob, actually did meet Booth in Canada—he would later brag that he "had cracked many a bottle of wine" with him[11]— and would, in fact, be a party to an aborted attempt on Lincoln's life a month before Booth struck successfully. Martin was also friendly in Toronto with Dr. Luke P. Blackburn, former chief surgeon in Sterling Price's division; the two men boarded at the same house. Blackburn was a native of Kentucky who had moved to Mississippi in the 1840s and won public commendation for his services during two yellow fever epidemics.[12] He and Martin discussed the feasibility of poisoning New York's water supply, but concluded that the amount of poison needed could not be obtained "without exciting suspicion." Headley, a modest, brown-haired younger officer—his beardless face struck some observers as feminine—tagged along with Martin wherever he went.

According to Commissioner Thompson afterward, it was Martin, "who having nothing else on hand" because of the failure of a plan to free Confederates from an Illinois prison camp, "expressed a wish to organize a corps to burn New York City."[13] Martin himself would later say he believed "the way to bring the North to its senses was to burn Northern cities."[14] The idea, however, had been fermenting for some time before Martin appeared in Canada. The election campaign in the North provided the catalyst: defeat of Lincoln became synony-

Colonel Jacob Thompson of Mississippi, head of the Confederate mission sent to Canada to initiate raids across the Union's weakest frontier, the more than one-thousand mile border between Canada and the United States. Courtesy of The New-York Historical Society.

Colonel Robert M. Martin, of Kentucky, leader of the Confederate band that tried to set fire to New York City. Courtesy of The New-York Historical Society.

Lieutenant John W. Headley, one of the Confederates who took part in the plot to burn New York City. Courtesy of The New-York Historical Society.

mous with defeat of the Union's war policy. The editorial in *The Richmond Whig,* many would later believe, was the signal to put the plan into effect.

It was an incredible scheme. Martin's small force was to be responsible for setting off a series of fires as a diversion while Copperheads seized Federal buildings and municipal offices, took control of the police department, freed prisoners from Fort Lafayette, and threw the Army commander in New York, Major General John Adams Dix, into a dungeon. By sunset, the Confederate flag would fly over City Hall! Following the success of the "revolution," a convention of delegates from New York, New Jersey, and the New England states was to be held in New York City to form a Confederacy that would cooperate with the government in Richmond and with the Northwest Confederacy that would also be set up.

The plan appeared valid to Thompson. The Draft Riots of July 1863, had indicated both how easily the city's embittered lower classes could be incited to riot and how ineffectual were New York's small police force and the token Federal detachment stationed there. Moreover, there was an active ring of Copperheads in the city, men of considerable power and influence. The Confederates reasoned that the Peace Democrats knew they would be persecuted if Lincoln was reelected, so that "They must yield to a cruel and disgraceful despotism or fight."[15]

Prominent among the New York Copperheads were the two Wood brothers, both congressmen. Before the war they had run a lottery concession in Louisiana. Fernando Wood, the older of the two, was an immaculately dressed, poker-faced corrupter who had risen on the shoulders of "two-penny" politicians to be elected mayor of the city three times. As mayor in January 1861, he had declared that if the South seceded "it behooves every distinct community, as well as every individual, to take care of themselves." New York, he had urged, should then become a "Free City."[16]

Wood's brother Benjamin published one of the most virulent anti-Lincoln newspapers, *The New York Daily News.* The *News* had been instrumental in fanning the hatred that led to the Draft Riots by suggesting that whites were being pressed into military service to free Negroes who would subsequently move north to take away their jobs. The *News*'s editor, Phineas Wright, a former New Orleans lawyer and plantation owner, was reputedly given $25,000 by Confederate agents to spread such stories.

There were other New Yorkers who could supposedly be trusted, too: James A. McMaster, editor and publisher of the weekly *Freeman's Journal and Catholic Register*; Representative James Brooks, co-owner of *The Evening Express* (and Fernando Wood's chief lieutenant); Rushmore G. Horton, editor of *The Weekly Day-Book*; and Hiram Cranston, proprietor of the New-York Hotel. In addition, it was believed that Governor Horatio Seymour, a misguided but sincere opponent of abolition, might aid the plan.[17] Seymour, among other things, was convinced that Lincoln Republicans were using the war to cement their power, and that the preservation of states' rights was the only way to prevent the emergence of a tyrannically controlled central government. Seymour had denounced the Emancipation Proclamation and called the draft unconstitutional.

As it was, the Peace Democrats were a strange mixture. Some were against the war because of the profiteering it had encouraged, others because personal liberties had been submerged. Still others feared the Republican party would swallow up their own, and there were those who were simply weary of war. In any case, Lincoln became the focus of their opposition: "despot," "filthy story teller," the worst of a bad lot. All the Copperhead arguments for peace, however, were imperiled by the mounting victories on the Union side. Even their presidential candidate, Major General George B. McClellan, had succumbed, abandoning the peace platform that the Democrats had forged when he, too, saw that the end was in sight. The only solution left to the Copperheads now was revolution.

McMaster, the publisher of *The Freeman's Journal*, was to be the liaison between the Confederates and the Copperheads. Their only other contacts in the city would be Larry McDonald's brother, Gus; Frank Clark, a former employee of McDonald's freighting company who now ran his own business; and a Captain E. Longmire of Missouri, who was already in New York conferring with McMaster.

Rob stayed in Toronto less than three weeks after his escape from Johnson's Island. Most of that time he was in seclusion with the others in the plot as a precaution—although the temptation to join in the banter around the bar in the Queen's Hotel, a rendezvous of Confederate exiles, must have been great. Headley remembered meeting nearly 100 soldiers and prominent citizens of the South within a few days of his arrival. "There was everything in the prospect in Toronto," he recalled, "to make the sojourn enjoyable."[18] Rob received money from Thompson for a new suit, food, and lodging, and had enough money left over to purchase a revolver and a small penknife.

Details of the plot were thrashed out in Thompson's suite at the Queen's Hotel, with Clay included in the final talks. Hines was to lead an attack on Chicago and Blackburn one on Boston to coincide with the raid in New York. Similar plans were afoot in Cincinnati and other cities.

Besides Rob, Martin, and Headley, the group going to New York would include five other men, all lieutenants: John T. Ashbrook, James T. Harrington, and James Chenault of Kentucky; John M. Price of Virginia; and a fifth man, whose name is unknown.[19] "Greek fire" was to be used. This was a mixture of phosphorus in a bisulfide of carbon that was commonly used in hand grenades. Igniting spontaneously on contact with the air, it had been employed earlier in an attack on shipping at St. Louis and in the St. Albans raid—but both times with unsatisfactory results. There was some question as to how to use it; however, the chemist who was preparing it was expected to provide the necessary directions.

The raid on St. Albans had created, according to Headley, "a profound sensation," alarming the people of the North from Maine to Minnesota—a "condition," the young Kentuckian said, "which was desired by the Confederacy."[20] The St. Albans raiders, led by Lieutenant Bennett H. Young, had been captured afterward by Federal troops on Canadian soil, and an international crisis had developed. Canadian protests resulted in Young and his men being turned over to Canadian authorities, who promised to prosecute them. Young, meanwhile, wrote a letter to *The Quebec Morning Chronicle* in which he defended his act in words that illustrated all too clearly the naive belief under which the New York expedition would also operate:

> I went there [St. Albans] for the purpose of burning the town and surrounding village as a retaliation for recent outrages in the Shenandoah Valley and elsewhere in the Confederate States. I am a commissioned officer in the "Provisional Army of the Confederate States" and violating no law of Canada.[21]

Jackson, Rob's roommate in Toronto, expressed similar feelings:

> We did things that one regrets being obliged to do; but we
> were responsible for our obedience, not our orders. We did what
> was commanded by our lawful superiors, and our actions were all
> legitimate under the horrible usages of war. The Federals fought
> us with fire and we fought them with fire; but it was a weapon
> that we did not love as did Sherman, . . . Sheridan, Butler, and
> others.[22]

Rob, for one, was thoroughly convinced that he was about to
engage in a legitimate act of war under Confederate orders. Martin, in
fact, carried with him a commission signed by Thompson, to be presented in the event they were caught as proof that they were acting
under official authority. Each of the eight Confederate officers was
given false papers for the trip. Martin was using his middle name,
Maxwell, as an alias, and would also go by the name of Drake. Headley also used his middle name, Williams, and was also known as
Smith. Rob's middle name, Cobb, was too well known in the North
thanks to "Cousin" Howell Cobb, now a Confederate general; instead, he sardonically chose the name of the Union Secretary of War,
Stanton. Rob also carried, as did Chenault, a letter of introduction to
Frank Clark. Martin secreted in the lining of his jacket Thompson's
commission and a letter of introduction to McMaster, and stowed in
his trunk the uniform and black-braided overcoat of a Federal officer.

On October 26, 1864—the day after Rob's twenty-ninth
birthday—the eight men, in civilian clothes, boarded a train in Toronto bound for the United States border. The phosphorus to start the
fires, they had been told, was not yet ready, but would be brought to
them by the chemist once they were in New York.[23]

chapter 9

he great characteristic of New York is din and excitement—everything is done in a hurry—all is intense anxiety," a guidebook of the time declared.[1] For a "magnificent panoramic view" of the city, it suggested climbing the steep steps to the tower of Trinity Church, 320 feet above the "Babel scene of confusion" on Broadway. Nearly 18,000 vehicles, it was estimated, passed along the thoroughfare. A visitor from England found it "crowded by cars, carts, omnibuses &c as at all times to render it difficult sometimes impossible to cross it."[2] Broadway, at the time, was synonymous with "patrician." The finest shops lined it: Lord & Taylor, Brooks Brothers, Knox the Hatter, Tiffany's.

Looking eastward from Trinity tower down Wall Street opposite, one saw, amid the closely packed banks and mercantile houses, the Treasury Building and Custom House. In the distance was the ferry that crossed the East River to Brooklyn. Turning northward, one saw Barnum's Museum, St. Paul's Chapel, the Astor House, City Hall, and—beyond City Hall Park—A. T. Stewart's Marble Palace, the city's largest department store. The Jersey shore was discernible across the Hudson to the west, over the top of the endless forest of masts along the docks. And to the south, finally, New York Harbor stretched like a carpet of water between the shores of Brooklyn, Staten Island, and New Jersey to the Atlantic Ocean.

Three times, fire had nearly razed the entire city. On September 21, 1776, the day before Nathan Hale was hanged, a blaze swept from Whitehall Slip up Broadway and Broad Street to City Hall, destroying all the buildings in its path, including Trinity Church. The British, who occupied the city, blamed it on American incendiaries. "The

Great Fire" of 1835 began on the evening of December 16 and continued to rage for nineteen hours in sub-zero weather. Nearly 700
buildings burned to the ground, including the Merchants Exchange
on Wall Street and what few structures were left in the Old Dutch
city. Virtually the same area was the scene of a similar fire on July 19,
1845, when 300 buildings were destroyed and thirty lives lost.

The city was so prone to flames that it was considered second only
to Constantinople in the world in point of the number of fires that
occurred each year. "You never pass a day without hearing the bells
going all over the city at least once a day, generally twice or three
times," the same English visitor noted in his diary. "When I first came
here I was surprised at the number of fires, but like the rest I very soon
got so use to it that the ringing of bells were nothing to me—I cared
not further."[3] Firefighting was in the hands of 125 volunteer companies, that, together, could assemble nearly 4,000 men. "It is a great pity
that their good name however is marred by the constant rows and
fights in which they are embroiled," the Englishman observed.
"Through these blood is often shed and lives sacrificed and all these
scenes arise from jealously [sic]."[4]

The volunteers' reputation had degenerated as the city expanded.
The upstanding businessmen who founded and became the first members of the various companies no longer had time to devote to fighting
fires. "The engine houses became loitering places for the idle and the
young and from which the young learned little except to become rude
in speech and imperious in manner," a buff complained. "It fostered
and brought forth a character very closely resembling the gamin in
Paris, familiarly known as the 'B'hoy.' "[5]

The firehouses, in effect, became social clubs, some of them luxu-
riously furnished. Such lavish attention was paid to the engines, hose
carts, and hook-and-ladder wagons, all of which were brightly colored
and embellished with paintings, that to be "dressed up like a fire
engine" became a popular epithet of dandyism. "Bunking" overnight
became widespread in the 1850s. It was encouraged by municipal officials as a way to speed the response to alarms, but the volunteers were
more interested in racing each other than in fighting fires. They insisted on dragging their cumbersome equipment through the city, instead of using horses. The difficulty was compounded by the wide
dispersal of the firehouses. There was only one pumper in all of lower
Manhattan south of Fulton Street, and but five to cover the heavily

built-up area around City Hall Park. As a result, most companies were responsible for responding to alarms in two of the city's eight fire districts.

An air of reckless abandon enveloped the city's social life, spurred, as the war dragged on, by the *nouveaux riches*: war contractors, most of them dishonest, who made no secret of their new wealth. Their critics described them by applying a derogatory label from the textile trade—the word used to describe the compound of refuse and sweepings that was rolled, glued, and smoothed into cloth for military uniforms—"shoddy," which fell apart in the rain or under the least strain. "Not to keep a carriage, not to wear diamonds, not to be attired in a robe which cost a small fortune, is now equivalent to being a nobody," *The New York Herald* lamented:

> The world has seen its iron age, its silver age, its golden age and its brazen age. This is the age of shoddy. The new brownstone palaces on Fifth Avenue, the new equipages at the Park, the new diamonds which dazzle unaccustomed eyes, the new silks and satins which rustle over loudly, as if to demand attention, the new people who live in the palaces and ride in the carriages and wear the diamonds and silks—all are shoddy . . . They live in shoddy houses. They ride in shoddy carriages, drawn by shoddy horses, and driven by shoddy coachmen who wear shoddy liveries. They lie upon shoddy beds, which have just come from the upholsterer's and still smell of shoddy varnish. They wear shoddy clothes purchased from shoddy merchants, who have erected mammoth stores, which appear to be marble, but are really shoddy. They set or follow the shoddy fashions, and fondly imagine themselves à *la mode de* Paris, when they are only à *la mode de* shoddy. Their professions and occupations are pure shoddy. They are shoddy brokers in Wall Street, or shoddy manufacturers of shoddy goods, or shoddy contractors for shoddy articles for a shoddy government. Six days in a week they are shoddy business men. On the seventh day they are shoddy Christians. They ride luxuriously to a shoddy church, where a shoddy clergyman reads to them from a shoddy Bible and preaches a shoddy sermon written on gilt-edged paper . . . Let us, then, enjoy the present, the park, the theatres and the opera, and leave the future to take care of itself. That is the sum of shoddy wisdom, and we shall not question such high authority.[6]

There was another side to the city—one you did not see from Trinity tower, or in the expensive stores along Broadway, or riding in Central Park, or at the amusement halls. As *Harper's Weekly* observed:

> A New Yorker contemplates his city with complacency. He moves among the busy streets down town, passes up Broadway, and looks with pride upon the long ranges of stately houses radiating from Madison Square. It is a very beautiful city, he says to himself, with satisfaction . . . That is certainly a just inference from the parts of the city of which we have spoken. But if the complacent observer will hear a few facts about the parts and people of the city that he has not seen in Wall Street, Broadway, or the Fifth Avenue, he will walk a little less proudly and speak more humbly. Of this population, 78,000 lives in damp, dark, dreary cellars, often under water, close to the most loathsome sinks, over-crowded, and reeking with filth and mortal disease. There is never sound health in them, and the constant sickness-rate ranges from 75 to 90 per cent.
>
> Of this population 500,000 live in tenant-houses. These buildings are of two classes—front and rear. Between them is the well-hole, as it is called, in which are the sinks and cesspools, from which the disgusting odor constantly penetrates every recess of the buildings with sickness and death. Every hideous form of misery and vice, hunger, murder, lust, and despair, are found in every corner. There is nothing that makes human nature repulsive or human life intolerable that does not abound in these tenant-houses.[7]

Most of those who lived in these hovels were foreign-born. There were more than 200,000 Irish, 120,000 Germans, and 50,000 from other European countries in the city, living astride what *Harper's Weekly* called "dusty avenues to wealth—these vestibules where fraud contends with honor for an entrance into the temple."[8] The Irish, many of whom emigrated to New York after the potato famine of 1848, were the most clannish of the foreign-born groups, intensely resentful of authority. Many of them were illiterate, and were forced to contend with the 10,000 Negroes living in the city for the most menial jobs. They openly scorned the blacks. They were not, however, alone in their anti-Negro attitude: prejudice extended to all social and economic levels. Negroes lived in separate communities and were never seen in public with whites except in the position of servants, which most of them were. Discrimination even extended to the city directory, which, when it listed a Negro, always followed his name with the note "(col'd)."

The tenement neighborhoods represented the seamiest side of the city; they were home to more than 600 brothels and 75 "concert halls" of ill repute, upwards of 8,000 liquor stores and saloons, and 3,300 prostitutes. The Bowery epitomized the worst of these areas—a maze of narrow, filthy streets and alleyways at whose center lay Five Points, an open triangle of space east of Broadway where Worth, Baxter, and Park streets converged. Gangs of toughs controlled it without interference from the police.

It was on just such "stews," the *Harper's Weekly* article concluded, that Fernando Wood and other politicians of his ilk fed.

On Friday morning, October 28, 1864, two men representing opposing factions of the Democratic party in New York held separate conferences within twenty blocks of each other. One, a Peace Democrat, was plotting the overthrow of the Federal authority. The other, a War Democrat, was pondering ways to maintain order in the face of reports of new rebel outbreaks.

At 5 Tryon Row, a block east of City Hall Park, James A. McMaster of *The Freeman's Journal* was welcoming three visitors from Canada who gave their names as "Stanton," "Maxwell," and "Williams."[9] McMaster had already received a note by mail from Jacob Thompson in Toronto alerting him to their arrival. He could match the handwriting against the letter of introduction that "Maxwell" now handed to him.

In the meantime, at his office at 49 Bleecker Street, between Mott and Mulberry, Major General John Adams Dix was discussing with his staff the wording of General Orders No. 80. Dix, commander of the Department of the East since the Draft Riots of July 1863, also had a message from Canada. It warned that Confederate agents were planning raids to coincide with the election eleven days away.

McMaster was a hulk of a man—six foot three, with a large face, broad forehead, a Roman nose. He had piercing eyes and spoke in a deep voice. Everything about him connoted power, and yet he was playing a somewhat ambivalent role. He was "chief manager" of the

New York Copperheads, but was on record as stating that he would not take an active part in the uprising once it started. It was a disturbing caution, and one that his New York colleagues exercised even more strongly.

To Rob and his companions, however, McMaster displayed no hesitancy—even when "Maxwell," who was watching the street outside the newspaper office's windows, seemed suddenly agitated; he thought he recognized the fat man who was walking on the other side of the street as someone he had recently seen in Toronto.

McMaster peered out the window. It was Young, he explained— "Old" Young, head of the city's detectives, who were often sent as "spies" with Federal authority into Canada.

The three Confederates must have exchanged worried looks because McMaster quickly suggested that they meet elsewhere the next day. (Longmire would join their talks tomorrow, Saturday.) Rob and the others agreed. For the moment, the three men could be reached at the St. Denis Hotel, at Broadway and 11th Street, but they planned to change quarters regularly to avoid detection.

General Dix was a stern-visaged, uncompromising native of New Hampshire, an Old Testament patriarch who wore a collar of whiskers under his chin. Sixty-six years old, he had had a distinguished career, noted for its integrity. Dix had first gone to war at the age of fourteen in 1812. Afterward, he studied and practiced law. He had held a succession of high appointive positions in New York State before his election to the United States Senate in the 1840s. President Buchanan named him Postmaster of New York in 1859 following a scandal in the department, and two years later appointed him Secretary of the Treasury to replace a secessionist.

One of Dix's first acts as secretary was characteristic. To a Federal revenue cutter threatened with seizure by Southerners in New Orleans, Dix wired: "If any man pulls down the American flag, shoot him on the spot."[10] He was as rigid regarding his own party and the Confederacy. A major prerequisite for healing Democratic wounds, he declared, was "a prosecution of the war with all the vigor that can be infused into it until the Rebellion is suppressed not for the subjugation of the Southern people, but for the overthrow of the leaders, who reject all compromise under the Constitution, and who should be expelled from the country or compelled to submit to the authority of the Government, and suffer the punishment due to their crimes."[11]

The general was, understandably, a worried man as the presidential election drew close. The Department of the East covered the New England States, New Jersey, and New York. Consequently, he was charged with protecting a major portion of the border with Canada, which was being increasingly pierced by Confederate raiders. To defend the area, Dix had only the most meager of forces—a combination of invalided veterans and unreliable state militia. His General Orders No. 80 indicated his concern:

> Satisfactory information has been received by the Major-General that rebel agents in Canada design to send into the United States, and colonize, at different points, large numbers of refugees, deserters and enemies of the Government, with a view to vote at the approaching Presidential election; and it is not unlikely, when this service to the rebel cause has been performed, that they may be organized for the purpose of shooting down peaceable citizens and plundering private property, as in the recent predatory incursions . . . at St. Albans. Against these mediated outrages on the purity of the elective franchise and these nefarious acts of robbery, incendiarism and murder, it is the determination of the Major-General commanding to guard by every possible precaution, and to visit on the perpetrators, if they shall be detected, the most signal and summary punishment . . .[12]

Dix ordered all Southerners within the Department of the East to register with the Army immediately, adding that

> those who fail to comply with this requirement will be regarded as spies or emissaries of the insurgent authorities in Richmond, and will be treated accordingly.[13]

Did Dix really believe all Southerners could be registered in the short time remaining before Election Day—if, indeed, they showed up at all? Observers guessed that there were anywhere from 10,000 to 50,000 Southern refugees—men, women, and children—in New York City alone.[14] General Orders No. 80 appears to have been little more than a bluff, couched in vague terms:

> Should any of these malefactors succeed in perpetrating their crimes, effective measures will be taken to prevent their return to Canada; and for this purpose special directions will be given, and suitable guards for the frontier will be provided . . .[15]

Dix did not have enough men to defend New York City, let alone the border with Canada. He was, however, pressing Washington for additional troops.

For the next six days, Rob and the other Confederate officers continued to meet secretly with McMaster and Longmire, unaware that reports of their plot were not only reaching Dix but were also being studied in Washington. Dix's General Orders No. 80 was carried by local papers on the weekend of October 29–30, but the conspirators apparently found in it no hint that the general knew the true nature of what was planned.

On Saturday the twenty-ninth, they met with McMaster and Longmire briefly. Another meeting was scheduled for Monday with Longmire—a tall, good-looking man who wore a moustache and goatee, and spoke with a twang.

McMaster, in the meantime, invited Rob and the others to dinner at his home on West 50th Street, off Ninth Avenue, on Sunday the thirtieth.[16] They spent the entire afternoon afterward going over details of the proposed uprising. McMaster openly talked about the Copperhead organization, at one point declaring that it had already enlisted "about 20,000" men and distributed smuggled arms among them. The uprising would start as soon as the Confederates had started a sufficient number of fires in various parts of the city to clog the streets with people and prevent any effective resistance. Copperhead commanders would then take possession of the city and all its approaches. The Confederates, in turn, promised "open, bold, and unflinching action when the hour arrived for crucial duty."[17]

Just before they were about to leave, McMaster told them he would ask Governor Seymour to send a "confidential agent" to confer with them. He was certain, he said, that the Governor would remain officially neutral and not use the state militia to suppress the rebellion. McMaster added that he would summon the Southerners once he heard from Seymour in Albany.

The meeting with Longmire the next day, Monday the thirty-first, was a perfunctory one. He was making arrangements to secrete the chemicals once they arrived but they had not as yet reached the city.

That afternoon, Rob went to the offices of Frank Clark, Larry McDonald's former employee, at 136 Fulton Street, near the heart of the city. He handed Clark a letter signed by McDonald:

> Allow me to introduce to you one of our college boys, about spending his vacation in the city. Of course, any favors or attention you can show him, do so and oblige, &c.[18]

Clark didn't ask any questions. He escorted Rob across the street to the Belmont Hotel and told the bookkeeper, a friend, that Rob was "a gentleman that wished to obtain a room there." It was only when Rob was signing the register that Clark discovered his name, "Stanton." At that point, Chenault entered the lobby. Earlier in the day, Clark had been handed a similar letter by Chenault and had helped to get him a room at the Belmont, too. Rob and Chenault acted as if they didn't know each other, and Clark—much to their amusement—introduced them to each other.

The eight young Confederates dispersed about the city in various hotels and boarding homes. Rob stayed at the Belmont Hotel for three days before moving to a rooming house at 89 Prince Street, between Broadway and Mercer. It was run by a widow, Mrs. Lydia P. Oatman, and her daughter, Mrs. Carrie Owens. At the same time, two of the other Confederates, Martin and Headley, made contact with Gus McDonald, a Southern agent, at his piano store at 358 Broadway. They used the side entrance on Franklin Place.[19] McDonald arranged to pick up their baggage, which was still checked at the train depot, and to cart it to his store, where it was kept for safety and convenience. While at his store, the two young Confederates met his niece, Larry McDonald's pretty, red-haired daughter, Katie. She worked there and knew all about her uncle's secret activities.

Martin and Headley, with time on their hands until they heard from McMaster or Longmire, decided to sightsee around the city. They had never been in New York before.

On Wednesday, November 2, Mayor Charles Godfrey Gunther of New York received an unusual telegram from Secretary of State William H. Seward:

> This Department has received information from the British Provinces to the effect that there is a conspiracy on foot to set

fire to the principal cities in the Northern States on the day of
the Presidential election. It is my duty to communicate this information to you.[20]

Seward sent similar telegrams to the mayors of Chicago, Buffalo,
Detroit, Cleveland, Albany, Philadelphia, New Haven, Providence,
Boston, Portland (Maine), and the Massachusetts cities of Ports-
mouth, Newburyport, and Salem.

McMaster could not have known about the telegrams when he
summoned Rob and the others to his office the next morning—
Thursday, November 3. The Confederates met with Governor Seymour's private secretary, who assured them that the Governor was
ready to cooperate by remaining neutral. The Confederates left the
meeting elated.

Later that afternoon, the text of Seward's telegram was made public. Even so, Rob and the others apparently still found nothing to
indicate that the Federal Government had damaging information.
However, the next morning, four days before the election, Major General Benjamin F. Butler—the devious, ambitious, vain, and pot-bellied
"Beast" of New Orleans—arrived in New York City. Rumors said he
was bringing 15,000 troops with him, to stem any disorders that might
accompany the voting.

The conspirators were shocked—and to their further dismay, Butler moved into the Fifth-Avenue Hotel. They decided to set up a
watch on the general's activities, hoping the rumors were false. They
soon proved true, however. Butler's personal entourage was so large—
he brought his wife and daughter along—that he had to leave the
Fifth-Avenue because it didn't have enough available rooms. He
switched to the Hoffman House, a new hotel a block north of the
point where Broadway cut across Fifth Avenue.

The Confederate officers lurked about the Hoffman House as it
took on the semblance of an Army field camp. Blue-uniformed officers and orderlies crowded its lobby, and sentries patrolled the corri-
dors. Horses were hitched outside, and dispatch riders rushed back
and forth through the entranceway and up and down the stairway to
Butler's suite of twelve rooms on the first floor. By a stroke of fate,
they were next to the rooms occupied by the corpulent, aging Win-
field Scott, who had retired as General in Chief of the Army shortly
after the outbreak of the war.

One room of the twelve was set up as a telegraph center, with an operator on duty twenty-four hours of the day. Sixty wires were strung into it, providing the general with direct contact not only with the War Department in Washington, but also with every major city in the state and every police station and polling place in the city.

Butler went into immediate consultation with Police Superintendent Kennedy, poring over maps of the city throughout the day. Kennedy was one of the few city officials whom Washington authorities trusted implicitly. The superintendent, on his own, had sent detectives to Baltimore in February 1861, to check on rumors of an attempt on Lincoln's life during his trip to the capital for his inauguration.[21]

Butler and Kennedy worked out a system of barricades to confine a riot, should one break out in the streets. Officers and scouts were selected to augment patrolmen at each polling place. All the city's volunteer firemen were put on standby duty. Chief Engineer John Decker alerted all bell-ringers in the fire towers to be on the lookout for fires, and to doublecheck against false alarms.

Although rumors had spread that as many as 15,000 soldiers were on their way to New York, Butler actually had less than 3,500 to work with. His request for 5,000 troops was turned down because the men were needed on the front lines in Virginia. The situation, in addition, was a delicate one. For one thing, most of the troops were New Yorkers who had already voted in the field by absentee ballot and could not enter the state on Election Day without voiding their votes.[22] Secondly, a show of force within the city itself was bound to be interpreted by anti-Lincoln elements as an Administration attempt to intimidate voters. As a result, the officers and scouts assigned to poll-watching duties were ordered to wear civilian clothes. Then, as the main body of troops arrived by ship from Virginia, Butler stationed them temporarily at Army posts on Staten Island and in Brooklyn. The posts, on Federal land, were not legally considered part of New York State.

Wisely, Butler demurred from accepting an offer to call out the state militia, reflecting that "if they were called out they would be under arms, and in the case of difficulty it was not quite certain which way all of them would shoot." Any armed forces in the confines of Manhattan on Election Day, he warned, would be treated "as enemies."[23]

As the day approached, Butler moved his men into position, setting up a cordon around Manhattan. He commandeered four ferry
boats and put his infantrymen aboard them; two were stationed in the
Hudson, the other two in the East River. Four swift tugs stood by with
steam up to carry messages back and forth, as needed. Artillery batteries, with their horses in harness, were on board a vessel on the Jersey
side of the Hudson. The general also positioned gunboats off the
Battery to protect the Federal buildings and Arsenal downtown, and
stationed a gunboat at High Bridge on the Harlem River to guard the
Croton Aqueduct link with the new reservoir on York Hill in Central
Park.

The Copperheads were thoroughly demoralized; many were afraid
they would be arrested. Only Horton of the *Day Book* and Brooks of
the *Express*, McMaster reported, wanted to go ahead with the plot.
The rest were wavering.

On Sunday, November 6, two days before the election, McMaster
sent for Rob, Martin, and Headley and expressed his doubts that the
plot could be put into execution. On the next day, he said the Copperhead leaders had held a conference and decided to postpone
action. The delay, he insisted, was only temporary: the plan would be
revived once the election went off without incident and the troops
were withdrawn.

That afternoon, however, reports reached New York that a number of Copperhead leaders and Confederate agents in Chicago had
been arrested. Then, when Election Day passed quietly not only in
New York but also in Buffalo, Boston, Cleveland and other major
cities, the Confederate band in New York was hard put to explain the
lack of concerted action.

It is impossible to pinpoint who was responsible for divulging the
various uprisings that were to have taken place on Election Day. The
Federal Government, in fact, had several sources of information. Its
most famous spy, Felix Stidger, had won the confidence of Copperheads in the Midwest. Another, Colonel Lafayette C. Baker, the notorious head of what he himself styled the Secret Service, was later
credited by one paper with finding out the details of the New York
plot. Secretary of State Seward had been warned by the United States
consul in Halifax. Charles A. Dana, Assistant Secretary of War, said

the conspiracy came to light in a letter intercepted in transit from Clay in Canada to Judah Benjamin in Richmond.[24] Headley, in his memoirs, blamed Hyams, calling him "the traitor or spy in our camp." Hyams, he noted, had been mysteriously absent from Toronto during the Confederates' sojourn in New York. Hyams also fits the description of one of the informers who leaked the operation to release the prisoners from Johnson's Island earlier in the fall, when Rob had been confined there.

McClellan won New York City, 73,716 votes to 36,687, but Lincoln took the nation, losing only three states. His victory, coupled with the battlefield triumphs of Sheridan and Sherman, completely dispelled the mood of failure on which the Copperheads had fed. On the local level, Copperheads in New York looked with foreboding on the future—especially since Fernando Wood, their leader, had lost his contest for reelection to the House.

Exasperated but persistent, the eight Confederates continued to watch Butler's comings and goings, hoping to persuade McMaster to take action while there was still time.

chapter 10

Rob stayed in seclusion at Mrs. Oatman's boarding house for more than two weeks, although the other seven Confederates were purposely moving regularly from one hotel or rooming house to another to avoid detection. Rob tarried because he was apparently having an affair with Ann Cullen, the chambermaid. There was always the danger of disclosure. At least one member of the West Point class of 1858 was on duty in the city—Royal T. Frank, attached to the Army recruiting office as acting assistant adjutant general. Moreover, Rob's old friend, Edwin H. Stoughton, was practicing law in New York, his Army career having washed out.

The days passed slowly, frustratingly, as the Confederates bided their time—and as their spirits sagged. By contrast, the mood around Butler's headquarters at the Hoffman House changed after Election Day from one of intense anxiety to one of light-hearted gaiety. The general began a round of social engagements, openly defying his many enemies in the city. He answered one threat—that he would be strung up from a lamppost if he appeared on Broadway—by taking a ride in Central Park and attending the opera, and he used the abusive letters he received as "cigar-lighters." "Truth crushed to earth," he announced, for all to hear, "may rise again, but they [the rebels] never will." At a banquet in his honor at the Fifth-Avenue Hotel, he boasted that "Peace hath her victories no less renowned than war, and of all the peaceful victories ever yet achieved in the interests of human freedom, that achieved in the peaceful quiet which most brooded over this land on the 8th of November was the greatest."[1]

The Confederates continued to badger McMaster, but the more they insisted on carrying out the plan the more vacillating McMaster became. To while away their time between meetings with the Copperhead publisher, Martin and Headley continued to tour the city. They took in the wit Artemus Ward at Dodworth Hall, and went by ferry to Brooklyn to hear Henry Ward Beecher preach. They also spent several nights in brothels.

Unknown to them, however, detectives were following them, for informers were continuing to visit the authorities. A "man from Richmond" appeared at police headquarters, saying he knew that $20,000 had been set aside to purchase phosphorus and to hire incendiaries.[2] He claimed to be acquainted with some of the conspirators, and offered to assist in ferreting them out if the Government would take care of his family. Ignored, the "man from Richmond" left the city in disgust. Chief Engineer John Decker of the Fire Department passed along a tip he received to the police but heard nothing about it afterward. A blockade runner got drunk in a saloon on Lispenard Street and talked of a plan that "would startle the community"; he said a hotel on Broadway was being used as a meeting place for rebel officers who were in the city to take part in it. Sergeant Young assigned two detectives to check out the story of a local resident who said that a plan to burn the city on election night had been postponed but was certain to be put into execution. He even gave a description of the conspirators, named the places to be set on fire, and provided other particulars. The detectives gave up trying to verify his story, however, concluding that it was a figment of the man's imagination.

The difficulty was, as the *Times* pointed out, that "the city is literally swarming with rebel adventurers, of an irresponsible and dangerous class." Young's nineteen-man detective force, swamped with work, could not begin to keep track of all the suspected Confederate agents. They apparently gave up following Martin and Headley after a week in which they could uncover nothing incriminating. At the same time, Detective Young returned from Canada, where he had gone to sound out post-election Rebel schemes. His report was relayed to General Dix, who, in turn, wrote the War Department on November 12 that he had decided to "let all the regulars return at once to Genl. Grant":

This decision has been influenced very strongly by the report of a very intelligent detective who returned from Canada this morning. He is confident there will be no more raids under rebel organization, though there may be small gangs of plunderers on the frontier . . .[3]

At last on Tuesday, November 15—the first snow of the season fell that day—Butler left New York to return to the front, "thus ending," the *Times* sighed with relief, "the movement on the part of the Government for the protection of New-York from the horrors of riots and bloodshed."

Rob and the others immediately pressed McMaster to agree to Thanksgiving Day, November 24, as the date for putting their plan into operation. Here was the chance, they insisted, to strike an effective blow at the North. They marshalled every argument they could think of: New York was now undefended, an attack on the city would relieve Lee in Virginia, there was still time to force peace on the North. McMaster hedged; he wanted time to think. Within twenty-four hours he had made up his mind—or rather William Tecumseh Sherman had made it up for him. More than 850 miles away in Georgia, Sherman set out with 60,000 troops from Atlanta, leaving that city in ruins, his destination unknown but profoundly feared. The Copperheads' determination collapsed completely. The defeat of the South, they believed, could no longer be stayed. McMaster withdrew from any further connection with the plan, which he now saw as doomed to failure.

Longmire was also growing reluctant. When the promised chemist never arrived from Canada, it was he who had arranged locally for a supply of "Greek fire" and also purchased quantities of turpentine and rosin. The Copperheads' withdrawal, however, threw a new light on the undertaking. The only thing that would be accomplished now, he said, would be the destruction of property and the loss of lives.

Rob and the other Confederates were dazed by the turn of events. An angry discussion took place. Price argued that they should return to Canada while they still could do so in safety. Rob was for carrying out their part of the overall plot—that is, for setting fire to the city. A new reason for carrying out their part of the conspiracy began to emerge: revenge. It was spurred by news reports that were beginning to reach New York detailing Union ravages in the Shenandoah Valley. Typical was a story in the anti-Administration *Daily News*. It re-counted how two divisions of Philip H. Sheridan's cavalry, under Grant's orders, had swept through the rich farmland, destroying more than 1,000 barns, scores of mills, hundreds of acres of unharvested corn, 300,000 bushels of harvested corn, 500 barrels of flour, more than 600,000 bushels of wheat:

> If two divisions of Sheridan's army have done all this de-struction, how much more shocking must be the total amount of that work done by the whole army! If in addition to this burning, breaking and destroying be added the plundering that has been carried out under the plea of subsistence off the country, the cruel ferocity of those outrages upon the inoffensive women, chil-dren, and old men of the Valley of the Shenandoah may well be regarded with an emotion of sickening horror.[4]

"Desolation," said the *News* in another article, "reigns in silence over the dismal scene."[5]

The fate of the people of the Shenandoah struck a responsive chord among the Confederates, many of whom had friends and rela-tives in Virginia. Rob, for his part, must have feared that a similar fate awaited his family in Louisiana. Stories were already circulating about the deprivations those remaining in Confederate Louisiana were suf-fering. The *Times*, for example, carried an account from *The Louisiana Democrat* of Alexandria under the heading, "Hard Times in Western Louisiana":

> The condition of affairs, of what was once the State of Loui-siana, is becoming really alarming. The long-dread Winter at hand, the town and country filled with a population whose pros-pects for a subsistence, at best, were precarious, but doubly so now by the action of the Government; hundreds of families, many of them those of soldiers, whose only means of living is the little store of Confederate money they, by the most pinching economy, had managed to save, is rendered worthless by the ne-glect of the Government in not providing the necessary facilities to enable them to exchange the old issue for the new. . . . Doubt-less there are a few among us who will be enabled to pass through the Winter without much actual suffering, but the majority, the

mass of the people, must and will be upon the verge of starvation
and freezing long before Spring. . . .[6]

The *Times* concluded with the comment, "This is about the average character of all the stories which refugees and 'intelligent contra-
bands' [former slaves] have to tell—a tale of want, misery, suffering."

Looking about him at the carefreeness, the luxury of a New York
virtually untouched by war, Rob urged that the small band go ahead
with plans to burn the city as "a lesson."

Martin, Headley, Chenault, Ashbrook, and Harrington agreed.
Thompson in Toronto had been told "he could expect to hear from us
in New York, no matter what might be done in other cities," Headley
said. "He seemed to approve our determination and hoped for no
more failures, and especially now when our last card was to be
played."[7]

Determined to succeed, Rob and his colleagues laid their plans at
a small cottage astride Central Park lent to Longmire—no questions
asked—by a Southern woman, a refugee. There they worked out the
details, deciding from the start to ignore Federal and municipal buildings because these were guarded.

The easiest places of access—and the glaring symbols of the
North's wealth—were the city's hotels. There were more than 125 in
the city, the most opulent of them on Broadway. The Astor House,
across from City Hall Park, was the grande dame of them all, built of
solid granite, with accommodations for 400 persons: the largest hotel
in the nation when it opened in 1836. In the years since, bigger and
more sumptuous hotels had been built, but the Astor remained popular with politicians, who liked to dine in the splendid restaurant in
the center of the lobby, where a fountain had once stood.

Moving north on Broadway one came to the St. Nicholas Hotel,
ideally situated at the corner of Spring Street near many theatres:
Bryant's, the Broadway, the Menagerie, Wood's Minstrels. Many of its
guests were from the entertainment world—the Booth Brothers and
Phineas T. Barnum, among others—but it had also been a favorite
stopping place for an unlikely assortment of Americans—"Stonewall"
Jackson, Stephen A. Douglas, Matthew Vassar, Horatio Seymour.

Built at a cost of more than $1 million in 1854, the St. Nicholas was six stories tall and divided into three wings, with 600 rooms that held upwards of 1,000 guests. Magnificent chandeliers, candelabra, and mirrors graced its halls and three dining rooms, and the corridors were completely carpeted. The hotel's most impressive feature was its lobby, 200 feet long and 60 wide, with a massive oak staircase at its heart that led to the suites above. It required more than 300 employees to run the hotel.

Nearby, next door to Niblo's Garden at Prince Street, was the Metropolitan Hotel, a huge brownstone edifice that boasted 13,000 yards of carpeting and 12 miles of water and gas pipes. The Metropolitan, which cost $1 million to build and handled 600 lodgers with ease, had steam heating, transoms over its doors to provide a rudimentary form of ventilation, and "sky parlors" from which lady guests could watch the promenade on Broadway below. The interior decorations—the fancy silverware included—cost $200,000. The Metropolitan, like a number of other hotels, was conducted on the European plan, with or without meals.

A few blocks farther north was the marble-faced Lafarge House, adjoining the Winter Garden Theatre. Considered an "elegant resort" for the "floating population of the New World," the Lafarge could accommodate more than 500 guests.[8]

Perhaps the most impressive hotel of all was the "New" Fifth-Avenue, facing Madison Square where Broadway crossed Fifth Avenue. It had rooms for 800 guests and a "perpendicular railway," an innovation especially popular with the elderly and female guests who did not like to climb stairs. The Fifth-Avenue's public rooms off its lobby were crowded with gold brokers and speculators. The hotel was considered most eligible for visitors from the South because it was near the railroad depots. As an extra added attraction in its attempt to lure clientele from the more centrally located hotels, the Fifth-Avenue included a fourth meal ("late supper") in its daily rate of $2.50.

Although the other hotels throughout the city were less ostentatious, they were almost always full, too—especially given the unusual comings and goings spurred by the war. Lovejoy's on Park Row opposite City Hall Park, which was large enough to have several wings, catered to transient businessmen and travelers enroute to other parts of the Union; it held 250 overnight guests. A block away, the Tammany, the meeting place of Tammany Democrats, was well known for its hospitality, and a favorite lunching spot for businessmen and their clients. The United States, on Fulton Street near the East River, was a creaky but comfortable old wooden hotel filled with merchants and ship captains. Businessmen in the Wall Street area lunched regularly at the Howard, one of the largest and best conducted of the older downtown hotels.

Rob and each of the others took four hotels as targets. Rooms were to be taken in advance wherever possible, and paid for in advance for one week. Some use of the rooms was necessary to avert suspicion, although it was common practice for merchants to rent lodgings in advance from which to take side trips to the suburbs on business.

On Friday, November 18, a crisp fall day, Ashbrook and Harrington moved into the St. Nicholas Hotel. Two days later, Headley took a room at the Astor, where it was decided further conferences would be held.

That same day, as a severe rainstorm that would last thirty hours began,[9] another unexpected arrival frustrated further action. Harrington, entering the lobby of the Astor on his way to Headley's room, thought he saw "Butcher" Grant in the lobby. He was right.

Grant, however, in contrast to Butler, was trying to keep his presence in New York a secret. He was on a shopping expedition with his wife following a brief visit to their children's school in Burlington, New Jersey. It was Grant's first visit to the city since his graduation from West Point in 1843. Although he didn't want his presence announced, word nevertheless soon spread across the city.

Surprisingly undaunted, the Confederates continued to take rooms in hotels around the city, although holding their target date in abeyance. On Monday, November 21, Rob and Chenault took rooms at Lovejoy's, and Harrington checked into the Metropolitan on the same day. Chenault also registered at the Howard Hotel the following day, after which he and Rob took rooms at the Exchange Hotel.

Grant left on the twenty-first. The Confederates learned of his departure two days later, when newspapers carried accounts of an interview he had finally agreed to. Sherman's drive through Georgia toward the sea, he said, "is one of the most momentous of the war. Its success will unquestionably inflict on the Confederates considerable injury." Grant believed that the "desolation of the country along the Federal lines of march will, no doubt, be complete for a certain width."[10]

His words served to buttress the determination of Rob and his friends to retaliate against the North. Longmire, however, backed out, "discouraged" when they told him they planned to set the city on fire "and give the people a scare if nothing else, and let the Government· at Washington understand that burning homes in the South might find a counterpart in the North."[11] Longmire left for the countryside until the raid was over. Before doing so, however, he gave the Confederates the name, description, and address of the chemist on Washington Place where the "Greek fire" had been secreted. The materials had already been paid for.

Martin again took a room at the Fifth-Avenue, but he and the others were now meeting regularly at Headley's room at the Astor, number 204. Headley had taken it under the name of "W. S. Haines." Afterward, the chambermaid would recall that the fireplace had been extensively used, in order to keep the room warm for his many visitors.

Thanksgiving Day—Thursday, November 24, 1864—was a day of jubilation and prayer throughout the North. The war seemed to most people to be finally headed toward a victorious conclusion. To match the mood, it was a lovely Indian Summer day, sunny and moderate. Church bell answered church bell, families dressed in their holiday best walked hand-in-hand near Castle Garden at the Battery, horses snorted with eagerness as they reached the wide path running from 59th Street to the Mall in Central Park. Everywhere, whipped by the light breeze, flags rippled gallantly.

Tension, however, gripped the occupants of room 302 at the Metropolitan Hotel. Eight men crowded into the modest chambers, summoned there by Martin, who had used stationery offhandedly picked up at McDonald's piano store to write the messages. The room was Harrington's, taken under the name of "James Simson, Rochester."

The Confederates discussed who would go to get the "Greek fire" that Longmire had arranged for—a dangerous mission. Martin resolved the debate by choosing his "assistant adjutant general," the boyish-looking Headley.[12] Everyone would meet at the cottage off Central

Park in two hours to test the phosphorus. None of them knew for certain how to use it.

Headley found the chemist's shop in a basement on the west side of Washington Place, off Washington Square. He was greeted inside by a stocky, bearded old man. All he had to do was to tell him that Longmire had sent him for his luggage. The old man handed a valise over the counter without saying a word. It was heavier than Headley expected: carrying it, he had to change hands every ten paces. He had made no arrangements for a carriage and could find none, so he walked until he reached a streetcar going up Bowery to Central Park:

> The car was crowded and I had to put the valise in front of me on the floor in the passway, as the seats ran full length on each side of the car. I soon began to smell a peculiar odor—a little like rotten eggs—and I noticed passengers were conscious of the same presence. But I sat unconcerned until my getting off place was reached, when I took up the valise and went out. I heard a passenger say as I alighted, "There must be something dead in that valise."[13]

When Headley reached the cottage, two men were missing—Price and the officer whose name is unknown. They had backed out at the last minute. That left only six to carry out the plan.

Inside the valise Headley carried were 144 bottles, each filled with four ounces of what looked like water. The bottles were sealed with plaster of Paris.

Some experimentation took place outside the cottage.[14] The "Greek fire" was supposed to burn on contact with the air, but it also had a built-in escape factor: it took several minutes for it to ignite after absorption. A wooden floor might be too hard to absorb the fluid, but the bedding and mattresses in a hotel room would serve perfectly. Moreover, the six Confederates also had rosin and turpentine to speed the process, if necessary, and matches could be used, too.

Most of the men had already taken rooms at several hotels; the bookings that remained on their lists would be taken care of the next day, if possible, before they held a final parley. Wherever they could, they would drop off supplies of "Greek fire" in advance; where that wasn't possible, they would take additional bottles with them.

Rob, with rooms already at Lovejoy's and the Exchange Hotel, also drew the Tammany and New England hotels. The latter was a few blocks north and east of Five Points, the heart of the Bowery. Chenault, who had also taken a room at Lovejoy's, apparently turned over his key to Rob in case Rob had time to start a second fire. Chenault was to start out from a second room he had taken in advance at the Howard Hotel, and was also assigned Handfield's Hotel, on the East River near a lumber yard. Martin, who was registered at the Fifth-Avenue, would take the Lafarge, St. James, and Belmont hotels, too. Headley took the Astor, where he was staying, the United States Hotel, and the Everett House. Harrington had a room at the Metropolitan Hotel and also at the St. Nicholas, where Ashbrook was residing. (The two apparently decided to meet at the hotel.) As for Ashbrook, he would be responsible not only for the St. Nicholas, but for the Lafarge House as well. A number of other hotels—the Brandeth House, the St. Denis Hotel, the Hoffman House, the Gramercy Park Hotel—were also targets.

The fires would be started beginning at 8 P.M. The early evening hour was chosen, Headley said, "so that the guests of the hotels might all escape, as we did not want to destroy any lives."[15] The fires would be confined chiefly to the business district along Broadway or other commercial areas, although Headley was also to set some along the wharves of the Hudson—both to confuse the Fire Department and to destroy the valuable cargoes there.

To carry the "Greek fire," the Confederates had more than a dozen satchels. All were black except one, which was russet-colored. They packed some of them with bottles of phosphorus cushioned with newspapers, old clothing, and boots, and decided to pick up the rest of the valises the following evening at 6 P.M. As the men began to file out, Rob turned cheerfully to Headley, excited by the prospect of action at last: "We'll make a spoon or spoil a horn."[16]

part 4

THE FIRES: REPRISE

Wake up Jacob, day's a-breakin';
Meat's in the pot an' hoe-cake's a-bakin'.

chapter 11

The day began bleakly.[1] Rain splashed from dark clouds, blown by a chill wind from the northwest. It made puddles out of ruts in the streets and ankle-deep dams where curb met cobblestone.

Rob was staying at the Exchange Hotel on Greenwich Street—"a hissing and a desolation, a place of lager beer saloons, emigrant boarding houses, and the vilest dens."[2] The hotel was between Reade and Duane streets. Its rear rooms overlooked the Hudson River docks two blocks away. Unless the weather changed, the plans would have to be delayed again.

It must have rankled Rob and the five other Confederates to read that morning's *Times*. Sherman's movements and marching orders in Georgia shared the front page with reports of Thanksgiving celebrations across the Union North:

IV. The army will forage liberally on the country during the march . . .

    Yesterday was more generally observed as a national holiday than any preceding Thanksgiving we remember . . .

V. To Army Corps Commanders is intrusted the power to destroy mills, houses, cotton gins, &c . . .

    The people of this city felt that it was a day of thankfulness and gratitude, not merely for the fatness of the annual turkey which graced the family table, but for the comparative prosperity in all things . . .

VI.   As for horses, mules, &c . . . belonging to the inhab-
             itants, the cavalry and artillery may appropriate freely and
             without limit . . .

             An exciting political contest has passed away and not
             left in its track the devastating effects of bloody strife, as
             many feared and a few hoped. Victor and vanquished
             burned their animosities, united in thanking God for the
             material prosperity of the country in the midst of a de-
             structive war . . .[3]

There was an extraordinary number of advertisements for amuse-
ments, for the 25th of November was a holiday—Evacuation Day,
commemorating the eighty-first anniversary of the day in 1783 when
the last British troops left New York City after the Revolutionary
War.[4] Stores and theatres were expecting large crowds—the stores in
particular, after having been closed on Thanksgiving Day. The evening hours would be especially busy. The first American performance
of Donizetti's new opera, "Don Sebastino," was scheduled at the
Academy of Music, "Artemus Ward among the Mormons" at
Dodworth Hall, "The School of Reform" at Wallack's Theatre.
Barnum's Museum was adding a performance in the evening at its
Lecture-Room, a melodrama from London entitled "Waiting for the
Verdict." The widely acclaimed "The Corsican Brothers" was being
performed at Niblo's Garden. The largest advertisement of all an-
nounced a unique attraction at the Winter Garden: Edwin Booth as
Brutus, Junius Brutus Booth as Cassius, and John Wilkes Booth as
Mark Antony in "Julius Caesar."
       By noon the rain had stopped and the sky had cleared.

       A few hours later, according to later newspaper accounts, Rob
made his way through the mid-afternoon bustle to the Tammany Hotel on Nassau Street at Frankfort. He was carrying a small black
satchel. Rob limped into the lobby and went straight to the desk. He
put the bag down by his feet and rang the tiny bell on the counter. A
clerk appeared from the office behind. Rob asked for a room for several nights. The clerk looked through a list. Room 108, an upper
bedchamber, was available. The clerk pushed the registration book
and a pen toward him. Rob wrote "C. E. Morse, Rochester."[5] The
clerk handed him a key, and Rob leaned down to pick up his satchel.

A porter came over but Rob waved him away, saying his bag was light. Rob apparently found a hiding place: a wardrobe would have sufficed, or he may even have stashed it under the bed. In any case, he secreted the satchel and left the room, locking it behind him. He put the key in his pocket and went back downstairs.

It had gone without trouble, just as it had at Lovejoy's and at the Exchange earlier in the week. Nevertheless, Rob was nervous as he rejoined the crowds in the street. He went to get a drink, putting off taking another hotel room until after the rendezvous at the cottage at six o'clock.[6]

It was about three o'clock when Headley walked into the Everett House at Union Square and 17th Street. He asked for a room but none was available. Headley picked up his bag and was about to leave—but then he turned back. He asked the clerk if he could leave his valise until the evening when he returned; perhaps there would be a room available then. The clerk couldn't promise a room, but Headley persisted. He swung his bag with ease across the counter, and the clerk put it behind the desk. Something inside clinked as the bag touched the floor.

From Union Square, Headley took a streetcar down Bowery, then walked the rest of the way to the United States Hotel at Fulton and Water streets, a block from the East River slips. Again, no room was available. Headley tried persuasion: he wanted to dine at the hotel, too, he said. The proprietor, John F. Carlton, told him to come back later; maybe there would be a bed then.

The sun was setting. Ashbrook had an hour and a half to get up to Central Park for the final meeting—enough time to take a room at the Lafarge House. He checked in as "J. B. Richardson, Camden, N.J." and was shown to room 104 on the third floor, facing Bond Street. He let a porter carry his valise, which was heavy. (An old cavalry boot added to its weight.) Ashbrook left the room a few minutes later after hiding the bag.

The tension of being in the city for four weeks, of waiting for so long, caused Martin to hesitate. He had walked from his room at the

Fifth-Avenue Hotel two blocks north and across the confluence with Broadway and was pacing the lobby of the St. James Hotel, wondering if he hadn't waited too long to register. The bookkeeper watched him curiously. Martin finally made his decision. He walked up and said he wanted to engage a room. The bookkeeper asked for how long. Probably a week, Martin answered. The bookkeeper slowly leafed through some papers. Martin fidgeted. He'd like to be shown it with as little delay as possible, he said. Just then, the proprietor, James L. Harway, walked up to greet his new guest. Martin mumbled a salutation and abruptly turned back to the bookkeeper. The man laid the registration book open on the counter. Martin took the pen he was offered and wrote slowly, in a childish script, "John." He paused, then added "Schools" in a slightly better hand, and finally, with a calligraphic flourish, "Md.": "John Schools, Md."

Yes sir, Mr. Schools, the bookkeeper said. *Room 84 on the third floor.* The porter would carry his luggage.

Martin hesitated again. The bookkeeper thought he was embarrassed by the apparently scanty wardrobe he carried. It was hotel policy to have the porter show guests up to their rooms, he explained. Martin relented. He handed the valise to the porter and followed him closely up the stairway. He took the bag away as they reached his room, telling the porter he would not need his services further. Once alone, Martin lit the gas jet. He hid his valise, then left the room and locked it. He still had to get down to McDonald's store to pick up the Federal uniform from his trunk there.

Rob met the others as arranged at six o'clock at the cottage. The Confederates completed packing the rest of the valises with bottles of phosphorus. They then stuffed their pockets with vials until their clothes bulged. There was a final runthrough of their plans, and a time was set at which to meet the next day—if everything went as scheduled.

"We were now ready," said Headley, "to create a sensation in New York."[7]

chapter 12

ob apparently took a streetcar down Bowery. As it passed Bayard Street, he decided to get off and start with the New England Hotel. It was a relatively small hotel—only 120 guests could be accommodated overnight—but he got a room. He signed the register as "Geo. Morse," again using the surname he had employed at the Tammany Hotel. He was shown to room 58 on the second floor.

As soon as he entered the room and closed the door, Rob began pulling at the bedclothes and mattress until they were in a pile on the bed. He threw a chair on top, to keep them from falling. He opened the carpetbag that he brought with him and uncapped one of the bottles he took from inside it. He poured the contents quickly over the pile. It saturated everything, so he put the second bottle from the valise in an already bulging pocket of his coat and tossed the bag onto the heap on the bed. He left the empty phosphorus bottle on the floor.

Less than five minutes later, Rob was limping hurriedly down the corridor, making for the staircase. He passed the night watchman without a word. The man stopped to watch Rob take the stairs almost at a run. Rob slowed his pace as he approached the desk below. He turned in his key, explaining that he was going out for a walk.

He had less than ten blocks to go from the New England Hotel to Lovejoy's. He had the keys to two rooms there—his own and Chenault's.

At that hotel, on Park Row opposite City Hall Park, Rob went immediately to his room, number 121, which he had taken four days earlier under the name of "William H. Warren, Schnectady." It was

Map shows the scope of the area of New York City imperiled by the Confederate attack. In addition to the fires set at the eleven hotels pictured here, a fire was also set at the New England Hotel in the densely populated Bowery district northwest of City Hall Park. There were also fires on the Hudson River docks near the one shown and at a lumber yard. *Map:* courtesy of The New-York Historical Society; *hotels: Frank Leslie's Illustrated Newspaper,* December 17, 1864. Reprinted by permission of the American Heritage Publishing Company.

four flights up, in the northeast wing. Rob repeated the procedure performed earlier at the New England Hotel, only this time he piled the bedding and the mattress in the center of the floor rather than on the single bed, which he judged as too narrow to hold it all. Before locking the door, he closed the windows and shutters. He reached Chenault's room, number 91 (taken under the name of "J. Jones, Schnectady"), in the southeast wing of the same floor, without passing anyone along the way. Again, he rapidly threw the bedding together and doused it with phosphorus. In his rush, however, he left unopened a bottle of phosphorus and two vials of turpentine that he had meant to pour onto the heap of blankets, towels, sheets, and drapes. He locked the room and headed for the stairs.

Chenault walked up to his room, number 44, on the fourth floor of the Howard Hotel on lower Broadway, without being seen. He had taken it three days earlier, signing in as "S. M. Harner, Philadelphia." He piled the bedding together in a heap on the bed, and flung a chair and the wooden washstand on top. He emptied two bottles of phosphorus on the pile, leaving one empty bottle on the bed and the other on the floor. He locked the door as he left, and passed by the desk downstairs again without being noticed. He walked out onto Broadway, in the financial district off Maiden Lane. He headed toward City Hall Park, apparently in order to catch a streetcar to the next hotel on his list. Somewhere in the vicinity of Park Row, however, he met Rob. As yet they could hear no fire alarms, so Rob suggested they see what was happening on Broadway: the other Confederates had had ample time to start some fires by now.

Ashbrook and Harrington were at the St. Nicholas Hotel on Broadway at Spring Street. Ashbrook was in room 139, in the middle building of the sprawling hotel. He had taken it a week earlier, registering as "J. T. Allen, Albany." To make certain his fire would spread, Ashbrook took a box of matches from his jacket and dumped them on the saturated mound on the bed, then tossed a sperm candle from the mantel onto it. He locked the door behind him, and headed downstairs to wait for Harrington.

Harrington, meanwhile, was in room 174 on the sixth floor of the front building, which he had taken the same day as Ashbrook, using the alias "C. S. Harrison, New Jersey." He finished dumping phosphorus on the bedclothes on the bed and left, locking the door. He went downstairs and joined Ashbrook as a well-dressed merchant passed by. "It's all right," Harrington said.[1] They both headed for the main door.

On reaching the street outside, Ashbrook and Harrington walked north on Broadway. After a block and a half they parted, in front of the Metropolitan Hotel. Harrington went inside the hotel, while Ashbrook continued on to the Lafarge House a little more than a block away.

"Mr. Nicks, Portville, Pa." was unsealing several bottles of phosphorus in his room, number 148, on an upper floor at the Fifth-Avenue Hotel. Martin put the drawers from the bureau, two chairs, and the bedding in a corner of the room and tossed rosin all about. He flung a box of six cartridges soaked in turpentine into another corner and scattered a dozen other cartridges throughout the room. He had two satchels—the one previously secreted in the room and the other he'd carried from the cottage. He left one bag, but also—carelessly—three sealed bottles of phosphorus.

Martin had only two short blocks to go to reach the St. James Hotel. He went up to room 84 on the third floor taken earlier in the day as "John Schools, Md." As at the Fifth-Avenue, apparently no one paid any heed to him or to the Federal overcoat he wore. Martin took the satchel from its hiding place, removed a bottle, soaked the bedding in phosphorus, and then scattered matches around the room. He threw the carpetbag into a corner, leaving in it several unopened vials of phosphorus. He picked up his other black valise and left, locking the door behind him.

His next assignment was the Belmont Hotel in the heart of the city—on Fulton Street, between Nassau and Broadway. On entering, he must have seen Lieutenant James M. Kellogg signing the register. Martin apparently also heard the clerk tell the officer that his room was not made up yet. The officer replied that he would return later after dining, and moved away. On an off-chance, Martin walked up the stairs to Kellogg's room (number 28) on the second floor and found it open. He undid the bed, tossing all the linens into a heap, then opened several bottles of phosphorus and poured them out.

Again leaving a carpetbag containing several sealed bottles, he has-
tened from the room.

Headley was at the Everett House on Union Square at 17th Street
by about 7:30 P.M. In his haste, he'd left his room at the Astor House
in midtown after soaking the floorboards with phosphorus instead of
dousing the bedding and furniture. He left his room at the Astor—
number 204, on the top floor, registered under the name of "W. S.
Haines"—with the night table, chairs, and washstand on top of the
mattress over the wet flooring. Headley also forgot to retrieve three
bottles of turpentine secreted in the room, and left a carpetbag without checking its contents. Inside it, in Martin's handwriting on Mc-
Donald's stationery, was the summons for the conference held at the
Metropolitan Hotel on Thanksgiving Day.

The clerk at the Everett was the same one who had been on duty
nearly five hours earlier. The clerk again told Headley there was no
room available. He returned the valise Headley had left. The Confederate could do nothing but leave.

He proceeded to the United States Hotel, at Fulton and Water
streets near the East River, where he'd also tried to get a room earlier.
As he reached there, at about 8:45 P.M., he heard in the distance the
sound of the first fire bells being rung. The tolling came from the City
Hall fire tower to the northeast.

Once inside the United States Hotel, Headley reminded its
owner, John F. Carlton, that he had sought a room a few hours ago.
Carlton, wary of burglars, was suspicious of the light bag Headley
carried. He said he didn't think a room was available. Determined,
Headley said he only needed a room for the night. Carlton gave in.
Headley signed the register as "William B. Brown" and was given
room 172 on the fifth floor. When he reappeared downstairs ten minutes later, Carlton grew suspicious again. He remembered Headley's
having said the first time that he would be staying for dinner. He
moved to intercept Headley but was too late: Headley had disappeared
through the door. Carlton debated whether to search his room for
burglaring tools.

Headley headed toward Broadway, five blocks west. By now, the
fire bells were sounding continuously from several parts of the city,
and helmeted volunteers were rushing with their engines, hose carts,

and ladder wagons in all directions. Crowds were gathering on the sidewalks as he reached Broadway. Headley wanted to see what had happened at the Astor. As he reached it he was baffled to find that no engines were there. Across the street, however, at Barnum's Museum, pandemonium had broken loose as men, women, and children rushed headlong from the building. He glanced at the clock on the City Hall tower. It read 9:15.[2]

When Rob and Chenault reached Broadway, they decided to hide for a while. Barnum's was on the corner. They entered, paying the thirty-cent admission. They went up the stairs to the fifth floor, passing by the exhibitions, until they reached a window high enough to see up and down Broadway. They stopped outside the Lecture-Room where a play was being performed. They heard the first alarm from there, followed almost immediately by a second tolling. Chenault was satisfied. He started to descend the stairs.

Rob paused, the liquor fuzzing his thinking. He began to follow Chenault, then stopped. "Just to scare," he said, taking a bottle of phosphorus from his pocket.[3] He threw it against the stairs. The bottle smashed. The phosphorus, smelling like garlic, drenched the wood and started to smoke and burn. Rob tossed another bottle in a stairwell as he hurried down the steps, but it failed to break.

Rob and Chenault parted on Ann Street outside, Chenault going on to the next hotel on his list, Handfield's. Rob stepped across Broadway, dodging between carriages.

Meanwhile, a fist fight broke out in front of Barnum's admission booth and almost immediately someone burst out of the door, shouting. A flood of people followed, running from the museum in a frenzy. Ladders appeared. Several children fell as their parents rushed with them in tow in the stampede. There were screams.

Fire engines blocked Broadway outside the St. James Hotel at 26th Street near Madison Square. The first alarm was sounded from here at 8:43 P.M. Outside the St. Nicholas Hotel, nearly twenty-five blocks to the south on Broadway, volunteer firemen were laying hose. A third alarm came within minutes from Barnum's Museum.

At first, the crowds along Broadway were slow to grasp the significance of the various alarms, but as the occupants of carriages passing up and down Broadway brought word of the fires at the St. James and St. Nicholas hotels and Barnum's Museum, terror spread from person to person. The rumble of police wagons added to the anxiety, as the patrolmen spilled from their vehicles and moved into the crowds, billyclubs grasped tightly in their hands. Where would the next alarm be sounded? Where was safe? Men ran frenziedly through the jammed streets toward their homes. The wooden houses in the vicinity of the fires were being evacuated, infants and valuables clutched alike in the arms of parents. The cries of suddenly awakened children brought the full horror into focus: the lives of more than half a million people hung in the balance.

Headley was on West Street. Rows of old clapboard buildings— ship chandleries, warehouses, grog shops—crowded one side. On the other, ship upon ship nestled along the docks thrust into the Hudson River, their bowsprits stretching over passersby. There were hardly any street lamps to light the way. Hidden by the darkness, Headley reached into his pocket and drew out several bottles and tossed them toward the wharves after first making certain that no one was in sight. He paused to do this between Franklin and North Moore streets, aiming for a barge full of hay that was tied to the dock. A block north, between North Moore and Beach, he threw several more bottles at stacks of hay piled on a bulkhead. He walked almost a dozen blocks north on West Street until he had another chance to throw two more bottles at a likely target—a lumber yard, with attached stable, at the corner of Clarkson Street.

Headley then headed back toward City Hall. As he turned onto Broadway he saw a familiar figure ahead of him, limping. Headley caught up with Rob easily. He slapped him on the shoulder from behind. Rob dropped to the ground, twisting as he did so, his hand reaching inside his coat for his gun. Headley laughed. Rob laughed, too. "He said," Headley recalled later, "he ought to shoot me for giving him such a scare."[4]

The two Confederates ducked into a store front and exchanged reports. Headley said he'd seen the panic at Barnum's and wondered what had happened, since it wasn't on the agenda. Rob gleefully told him: Coming down the stairwell after hearing the first alarm he cleared a turn without anyone in sight. He thought it would be "fun" to throw a fright, he said. The bottle had cracked like "an egg."

Ashbrook, meanwhile, was fumbling through his room at the La-farge not far away, searching for matches to light the gas jet. Ashbrook was in room 104 on the third floor facing Bond Street, which he'd taken that afternoon as "J. B. Richardson, Camden, N. J."

The servant girl he passed in the hallway had told Ashbrook he could find matches inside the room, but Ashbrook had looked in vain. He poked his head into the corridor and called for her. She entered his room without speaking, pointed to a box of lucifers on the mantelpiece, took one out, and lit the gas for him. Ashbrook mum-bled an embarrassed thanks, and closed the door after her. She passed the door several times in the next twenty minutes and could see the reflection of the gaslight through the open transom. Then she heard the key rattle. Ashbrook appeared, stepped into the hall, locked the door behind him, and departed from the stairs. Passing the room a moment later, the girl concluded that he'd forgotten to turn off the gas. She groped in her apron for the master key when a bright light in the transom lit up the hall like a bolt of lightning.

Volunteers pulling a fire engine raced to the Lafarge. Suddenly there were shouts from the Winter Garden Theatre next door. A crush of fashionably dressed ladies and gentlemen burst from its exits. Sev-eral were shouting excitedly: "Fire! Fire!"

A similar scene was taking place two blocks south at Niblo's Gar-den, next door to the Metropolitan Hotel. Harrington had gone up to his room, number 302, after leaving Ashbrook. The room, taken un-der the name "James Simson, Rochester" four days earlier, was on the top floor. Harrington had the russet portmanteau with him. He sprayed the bedding with a bottle of phosphorus, and poured another into a bureau drawer. He left a third, unopened, in the bag, along with the pair of boots, a pair of pantaloons, and a pair of prunella gaiters he had included in order to disguise the weight of the luggage. The phosphorus began smoldering almost at once.

As Harrington left the hotel, a Southern woman discovered the fire and told a chambermaid. The maid ran downstairs to inform the hotel proprietor, Simeon Leland. As the alarm spread, word reached Niblo's Garden, fear gripping the audience. The dreaded cry "Fire!" spread throughout the theatre.

Rob and Headley pressed south on Broadway, elbowing their way through the crowds. The huge swells of people now on the streets were wild with excitement. Rumors were shouted from street corner to street corner: reports of fires at Wallack's Theatre and the Academy of Music, stories of hotel owners who had been turning away strangers seeking lodging. And then the most fearful rumor of all: "A Confederate attack!"

The two Confederates decided to part. They could meet the next morning at the Exchange Hotel, where Rob and Chenault were staying. Rob still had two hotels to attend to.

Headley was troubled as he continued through the crowds. There seemed to be no rhyme or reason to explain why the fires he and Rob had set had not taken hold, nor any explanation why those that had apparently caught on did not turn the hotels into wild bonfires. He was also confused by the conduct of the volunteer firemen. He hadn't seen any of their usual brawls break out. The Confederates had counted on the well-known rowdyism of the companies to aid in the confusion. Someone must have alerted the authorities. Also, something was wrong with the phosphorus. Longmire or the chemist must have "put up a job on us after it was found that we could not be dissuaded from our purpose."[5]

Within quick succession five new alarms were sounded—from the United States Hotel at Fulton and Water streets, the New England Hotel ten blocks away, Lovejoy's across from City Hall Park, along the Hudson River docks, and across town at the Belmont on Fulton Street.

Now that they grasped the full scope of the incendiary attack, police and fire department officials, working in unison, sent detachments and equipment in answer to each new alarm—the police to restore order and hunt for the arsonists, the volunteer firemen to fight the blaze and, if possible, trace its source. In the midst of what seemed to many to be chaos, the more than 5,000 policemen and volunteers acted with an alacrity and sureness that did much to calm the frightened citizens. Rage soon outweighed fear, and a new cry went up: "Find the rebels! Hang them from a lamppost! Burn them at the stake!"

Only Rob and Martin continued to carry out their assignments. They were in hotels across the street from one another as midnight approached—Martin in his sixth-floor room at French's Hotel at Chatham and Frankfort streets, Rob in the Tammany Hotel, ten paces away across Frankfort Street. Rob's room, number 108 on an upper floor, had been taken earlier in the day as "C. E. Morse, Rochester."[6]

Rob was drunk. After leaving Headley on Broadway, he'd apparently stopped again at a saloon. Carelessly, then, he did not notice that the shutters on the window of his room were open. He poured phosphorus on the bedding from a bottle labeled "Spirits of Turpentine." Deciding not to wait for the phosphorus to work, Rob bent down with a piece of flaming paper. There was a brief flare. Rob hurried to the door and went out. As a doublecheck, he looked back inside the room. The fire had gone out. Rob reentered the room and leaned down again, now with a match in his hand. This time, the entire room seemed to light up. Rob got away as quickly as he could, closing the door behind him.

Across the street, the bookkeeper and the porter at French's Hotel were racing down the stairs from the porter's quarters. The porter, who'd been showing the other his new revolver, had a clear view of Rob, but the thought never seemed to cross his mind to use the gun, even though it was obvious that arson was being attempted.

By the time the bookkeeper reached the Tammany to give the alarm, the building was filling with smoke and guests were escaping into the street. A fire engine was already there. As the bookkeeper searched the crowd for Rob, two firemen came out of the hotel. One carried a crying child in his arms, the other an unconscious woman in her nightclothes. The bookkeeper turned back to French's Hotel, suddenly recalling the missing silver leaf on Martin's hat when he had registered shortly before. That, and the fact that the officer had spoken with a distinct Southern accent, prompted him to tell the porter to get his revolver and keep a sharp watch on Martin's movements: "Shoot if necessary." Then, the bookkeeper went to get the hotel proprietor, Richard French.

Martin, hearing the commotion from the street, opened the shutters and looked out. Bedding and sheets were being thrown like flaming torches from the Tammany Hotel across the way. He went to his door and peered out. The porter saw him, and warned Martin not to leave his room because his own actions were suspect. "You must be mistaken," Martin said in an injured tone. "I don't want to be disturbed. Get out of the hall." Then French, the proprietor, came down the corridor. "I think it best you leave," he said to the Confederate. "Do you have any fear of your hotel being set on fire?" Martin asked. "No," said French, "but I'd like you to leave. Please see the cashier and get your money back. I won't let you stay under any consideration." Martin, chagrined, went back inside his room, got his overcoat and hat, and emerged. He went downstairs. Several guests went up to French after Martin was out of sight and cautioned the hotel owner that Martin's overcoat pockets bulged as if he was trying to conceal something. One said Martin ought to be stopped and searched. French thought a moment and agreed. He followed Martin down the stairs, planning to head him off at the cashier's window, but was too late. Martin had left the hotel.

Martin walked down Broadway. Apparently tired, he stopped after a few blocks and entered the National Hotel on Courtlandt Street. The clerk was discussing the fires uptown with some guests as he came in. Martin flushed when he heard what they were talking about. The clerk noticed his embarrassment. He gave Martin a room on the first floor but warned the watchman to keep an eye on the new guest. Martin left a call to be awakened at six in the morning.

After walking for several hours, Rob returned to the Exchange Hotel on Greenwich Street. Chenault was in his own room, apparently asleep. Exhausted and drunk, Rob went to bed also.

The alarms kept ringing from one end of the city to the other throughout the night, but the worst fears were quelled as it became apparent that all the fires had been checked—indeed, that in some cases there had been no fire at all. Although crowds quickly formed whenever a new alarm was sounded, the majority of the people gradually turned toward their homes after midnight, relieved but still on edge. The possibilities of what might have been kept many from sleeping that night.

The city had been spared by luck—or, rather, by a dozen instances of luck. In some hotels, as on the docks, the phosphorus simply smoldered for hours; the oxygen it needed to feed on was cut off from the closed rooms. Headley blamed Longmire and the chemist, and seems not to have considered the possibility that he and the other conspirators had blundered.

No lives were lost, no one—incredibly—even seriously injured, despite the panics at Barnum's and the theatres. The most damage done was to the St. Nicholas Hotel, where Ashbrook and Harrington had both set fires. It cost $10,000 to repair the damage there.

New York had escaped destruction, but it was frightened. And its mood was ugly.

chapter 13

ob and Martin sat in the parlor at the Exchange Hotel, reading the morning papers. The accounts were sparse and incomplete, but both the *Times* and the *Herald* headlined that the fires were a "Rebel plot." The *Times* further reported that a bag containing phosphorus found at one hotel had burst into flames on being opened. "The police," the *Times* added ominously, "are said to be on the track of several suspected persons."[1]

A newcomer entered the hotel. He looked familiar. It was Young—"Old" Young, head of the city detectives.[2] He went up to the hotel desk and spoke to the man there for several minutes, then walked over to the banquette and heaved his heavy bulk into the seat beside Martin. Martin, still in uniform, was engrossed in reading the *Times*.

To Rob, all the persons lounging in the parlor looked like detectives. He was sure they would be caught and "expected to die then."[3] Martin, meanwhile, was talking with Young and did not appear concerned. Why hadn't Young arrested Martin, Rob wondered—and himself?

A patrolman entered the parlor and walked up to Young. The detective got up wearily to speak to him, then followed the patrolman from the hotel. Martin turned to Rob—with a smile that seemed to say he'd fooled him!

Rob and the others dispersed, planning to meet again at the cottage at six. Martin and Headley went to eat at a restaurant on Broadway at 12th Street.[4] Headley shoved the latest editions toward Martin.

Everyone else in the busy restaurant was also reading the papers, but Headley felt uncomfortable. He insisted to Martin that they take a streetcar up to Central Park.

Headley was growing increasingly nervous. According to the *Evening Post's* third edition, the police so far were on the wrong track. They had made several arrests: a woman from Baltimore, an ex-Confederate soldier, an Army lieutenant. What disturbed Headley, however, was the description given by the clerk at the United States Hotel: "William B. Brown," who'd taken room 172 on the fifth floor where a fire was discovered, was "modest and genteel in appearance."[5]

Martin wanted to return downtown to get his baggage from McDonald's store and eat supper. Headley hesitated, but Martin, apparently buoyed up by his experience with Young, persuaded Headley that there was nothing to worry about as far as the police were concerned.

The two left the park about four o'clock, and hailed a hack. As they passed Union Square, Martin told Headley to go on to the restaurant to order supper while he dropped by McDonald's. The hack stopped at the piano store at Broadway and Franklin Place, and Martin alighted. He started down the two steps into the vestibule when he saw Gus McDonald's niece, Katie, at the window. She looked panic-stricken. Behind her, their backs to the street, Martin could see several men talking with McDonald. Katie put her hand, palm outward, before her face and waved Martin away. The Confederate turned instantly, and ran to overtake Headley in the hack. He caught up with it quickly and banged on the door. Headley ordered the driver to stop. Martin looked pale as he sat down. He didn't say a word and tried to appear casual as he looked back over his shoulder through the oval rear window.

The fourth edition of the *Evening Post* carried the story, tacked onto its earlier accounts. The police, it said, had made "an important arrest," a man in whose possession was found "the baggage of the chief conspirator and one hundred and twenty dollars in American gold. He was the confidant of the conspirators." The police believed the culprits had already left the city, it said, but "have full descriptions of several of them."[6]

Martin was worried now, too. He and Headley decided to get out of New York and back to Canada as soon as possible. They left the restaurant after reading the *Post*'s fourth edition and returned to Central Park, wondering if any of the others would make it. They reached the cottage at six, and were relieved when Rob and the others showed up also. Each had been certain the others had been picked up by the police. All agreed they had better escape from the city immediately. There was a northbound Hudson River Railroad express at 10:40 P.M. According to the train schedule, sleepers were open for boarding at nine at the 30th Street depot on 10th Avenue. It was decided that they would board as soon as they could. In the meantime, those who had baggage would retrieve it and all would meet at the Exchange Hotel.

The ticket windows opened at eight. Ashbrook and Harrington were selected to pick up the tickets, apparently because they'd been residing at a boarding house on a secluded street in Toronto and were not too well known in that city, where spies and detectives were always hanging about. Sleeping-car accommodations were available only as far as Albany, but they took them.

When Ashbrook and Harrington rejoined the others at nine, all six men went to the depot. The sleeping car was on a siding. The six slipped into it without being noticed and went directly to their individual berths—but they did not undress. Martin waited for the porter to pass through, then cautiously scouted the car. He went down the aisle, pausing by each berth with last-minute instructions: If anyone came to search for the Confederates, he'd "start the ball" and they would fight it out. There was an exit at the rear of the car. They were to get lost in the crowd outside if anything happened.

A locomotive and coaches backed into the station and hooked onto the sleeper. A swarm of passengers came down the platform lugging packages and valises. Among them were several men without baggage, obviously detectives. They scrutinized everyone boarding the train.

At 10:40 P.M. a whistle shrieked. With a final hiss of steam, the train began to pull slowly from the station into the dark night.

Rob and the others waited an hour before getting undressed, convinced by then that no detectives were on board the train and searching the cars. Finally, they slept, as the train sped north. The six Confederates arrived in Albany at six in the morning. There were no through trains on Sunday to Niagara Falls or the Suspension Bridge, so they took rooms at several hotels and spent the day in them. Late in the evening a sleeper came through bound for the border. They took it, and each must have breathed a sigh of relief as they crossed the bridge into Canada before dawn. By the afternoon of Monday, November 28, they were back in Toronto, safe—or so they thought.

part 5

THE CHASE

\

O Lord, dear Father, guide us through the shiftin' scenes of life
And finally take us somewhere, Lord, where there won't be no
  sickness an' sorrow,
Somewhere in the sweet Beulah Land, just somewhere, Lord.

chapter 14

On Saturday night, November 26, 1864, a petty thief was caught in the act of stealing a coat from the rack outside the dining room of New York's St. Nicholas Hotel.[1] The thief bolted for the front door, plunging through the glass. Two house detectives seized him as he staggered to his feet. They took him back inside the hotel and into the business office. Word of his capture spread rapidly throughout the hotel, but was distorted as guest told guest. A large, angry mob soon gathered outside the office, convinced that the thief was one of the incendiaries who had tried to set the St. Nicholas on fire the night before. Cries of "Hang him! Hang him!" filled the lobby. "It is evident," the sensation-oriented *Herald* commented in its report of the incident, "that no mercy would be shown to a culprit who might be detected in an act of incendiarism. The nearest lamppost would be the only tribunal that would be invoked."

New York City, shaken out of its holiday weekend mood by the night of terror, recoiled at the thought of what might have happened—the loss of life, on a scale too horrible to contemplate, the destruction of thousands of buildings and homes, the obliteration in one stupendous holocaust of the greatest city in the nation. The city thanked God for its deliverance—and lusted for revenge.

The obscurity and mystery which enveloped the fiendish attempt made on Friday night to set on fire the principal hotels, and through them the city and shipping in the harbor is gradually being dissipated, and as the fearful proportions, diabolical character, and remarkable daring of the plot become apparent, the consciousness that for the moment the danger is past, and

127

that a kind Providence has averted the fearful and heartrending
calamity which was hanging over us should prompt all to renew
thanksgiving to the Maker and Preserver of all.

Thus began the news story in Horace Greeley's *Tribune,* which
continued:

> The mind cannot altogether avoid reverting to the scenes of
> horror which must have been enacted in the lofty and crowded
> hotels, which were attempted, the fearful loss of life, the wide-
> spread nature of the conflagration resulting from the size of the
> buildings in which it originated, the combustible nature of their
> contents, and the utter powerlessness of the Fire Department,
> although assisted by the united efforts of the populace, to cope
> with a conflagration starting from so many points, without feel-
> ing convinced that a catastrophe was imminent, without parallel
> during late years, and only to be compared in magnitude to the
> earthquake of Lisbon, the great fire of London, the burning of
> Rome, or the destruction of Pompeii and Heroulaneum [sic] . . .

The rival *Times,* calling the plot "one of the most fiendish and
inhuman acts known in modern times," declared:

> The plan was excellently well conceived, and evidently pre-
> pared with great care, and had it been executed with one-half the
> ability with which it was drawn up, no human power could have
> saved this city from utter destruction . . . the best portion of the
> city would have been laid in ashes.

Frank Leslie's Illustrated Newspaper—noting that the property immediately jeopardized was valued at $15 million, and that the hotels
alone held 5,000 guests—said that the fires, if successful, would have
been a "more terrible blow to the Union cause than the defeat and
pursuit of Gen. Grant's army to the fortifications of Washington."

All the newspapers in the city, pro-Lincoln and Copperhead alike,
reacted to the plot with shock: "the most diabolical attempt at arson
and murder of which there is any record in the history of our country,"
"among the most gigantic crimes of history," "It makes one shudder to
contemplate what might have been the result . . ." Their concern was
borne out by the report of Fire Marshal Alfred E. Baker, who said that
in his many years of investigating incendiary fires, "neither in their
audacity nor in the difficulty of arriving at a detection of the perpetra-

tors, have I met with any series of events which caused me so much labor and anxiety as the attempts which were made to fire our principal hotels."[2] Baker had the contents of two bottles of phosphorus found at the Fifth-Avenue Hotel quickly analyzed:

> The preparation was found to be phosphorus dissolved in sulphuret of carbon. I had some of the mixture prepared, and found that by dissolving two parts of phosphorus into four parts of sulphuret of carbon the exact results were obtained. By saturating muslin or paper with it, I found that a blaze was produced in from four to eight minutes.[3]

Baker believed that the plot failed "not from any want of courage on the part of the conspirators, but from miscalculations as to the use of the combustible materials employed":

> The chemist had done his work sagaciously, but in carrying out the plan a blunder was committed which defeated the anticipated results. In each case the doors and windows of the room were left closed, so that when the phosphorus ignited, the fire only smoldered from the want of oxygen necessary to give it activity, thus affording an opportunity for its detection before much harm was done . . . Happily, as I have shown, this fiendish plan was defeated by one of those slight miscalculations which so often interpose to frustrate the designs of evil-minded men.[4]

"Here was their grand mistake," the *Tribune* agreed, "and it is no doubt owing to this principally that New York is not in flames at this moment."

The fire marshal was certain that "the whole scheme was concocted by Southern emissaries." Not everyone agreed, however. Benjamin Wood's Copperhead *Daily News* suggested that the attempts might have been an Administration plan to punish anti-Lincoln New York. The *Herald* retorted by accusing rival newspapers of "fomenting all the revolutionary and rebel elements to the point of insurrection." The *New York Leader*, a Democratic organ, tried to reason with both. It was "inexcusable," it said, to call the plot a "Republican hoax":

> Suppose the plot had succeeded . . . would the sight of the charred bodies of thousands of our best citizens, their wives and their innocent children, have provoked a smile?

Like Baker, however, most newspapers believed Southern sabo-
teurs were to blame, rejecting another theory that the city's criminal
element might have initiated the fires as a prelude to wholesale loot-
ing and plundering. The *Times* asserted:

> Rebels and rebel abettors, it is easy to see, have grown des-
> perate in their last frantic struggle of resistance to lawful Govern-
> ment. Their regular armies are melting away like snow before the
> sun . . . A despairing wail is heard from one extremity of rebel-
> dom to another.

The *Times* declared that irregular bands of Confederates who turn
out to be "belligerents" with military commissions "are but parts of
the same scheme of desperation." As to the charge that the plot was
an Administration trick, it snorted, "This is carrying impudence into
absolute senselessness"; that Government agents set the fires "is an
amazing perversity."

Some Copperhead newspapers, hoping to head off any acts of
vengeance directed against the South, were surprisingly candid. If it
were true that Confederate guerrillas and escaped prisoners were responsible, Rushmore G. Horton's *Weekly Day-Book* reasoned, "it is
undoubtedly intended as a retaliation for the wholesale destruction of
property in the Southern States." The *World* said, "The infernal deed
would have, in a manner, avenged the shelling of Charleston, the
destruction of Atlanta, and the devastation in the Shenandoah valley
by Sheridan's troops." The *World* believed that "the attempt was made
by men identified with the Southern cause, and was prompted by a
mistaken zeal in that direction." On the other hand, the Richmond
Government could not be blamed:

> Be the incendiaries whom they may, dismiss as absurd, un-
> generous and unjust, the idea that the Confederate authorities,
> or the Southerners, as a people, are accomplices in the act, or
> that they originated, or encouraged it in any way, or that they
> will indorse it. If perpetrated by Southerners, it was, probably, by
> a few, rendered desperate by personal grievances, impelled by the
> memory of their individual losses in kindred or property, and
> acting upon their own responsibility . . .

McMaster of *The Freeman's Journal* could, of course, identify the
arsonists, but only by jeopardizing himself. He was, however, revolted

by what had occurred, although sympathetic of the motive. He also strove, like the *World*, to exonerate Richmond. "It would, irrespective of the *crime*," he said, "be most *unwise*, and the Confederate Government is not composed of fools! . . . the city of New York is known to be *crowded* with people who are opposed to the war. Can it be dreamed that the Confederate Government wanted to burn up the wives and children of these opponents of war? . . . Can it be imagined that the Confederate Government wished to rouse to wrath, and to revenge, a population that, as to the majority of it, desires to be friends with the South?"

The plot, McMaster went on, was too well-conceived to be the work of thieves. Had it occurred before Lincoln's election, he said, it might well have been thought an Administration attempt to instill martial law, but it had not. McMaster, all-knowing, said the answer lay elsewhere:

> What commends itself to our judgment, as the explanation of the affair, is that this "plot" was gotten up by the agents of *no* government, and was managed by no experts in the arts of felony. We form the theory of it, that it was the work of a company of men from Virginia, Georgia, Alabama, Mississippi, Louisiana, Tennessee, Kentucky, Missouri—men, probably, whose hearts have been burnt to ashes by horrible outrages committed on their mothers, sisters, wives, daughters—perhaps on their own persons . . . *Such* men, rendered irrational by wrongs afflicted, would be the ones to say, "Kill! kill! strike! strike!" . . . Passion, not reason, seems to have been their guide! They were the "John Browns" of the South, except that, probably they were not *fancied* wrongs of *others*, that crazed them! For the honor of human nature, we are glad to think they must have been crazy men! . . . Human nature revolts at the idea of what they attempted.

McMaster then washed his hands of the entire scheme:

> The soldiers, or the men, proved to have committed these acts of vandalism, should, mutually, be given up to the people outraged, to be tried and punished by the laws of the land!

This call for vengeance echoed loudly—and passionately—in both Administration and anti-Administration newspapers. "It was suggested," Benjamin Wood's Copperhead *Daily News* said, "that if they had been captured, they should have been confined in the cage, with the boa-constrictor as a proper punishment for their wrong-doing."

The *Herald* said that "it was confidently hoped that some avenging Nemesis will point a finger to their hiding place, and the citizens of New York will eventually have the gratification of witnessing the severest penalty of the law inflicted upon the scoundrels." The jeremiad continued:

> The wretches who would have destroyed all our principal hotels but one by fire, and caused the death of their harmless occupants, deserve no pity, and should they be detected, as we have no doubt they will be, should be hung up in as brief a space as possible and as soon as the law will permit.

Revenge, it seemed certain, would take precedence over justice if the conspirators were ever caught.

chapter 15

ohn D. Allison sat in stunned silence. Sergeant John S. Young of the city detective force had just left his cell at police headquarters after telling Allison that his "chances for living were slim"—that he "would be hung in one or two days."[1]

Allison, a former member of Morgan's command, had been released only twelve days earlier from Fort Lafayette after convincing Federal authorities that he was a citizen of Britain. He'd spent the next week and a half running into "many old friends and many of [his] late prison companions," trying, he noted in his diary, to raise enough money to return home to Kentucky and otherwise "seeking enjoyment in drinks, drives, Billiards Etc. Etc. At night visiting various places of Amusement, Etc. Etc." On Friday, the twenty-fifth, Allison went to the St. Nicholas Hotel to meet some friends for a few games of billiards. He was near the clerk's office when the fire alarm sounded. Allison stayed about an hour, leaving when he heard that the hotel he roomed in, the Lafarge House, was on fire also. He went to the Lafarge, where the fire was soon put out, and finally, about eleven o'clock, took supper and had a smoke. He retired about midnight.

> A rap was heard at my door. I opened it—two persons both strangers entered, asked if my name was A., told me I was their prisoner. Told me to dress, which I set about doing at once. I observed that they picked up each article of my apparell & smelled them separately. My valise they went at with the same gusto a hungry hound would at a rare beef bone. They opened each package & smelt it. Being dressed by this time I went down

with them got into a closed Coach & was driven to (as I afterwards learned) the Police Hd. Qrts. I was domiciled in a small room with a boy and man (Ward). Now my Captors commenced questioning me as to the fire, and finally told me I was an incendiary. All night crowds of men were being ushered into the room to see if they could recognize me.

All day Saturday, November twenty-sixth, the identification procedure continued, until Allison believed the numbers of persons "calling to see me must have amounted to an hundred. They stared at me in utter wonder." After Young visited him, Allison was shocked into numbness. "All the feelings that ever passed over one to be executed in a few hours, I experienced." Still there was no letup. "The crowd of visitors continued to a late hour." Worse, there were reports of rewards being offered for the capture of the conspirators.

> Here was my greatest fear. I concluded that in a place of this size many could be found to swear that I was the offender, that they might secure the reward.

Allison had cause to be frightened. He was the prime suspect in the plot to burn New York City.

The magnitude and complexity of the plot were baffling enough to Police Superintendent John Alexander Kennedy; he also had to sort out fact from rumor, and a perplexing rash of stories was being reported. General Dix was forwarding from his office nearby all the letters received from anonymous sources; "Loyal Citizen," "Loyal Man," "A Patriot."[2] They identified what amounted to scores of Southern refugees as "still a rebel," "a notorious rebel," "disloyal," or simply "suspicious."

The newspapers were carrying accounts that ranged from the meticulously accurate to sheer nonsense. Although the *Herald*, for example, ran a description of "William B. Brown," the occupant of room 172 at the United States Hotel, that fit Headley to a tee— unobtrusive, "rather effeminate-looking"—the *Times* described the same conspirator as having been disguised in a wig and whiskers and offered the opinion that all the others were disguised, too. "W. L. Haines," the occupant of room 204 at the Astor House (again, Headley), was identified by two papers as a chemist and telegraph operator who'd once been confined at Fort Lafayette. The *World* wondered whether a gang of "ruffians" who'd recently bragged to other passengers on a streetcar that they belonged to Mosby's guerrillas were, in fact, the men who'd set the fires. It was even said that George H. Sanders and Jacob Thompson had been in New York in disguise to direct the fires.

There was widespread fear that another serious attack might be attempted. This was pointed up when a carpenter named William Campbell called at Army headquarters on Saturday carrying two boxes containing some curious-looking cylinders. Officers immediately identified them as "torpedoes." Campbell said a tall, black-haired stranger had brought the torpedoes to his shop to have boxes made for them, but had never returned to pick them up. (A few days later, a torpedo was found on a Long Island Sound freight steamer.)

Any fire of unknown origin was immediately blamed on Southern arsonists. Incendiaries were held responsible for starting a fire in a storage room at the International Hotel on Monday, the twenty-eighth, as well as two blazes at lumber yards in the next two days. Even a fire in the basement of the Bancroft House on the night before the plot was blamed on the conspirators.

Officials in Washington reacted by placing extra guards on all Government buildings, hotels, and other "important structures" in the capital. The War Department Rifles, a volunteer militia, was called up to double the available guard, and the Treasury Guards were alerted for possible duty in case of an emergency. A mysterious report from Rochester, New York, referred to 150 rebels waiting to set fire to a number of principal cities by means of combustible "preparations" that were easily ignited by "slow matches."

Additional guards and watches were also posted at all hotels and Government buildings in New York. The Brooklyn Navy Yard restricted visitors and tightened its security regulations with the warning that any loiterers would be arrested, and any idle workers dismissed out of hand. A number of door keys to hotel rooms were found at various places in the street and identified as having come from some of the hotels where fires had occurred.

Meanwhile, Hiram Cranston, the proprietor of the New-York Hotel and a well-known Copperhead, was trying to allay the suspicions that had developed because his hotel had been spared. In answer to a letter from "Inquiring Mind" printed in the *Times*, Cranston asked why Stetson of the Astor House had not been accused of complicity when it was learned the Astor House was the rendezvous point of the conspirators. "Will you oblige me," he added, "by asking 'Inquiring Mind' if I cannot convince my fellow-citizens of my 'loyalty' in some other manner than by setting fire to my hotel."[3]

Meanwhile, Superintendent Kennedy came to the conclusion that "the most vicious of the gang" had fled to Canada. Several promising arrests made on the night of the fires had not panned out. The woman from Baltimore was freed and allowed to return home after proving her story that she had been making the rounds of several hotels in search of a clerk from A. T. Stewart's department store. James M. Kellogg, the Army lieutenant who'd registered for the room at the Belmont Hotel, had also convinced the police of his innocence. Two young Southerners who had been picked up on Monday because they weren't registered also had unimpeachable alibis. That left only Allison and McDonald, both of whom denied any connection with the plot. The police superintendent considered picking up one of the better-known Copperheads in the city for questioning in hopes of cracking the case. In the meantime, he planned to see Dix about sending some of Young's "shadows" to Canada to try to trace the conspirators.

On Monday, November 28, New York Mayor Gunther announced a $25,000 reward "for the arrest and conviction of said incendiaries, or either of them." The County Board of Supervisors, however, set the reward at $5,000. Its resolution, adopted unanimously, declared:

> The commission of so great and extraordinary a crime, endangering the lives and property of hundreds of citizens of this County and their families, demands prompt action on the part of the County authorities to secure the arrest of the perpetrators.[4]

Some papers reported erroneously that the reward would amount to $25,000—perhaps confused by another reward offer. That same day, the Hotel-Keeper's Society met at the St. Nicholas Hotel. A number of members had hastily assembled the previous Saturday and agreed to a $3,000 reward, but this was considered too little. Consequently, the sum was upped to $20,000: $5,000 for the first arrest and conviction, $3,000 for the second, $2,000 for the third, and $1,000 for each additional arrest and conviction—in effect, thirteen rewards, one for each hotel set on fire.

The number of Southern refugees who appeared at Army headquarters on Monday to register increased beyond all expectations. The queue was long, and some of the better-fixed registrants were paying $5 for a place near the head of the line. Colonel H. Z. Haynau, who was in charge, was cross-examining everyone so thoroughly that only eighty were questioned and registered on the first day. Haynau was jotting down the age, place of birth, business, and former and present residence as well as a personal description of each applicant. (None, however, was being required to take the oath of allegiance.)

Major General John Adams Dix was composing a message to Secretary of War Edwin M. Stanton that evening, after conferring with Superintendent Kennedy. Dix believed that Allison was definitely one of the conspirators, and that the others had already fled to Canada. Kennedy's chief of detectives, Young, had put together a list of those who'd taken rooms at the hotels, aware, though, that they could very well be aliases. The best description so far was of the one who'd set the fire at the New England Hotel: "Geo. Morse," a respectable-looking man, bearded, about thirty-five years old, with light hair and a florid complexion, wearing a gray coat, and who walked with a pronounced limp.[5]

Dix's message to Washington spelled out his intentions:

> I have been very busy with the Police in the investigation of the diabolical attempt to fire the City. Most of the parties immediately concerned left the same night. We have much valuable information and I hope to be able to convict a man now in custody. Distr. Att. A. Oakley Hall who is acting very zealously thinks he will be able to furnish the Secy. of State with sufficient evidence to demand one of the conspirators who has reached Toronto under the extradition treaty.[6]

Dix's expectation that Canada might cooperate with the United States was apparently based on newspaper reports indicating that, as a result of recent Confederate activities, Canadians—once neutral and sympathetic to Southerners—were now disenchanted with the Confederacy.

As Dix's wire was tapped out to Washington, three city detectives left by train for Canada.

chapter 16

Jacob Thompson, the Confederate commissioner in Toronto, had much to explain as he prepared a lengthy report on his activities in Canada for Secretary of State Judah P. Benjamin in Richmond. The effort to set up a Northwest Confederacy, he wrote, had been stymied because "the vigilance of the Administration, its large detective force, the large bounties paid for treachery, and the respectable men who have yielded to the temptation, added to the large military force stationed in these States, make organization and preparation almost an impossibility."[1]

The plan to seize the *Philo Parsons* and free the prisoners held at Johnson's Island had been "well conceived, and held out the promise of success," but as result of its failure two of the three principals in the project were in prison: Captain Charles H. Cole, who had been betrayed before being able to get the officers of the warship *Michigan* drunk, was himself a prisoner on Johnson's Island now, and acting master Bennet G. Burley, who had aided John Yates Beall in seizing the *Philo Parsons,* had been arrested in Canada and was fighting extradition to the United States. Thompson was sure he could prove that Burley had acted under orders and would be released—"but it may lead to my expulsion from the provinces; at least I have it from a reliable source that this last proposition has been pressed upon the Canadian authorities, and they have considered it."[2]

Thompson, inferring—as he put it—from Benjamin's latest "personal" run in the *New York Daily News* that Benjamin wanted him to remain in Canada, was still optimistic that something could be done to hinder the Northern war effort. Peace Democrats in the Midwest, he believed, could yet be swayed to rise up in revolt. "The feeling with the masses is as strong as ever; they are true, brave, and I believe willing and ready, but they have no leaders." Lincoln's election, he conceded, had "so demoralized the leaders of the order of the 'Sons of Liberty' " that a new organization under new leaders had become an absolute necessity. This was now being formed "with great vigor and success" under the new title of the "Order of the Star."[3]

As for the plot to burn New York, the former Mississippi congressman called it "a most daring attempt." Its failure, he implied, was the fault of the conspirators, who had decided to use phosphorus to carry out the arson:

> Their reliance on the Greek fire has proved a misfortune. It cannot be depended on as an agent in such work. I have no faith whatever in it, and no attempt shall hereafter be made, under my general directions with any such material.[4]

Having thus shifted the blame for the plot's failure onto someone else, Thompson crowed that the attempt had nevertheless "produced a great panic, which will not subside." Such a reaction would go hand in glove with his newest scheme. Thompson, out of touch with reality, was already concocting a proposal to present to Richmond—a complex movement of Southern armies to draw Sherman from Georgia and Grant away from Petersburg and Richmond by relocating the Confederate government in Wheeling, West Virginia, and throwing up a 100-mile line of Southern troops north to Lake Erie.

At almost the same time that Thompson was writing his report to Benjamin, the newspapers in Richmond began recounting the details of the New York plot, based on gleanings from the Northern papers. Richmond citizens first learned of the conspiracy in a short, one-paragraph account quoting the *New York Herald* on Tuesday, November 29. The next day, the Confederate capital's newspapers carried the *Washington Chronicle*'s report of Allison's arrest and Dix's determination to find the conspirators and speedily punish them. The *Richmond Daily Examiner* stoutly proclaimed the Confederate Government's innocence in the attempt to burn New York:

> Although, therefore, we wholly deny that there was any "rebel plot" to destroy New York, and that these States, or this

Confederacy had any complicity whatsoever with that transaction,—yet if New York were burned down, together with Boston and Philadelphia, by vengeful and desperate men who have been burnt out of house and home themselves, the incident would be soothing to every well-regulated mind.[5]

In a turnabout from its own exhortation to burn New York, the *Whig* surprisingly chastised Thompson—supporting the idea that once Election Day had passed in the North, the Confederate government, fearful of what might happen to beleaguered Richmond, did not know about (or else shied away from) the plot being put into operation. The *Whig*'s editorial on December 2, entitled "The Man With the Black Valise," declared:

We are rather sorry that the man with the black valise commenced his operations in New York . . . it is not against the commercial metropolis of Yankeedom that Southern hostility is at this movement [sic] directed. If there is any place in the North that ought to be spared, that place is New York. Not that its population is overtly friendly to us, but that it is undeniably hostile to Lincoln and his Government . . . We hope, therefore, that the gentleman of the black valise will resolve to let New York alone, and turn his attention to cities more eminently deserving of it—Boston, for instance, or Philadelphia. The destruction of places like these would be something like an approximate equivalent for the atrocities that Yankee armies have committed in the South . . . It is a pity that they had not made the discovery *sooner*. The man with the black valise is among them, and will not be exorcised. He is ubiquitous. He can be at eight different New York hotels in one night; and there is no reason why he should not be in half a dozen Yankee cities at the same time. . . .[6]

Clearly, Richmond—like the Copperheads in New York—was washing its hands of the conspiracy.

chapter 17

The relief on returning safely to Canada was soon dispelled for Rob and his friends. Within two days they were forced to go into hiding. The night of their arrival back in Toronto, on Monday, November 28, Martin and Headley went immediately to Thompson at the Queen's Hotel to report.[1] Headley told Thompson of his suspicions about Hyams, Thompson's confidant and courier, and when Hyams returned to Toronto the next day they treated him so coldly that he finally left the city.

The following day—Wednesday, November 30—Katie McDonald arrived unexpectedly, in company with James Horton. Horton's brother Rushmore, the editor of The Day-Book, had been picked up by the police in New York for questioning and was being held with Gus McDonald in the city prison. Katie and James Horton appealed to Thompson to furnish them with sworn testimony that neither man was involved in the plot.

Later, Horton took Thompson aside to tell him startling news. He was certain that several men he'd spotted taking rooms at the Queen's Hotel were detectives from New York. A friend of Thompson's confirmed Horton's information shortly afterward with the report that the new arrivals "had casually inquired" of him about four men whose descriptions fit Rob, Martin, Headley, and Ashbrook. Thompson left immediately, in a snowstorm, for Headley's boarding house, to inform the Kentuckian of this development. Larry McDonald, Katie's father, found a small cottage for rent in the suburbs of Toronto and took Headley there to stay with him. They avoided being seen at restaurants by cooking their own meals.

Rob, meanwhile, was rooming again with Edward A. Jackson, the escaped prisoner of war from Mississippi. He also befriended Judge S. V. Mitchell, former aide to Brigadier General William Terry of Virginia. About this time, too, he apparently shaved off his beard. With nothing much to do, Rob wrote several letters to friends left behind two months ago at Johnson's Island, bragging about the part he had played in the attempt on New York.

Like Rob and Headley, the other four incendiaries—Martin, Ashbrook, Chenault, and Harrington—also went into seclusion, either in Toronto itself or in its suburbs.

Back in New York, General Dix waited for news from Toronto. Three city detectives were in the Canadian city seeking information. Their first report, relayed to Dix by Sergeant Young, made it clear that most of the conspirators had once served with Morgan's cavalry. Hoping to get help in identifying the Confederates, Dix wired Columbus, Ohio, on December 3. Captain Thomas H. Hines, head of military operations for the Confederate commissioners in Canada, had been held along with Morgan and several other officers of Morgan's command in the penitentiary there in the fall of 1863. (They had subsequently escaped through a tunnel.) Dix asked the provost marshal in Columbus to "Please send some one here immediately who is acquainted with Capt. Hines and others of Morgan's men."[2]

Superintendent Kennedy, in the meantime, decided to send more men to Canada to press the hunt. Young himself was going, along with two more detectives, James P. Bennett and Christian B. McDougall.

On December 12, a sentry trudging through the snow in the prison yard at Johnson's Island found a letter stuffed into the outgoing letter box. The envelope was addressed to the superintendent of the prison camp. It was unsigned.

> Sir: It having come to my attention that one Mr. R.C. Kennedy, a Lieutenant [sic] of the Confederate army, who escaped this prison some time since, was in N.York at the time of the burning of some hotels which recently occurred. I have seen two letters from said Kennedy recently both of which I think can be

found at any time. Kennedy is bold and acknowledges to have had a hand in the burnings. He is in Toronto C.W. at present and can if desired be induced to come to Brooklyn or N.York City at almost any time. Where he might be apprehended if desired. Kenedy [sic] is under an assumed name which I cannot recall at present, but is contained in a letter recently received in my room. All that is in my power will be done at your request, to ferret out this or any other similar case within my knowledge. You will please let no one know of this correspondence who would convey it to any of the prisoners. Should this be of value to you, you can know the writer by putting a note on the bulletin board marked XX in which you need not mention what subject is embraced.[3]

The opportunity, Thompson apparently believed, was too valuable to let slip. He'd received word from Sandusky that seven Confederate generals were to be removed from Johnson's Island in mid-December for transfer by train to Fort Lafayette in New York Harbor. Thompson hoped to waylay the train and free the officers.[4]

On Sunday night, December 11, the first of ten Confederates who'd agreed to the venture left Toronto in pairs for Buffalo. The rest followed the next night.

Taking part in the scheme were Rob, Martin, Headley, Harrington, Ashbrook, and five other Southern soldiers: Charles C. Hemming of Florida, whom Headley had recently befriended, and who was living with Headley and McDonald in the suburban cottage; George S. Anderson, an eighteen-year-old private who had served briefly as Martin's courier when Morgan was still alive; Farney Holt of Memphis; W. P. Rutland of Nashville; and John Yates Beall, leader of the group that had seized the *Philo Parsons.*

On December 15 the ten men left the Genesee House in Buffalo. Martin headed by train for Erie, Pennsylvania, to scout ahead, while the others dropped off at Dunkirk, on Lake Erie, not far from Buffalo. They planned to capture the train carrying the Confederate generals between Dunkirk and Buffalo, derail its coaches, and run the engine and Express car closer to Buffalo before derailing them, too.

Martin arrived on the eastbound train at Dunkirk as scheduled, but with word that the generals were not on board.

The next day—Friday, December 16—the Confederates decided to stop the next eastbound train to try to get information. They met in the suburbs at five o'clock, parking a sleigh they had rented in the deep snow amid a clump of trees. As the eastbound train came toward them in the darkness, they dragged a long iron rail from beside the roadbed and lay it across the tracks. The train came roaring on as they labored in the cold wind to fasten the rail to the tracks. It was too late: the locomotive engaged the rail and pushed it fifty yards before the engineer stopped the train. The Confederates didn't wait around. They fled back to the sleigh and returned as fast as they could to Buffalo, where they hoped to catch a train over the Suspension Bridge into Canada.

Upon reaching the New York Central Railroad depot, the gang broke up into pairs. A train bound for Canada came through. Rob, Ashbrook, Holt, and Rutland boarded it. Headley and Martin, however, decided to take a hotel room for the night. They caught up with the others in Toronto the next day. Harrington and Hemming also made it back safely.

Beall, meanwhile, was concerned about Anderson. Cold and ill, young Anderson fell asleep in the depot restaurant. Beall stayed by his side. He was sitting next to Anderson when a police officer from Niagara City on special border patrol duty saw them. Believing they were escaped prisoners of war, the policeman approached with his hand on his pistol.

The latest failure scotched all further raids from Canada. Thompson, faced with increasing difficulties with the Canadian authorities, was obtaining passports for those Confederates who wanted to return to the South, as well as providing them with money for transportation.

At the same time, Young's detectives were fanning out.[5] Some stayed in Toronto, while others headed for Port Huron and Detroit to cover the Canadian border with Michigan. Several had wormed their way into Larry McDonald's confidence by posing as Southern sympathizers and friends of the men who'd tried to burn New York, going so far as cursing Lincoln and spitting on the Union flag to "prove" their sincerity. A meeting was arranged between Young and McDonald on Christmas night. When McDonald failed to show up in Lewiston on the American side, Young returned to Niagara Falls, leaving a message that he could be reached at the Central House there. At midnight, a messenger from McDonald arrived. Young, who had apparently hoped to lure him across the border in order to arrest him, had no choice but to accompany the messenger into Canada.

With amazing naivete, McDonald fell for Young's ruse. The detective, feigning concern for his Confederate friends, was able to draw from McDonald an almost complete account of the plot, that the city "was to be wrapped in one dazzling conflagration." More important, McDonald, in all candor, told Young that only six men were responsible. He apparently also let slip the knowledge that several of the men were preparing to return South.

Rob's roommate, Jackson, was planning to run the blockade by ship from Halifax with eleven other former prisoners of war. Rob, hoping to return to Joe Wheeler's command, felt the route was too dangerous because of the Federal fleet off Wilmington, North Carolina—one of the few Southern ports still in Confederate hands. He and Ashbrook decided to cross the border into Michigan and work their way south through Illinois into Southern territory. On December 24, with Thompson's assistance, Rob obtained a passport issued by R. J. Kimball, the United States Consular Agent in Toronto. It was made out in the name of "Richard Cobb—27—Rock Island, Ill." who "makes oath before me and says that he is not engaged in, nor will he become engaged in, aiding or abetting in the Rebellion in the United States in any manner whatsoever."[6]

There was a last get-together of the Confederates in St. Catharines.[7] Rob was there, as well as Ashbrook, Headley, young "Judge" Mitchell, and George B. Eastin of Morgan's command. John M. Price, who'd backed out of the attempt on New York at the last moment, showed up, too; he was also planning to run the blockade. No one accused the Virginian of cowardice. Rob, in fact, filled him in on all the details of the incendiarism, including his setting of the fire at Barnum's Museum. Rob must have been especially excited at the prospect of returning home after his adventures of the last three months: the escape from prison camp, the fires in New York, the escapade against the train. Apparently in high spirits, he sang an old Irish ditty for the others. The song was a favorite with thieves and murderers about to be executed:

"Trust to luck, trust to luck,

Stare Fate in the face,

For your heart will be easy

If it's in the right place . . ."

Two days later, on December 27, Thompson had Rob sign in his own name a "Certificate of Citizenship" to help get him through the Southern lines:

> Personally appeared before me, at my office in this City, Robt. C. Kennedy who being sworn, upon his oath says, that he is a Citizen of the State of Louisiana, and a soldier of the Armies of the Confederate States of America. Being desirous of returning to the Confederacy, he makes this application for means to enable him to do so.
>
> Signed before Mr. Wm. L. McDonald, Transportation Agent for Escaped Prisoners.

To help Rob pay his expenses inside Confederate territory, Thompson gave him a $20 Confederate bill as well as some gold to cover travel costs until he reached the South. Rob also signed in his own name a document prepared by Thompson. He was assured it would protect him against being held as a spy if he were caught.

> I do solemnly pledge my word of honor as a Confederate soldier that I will use all due diligence consistent with my personal safety in returning to the Confederacy and will promptly report myself for duty to the nearest commanding officer and will make a true return to the Paymaster of my regiment of all sums advanced me or received from the Government Agents at this place.

Rob ripped off the edge of the lining of his gray jacket. He hid the papers inside together with the $20 Confederate bill and an old quartermaster's receipt he had been carrying since his service with Joe Wheeler: dated August 31, 1863, it was for one month's pay ($130) and bore his name and rank.

As Headley observed, "It seemed almost impossible for a Confederate to leave Canada for the South without being followed by detectives."[8] Two New York detectives spotted Rob and Ashbrook as they went up to the ticket window of the Grand Trunk Railway on Wednesday, December 28, to purchase fares for the trip west to the St. Clair River and into Michigan. After they'd left, the detectives went up to the ticket seller, ascertained the destination of the two Confederates, and went to a telegraph office to wire Detroit.

That night, Rob put on a dark pair of pants and a black overcoat over his gray suit. He tucked his revolver into his belt. Then, he left his boarding house and went to meet Ashbrook at the depot. Once on the train, they went through the coaches looking for seats, but couldn't find two together. Finally, Ashbrook sat down beside a window in the rear of a car and Rob in the front, probably near the stove. Both apparently fell off to sleep soon after the train left on its overnight trip.

Two New York detectives, James P. Bennett and Christian B. McDougall, had been in Detroit several days, staying at the Biddle House. Each day, they went to the railroad station to watch the passengers disembark from the four trains that came from Canada, at 7 and 11 A.M. and at 5 and 11 P.M. On the night of December 28 they received a wire from Toronto. The two detectives immediately headed for the rail junction three miles outside Detroit.

Snow covered the fields outside as the train reached the border with the United States. A cursory inspection of passports followed. Soon after the train resumed its journey, Ashbrook saw the detectives. The two men walked slowly through the cars. Ashbrook tried to get Rob's attention. Rob saw Ashbrook gesturing, but must have misinterpreted his meaning. He apparently went back to sleep, unsuspicious.

Ashbrook, however, grew panicky. He heaved at the latch of his window and pulled it up. A blast of cold air shot into the coach. Ashbrook thrust himself through the window and fell into the deep snow outside.[9] Somehow, the detectives up front didn't notice. (A passenger must have quickly closed the window after Ashbrook's departure.)

Bennett and McDougall were the first out onto the platform as the train pulled into Detroit. They stood by a pillar, watching as the other passengers disembarked.

Rob took his small suitcase and left the car. He and Ashbrook had planned to stay in Detroit until they could find a train south. It is possible that they had also decided to break up at the station and meet elsewhere afterward, because Rob evidently suspected nothing when he did not see Ashbrook on the platform. He walked through the station and into the street.

Bennett elbowed his way through the crowd at the depot to get ahead of Rob while McDougall followed him from behind. Rob had walked about thirty paces along the street when he heard a voice. He stopped and turned. McDougall approached and asked if he had a pass. As Rob answered affirmatively, Bennett, now behind him, edged near the curb.

"What's your name?" McDougall asked.[10]

"Richard Cobb."

Rob took the passport from his coat and offered it to McDougall. The detective didn't even look at it.

"Your name is Stanton," he declared.

Rob instantly reached inside his coat for his gun, but Bennett was upon him before he could grab it, pinning his arms from behind. Rob pleaded for the detectives to give him a chance: the gun and ten paces. Both ignored him. Rob squirmed as McDougall handcuffed him. Bennett reached inside Rob's overcoat and pulled out the gun. Rob cursed: *He was sorry he didn't get a chance to shoot Bennett and McDougall; another second and he'd have gotten both of them.*

McDougall escorted Rob to the detectives' room at the Biddle House. Bennett stayed a while at the depot looking for the second Confederate who, according to the telegram, was traveling with Rob. He returned to the hotel to find Rob in his underwear, pushed into a chair. McDougall was beginning to go through his clothes. Suddenly, McDougall felt something in the jacket. He ripped the lining apart and pulled out Rob's papers and the $20 Confederate bill. McDougall began to read the papers.

Rob offered to pay for his freedom: *He had plenty of money. Nobody would ever know. What did it matter to them?* The detectives did not answer.

Rob, his clothes back on and handcuffed, was taken to the House of Correction and placed in a cell, still manacled. He heard Bennett tell a guard to be careful: the prisoner had tried to shoot them. They'd be back for him when it was time to leave for New York.

There was a slight bulge from an inside pocket of Rob's suit that McDougall had overlooked. Still hidden inside were several gold pieces and the small penknife Rob had purchased in Toronto.

As the new year of 1865 began, Bennett and McDougall escorted Rob aboard a train headed east. He tried to find out what they had in the way of evidence against him, but neither detective would talk. Warily, Rob asked if it had anything to do with the fires in New York. *Why?* Bennett asked. *Did he know anything about them?* Rob snickered, but said nothing further. He waited until their attention was distracted and then tried to pry the coach window open, but Bennett and McDougall seized him before he could get it up.

Rob spent the rest of the trip alternately cursing the detectives and waving his handcuffed hands defiantly at the other passengers.

"These are badges of honor!" he cried out. "I am a Southern gentleman!"[11]

part 6

THE TRIAL

King Jesus was a preacher;
He spoke in Palestine,
Proclaimed to all the nation
His power to redeem.
All de days of my life, ever since I been born,
I never heard a man speak lak dis man befo'.

I never heard a man speak lak dis man befo'.
All the days of my life, ever since I been born,
I never heard a man speak lak dis man befo'.

He spoke over in Jerusalem;
His parents they were gone;
"I want to ask some questions,
I'm from my Father's throne."
All de days of my life, ever since I been born,
I never heard a man speak lak dis man befo'.

He spake at the grave of Lazarus,
When a congregation met;
The Lord God folded up His arms;
I'm told that Jesus wept.
All de days of my life, ever since I been born,
I never heard a man speak lak dis man befo'.

He spoke to the Jewish nation,
"I am the solid rock;
Behold I am your Saviour,
I stand at the do' an' knock!"
All de days of my life, ever since I been born,
I never heard a man speak lak dis man befo'.

chapter 18

A s Rob was being taken to New York under guard, a Confederate he had served with in the raid on the train outside Buffalo sat in a cold cell at police headquarters on Mulberry Street: John Yates Beall. Their lives had touched before—and now they were irrevocably interwoven. Beall had a small, leatherbound notebook in which, with a stubby pencil, he chronicled what was happening to him:

> Thursday, Dec. 29, 1864. I purpose to keep in this little book a daily account of my imprisonment as far as I can . . .

> The Christmas of '64 I spent in a New York prison! Had I, 4 years ago, stood in New York, and proclaimed myself a citizen of Virginia, I would have been welcomed; now I am immured because I am a Virginian, *tempora mutatantur, et cum illis mutamus.*[1] As long as I am a citizen of Virginia, I shall cling to her destiny and maintain her laws as expressed by a majority of her citizens speaking through their authorized channel, if her voice be for war or peace. I shall go as she says . . . What misery have I seen during these four years, murder, lust, hate, rapine, devastation, war! What hardships suffered, what privations endured! May God grant that I may not see the like again! Nay, that my country may not! Oh, far rather would I welcome Death, *come as he might!* far rather would I meet him than go through four more such years. I can now understand why David would trust to his God, rather than to man . . .[2]

Beside Beall, on the cot that served also as his chair, lay a New Testament.

Since I have been placed in this cell I have read the Scrip-
ture, and have found such relief in its blessed words, especially
where it speaks of God's love for man; how He loved him, an
enemy, a sinner, and sent His Son into the world to save His
enemy . . .[3]

Beall—he pronounced his name "Bell"—was a stoutly built man
of Rob's age and height.[4] He had brilliant blue eyes, long brown hair,
and a light moustache and whiskers. Beall was a native of Walnut
Grove in the Shenandoah Valley, his family wealthy and influential
plantation owners. A graduate of the University of Virginia and an
Episcopalian, Beall was so devout that he had never played billiards in
his life. His military career began when he joined Botts Greys, a
volunteer unit in the Valley, at the time of John Brown's raid at Harp-
ers Ferry. He accompanied the unit when it was turned over to the
Confederate States as a brigade of the Army of Northern Virginia.
Wounded early in the war by a shot that broke three ribs, Beall was
subsequently discharged. Upon recovering, he joined the Confederate
Navy as a privateer, conducting numerous raids on Federal transports
and lighthouses in the Chesapeake Bay area. Captured and put in
irons in November 1863, Beall was later exchanged after the Richmond Government instituted retaliatory measures on Union prisoners. He appealed immediately for "special service" and was sent to
Canada to aid Jacob Thompson, volunteering to lead the unsuccessful
expedition to free the 3,000 Confederate officers held at Johnson's
Island. That had been followed by the fiasco in trying to derail the
train outside Buffalo—and his capture.

As yet, the police and Federal authorities had no idea of his real
identity, although they suspected that the name he went by—Baker—
was an alias, and—erroneously—that he had been involved in the
attempt to burn New York. Anderson, arrested with him in Buffalo,
was being kept in the House of Detention for Witnesses, a few blocks
south on Mulberry Street from police headquarters.

Detective James J. Kelso was in charge at headquarters in Young's
absence when Beall was brought there. Determined to learn "Baker's"
true identity and to determine whether he was involved in the incendiary plot, Kelso had Beall paraded in a lineup before witnesses—but
without success. He then asked the turnkey who attended the cells at
night to try to trick Beall into a compromising statement. The turnkey, Edward Hays, a former Navy Yard laborer and saloonkeeper who'd

taken the job at police headquarters the previous April, was briefed by Kelso to win Beall's confidence.

> Dec. 30th. Last evening the doorman brought me a "Book of Common Prayer" for $1.00, and it was and will be a source of great comfort to me . . .[5]

"There's a good deal done for money."

"It would be worth $1,000 in gold to get me out of here. Can you arrange it?"

"You must be in big trouble to pay a thousand. Did you have anything to do with those fires?"

"I didn't have a hand in them, but I know who did—they're all up in Canada."

Perhaps, the turnkey suggested, if he carried a message to them, told them Beall needed help—.

Beall poked several letters through the grating. Mail them. He had money to pay.

Hays took the letters and a coin Beall offered. He left through the thick iron door at the end of the passageway and headed upstairs to Kelso's office, pocketing the coin on the way.

Beall continued his diary for three more days:

> Dec. 31st. This year is gone . . . To-day I complete my twenty-ninth year. What have I done to make this world any wiser or better? . . . Will I see the year 1865 go out; or will I pass away from this world of sin, shame and suffering?
>
> Jan. 1st, 1865 . . . Oh this war! This far on life's way I have lived an honest life, defrauding no man . . . I saw grandfather and father die; they both took great comfort from the thought that no one could say that they had of malice aforethought injured them. Better the sudden death, or all the loathsome corruption of a lingering life, with honor and a pure conscience, than a long life with all material comforts and a canker-worm of infelt and con-stant dwelling dishonor; yea, a thousand time . . . .
>
> Jan. 2nd. Last night was called out, and a search made of my room and my person . . . I do most earnestly wish that I was in Richmond. Oh for the wings to fly to the uttermost part of the earth. What would I do without Bible and Prayer-book, and the

faith taught in them, best born of God, the fount in every bless-
ing? That faith nothing can take away save God.[6]

That same day, Beall was transferred to Fort Lafayette.

Rob entered the narrow passage.[7] It was cold. The walls were of
brick, the floor of stone. A lone stove sat at the end of the passage, off
of which were four cells. Two dirty, double-grated windows provided
the only light during the day. The turnkey unlocked the rusty iron
door of one of the cells. The cell was eight feet long and five feet
wide. A pail of water and a small sink were pushed against the far
wall. There was no window. As yet, Rob had no idea that Beall had
preceded him and was now imprisoned elsewhere.

Apparently dirty and disheveled, a stubble of beard on his face,
Rob stood in a room several flights above his cell as a number of
persons paraded past him, peering closely at his face. So far, no one
had been able to identify him.

The police were apparently already certain he was one of the
incendiaries: his limp was the give-away. Perhaps the lack of a full-
grown beard was the reason that no identification had been made.
The police must have thought so: they decided not to let Rob shave.
Meanwhile, there was news of another suspect being caught—a man
so frightened that he was sure to talk. His name was John Price. From
Virginia. Rob was not told of his arrest.

Hays was again playing the role of informer. This time, with Rob.
"I once got offered $1,500 in gold to let a prisoner go."
"Would you free me for that?"
"You don't have that much, do you?" the turnkey asked. "I could
take it right now."
"No," Rob answered, "but I know where I can get it. Would you
deliver a letter for me?"
"Sure, if there's something in it for me."
"I'll need a pen and some paper and envelopes."

> In prison Mulberry St. N.Y.
> Jan. 11th 1865

Mr. Hiram Cranston

Dear Sir

I do not know you personally but have heard of you & address you in my hour of need. I am a Capt in C.S.A. & belong to the 1st La. Infantry (Gladden's old Regt which you perhaps recollect). I have been arrested & am to be tried by court-martial for attempting to fire this City. This is what I learn from indications. I have not been informed of the nature of charges against me.[8] Whatever may be the result of the trial, there is at best a long imprisonment before me. I can be released by paying fifteen-hundred ($1500) dollars in gold—as the bearer can inform you. Will you advance or raise it for me? The C.S. Agent in Canada, Hon. J. Thompson I know would cheerfully refund the amount— and I and my Father have ample cotton for twenty-six times the sum. I know this is a strange request to make of an entire stranger, but consider my life at stake—$1500 is but a paltry sum to pay for it. If you could only visit me I could satisfy you of my ability to make *all right*. Let me have an answer by bearer— verbally if you think best.

Please burn this as stationery is dangerous.

Very respectfully
Yr. obt svt
Robt. C. Kennedy
Capt 1st La Infty[9]

Cranston, the proprietor of the New York Hotel, was an unknown commodity and might not want to get involved. Rob decided to try another Copperhead as well. Surely Representative Benjamin Wood, publisher of the *Daily News*, could be trusted. Rob had not yet been told of the charges against him, but he must have wanted to make his appeal sound more urgent. It was one of a string of mistakes he was to make.

In prison. Mulberry St.
Jany 11th 1865

Hon. Benj. Wood

Dear Sir

I am a prisoner in the hands of my enemies, to be tried by court-martial as I am informed, for attempting to fire this City. I can be released for $1500 in gold as the bearer can inform you. Can you advance it for me? I could refund it as soon as I reach Canada as Hon. J. Thompson or my friend Mr. S.V. Mitchell *I know* would cheerfully furnish the means to do so. I live in Louisiana Claiborne Parish—not yet overrun by the Federals. If I could *only* see you I am satisfied I could convince you of my ability to make it all right.

Consider my life is at stake. Please answer per bearer verbally if you think best.

Respectfully
Your obt servt.
Robt. C. Kennedy
Capt. C.S.A.[10]

"Cranston will furnish the money," Rob told the turnkey, "but make a strong case to Wood, too. Tell him the money will be returned from Canada."

"You have high-up friends," Hays said.

"I need them. You people are trying to implicate me in those fires."

"Did you have anything to do with them?"

"No!"

The next morning Hays delivered the letters to Superintendent Kennedy, who immediately arranged to see General Dix. A break in the case seemed near.

The letter to Cranston apparently appeared innocuous to Dix: Rob apparently did not know him. They'd hold onto it, and concoct some story for Rob's benefit.

As for Wood, a copy of the letter would be made before sending it to him—Rob hadn't said anything in this letter about their being strangers. Dix asked an adjutant, Captain Edward W. Hooper, to copy the letter; the original was to go back to the superintendent.

In the meantime, there was the matter of Beall. There was enough evidence to try him for seizing the lake steamer and attempting to derail the train upstate. It would be best to keep Beall and Rob separated.

Later that morning—Thursday, January 12—Hays went to Wood's office at the *News*, 19 Park Row. The Copperhead editor opened the letter Hays handed him. His eyes lit up in wonder as he read it. "I don't recognize such business," he said. "I just run a paper." Wood tore up the letter and turned away from Hays without saying more.

Hays returned to police headquarters. After reporting to Superintendent Kennedy what had happened, he went down to the cells.

"Cranston would not give me any money," the turnkey lied to Rob. "Said he could not get that much. The same thing was true of Wood."

"Damn such men that let on that they are sympathizers with the South and would help them."

Rob swore several times.

The turnkey suggested trying someone else.

"I know McMaster, the editor of *The Freeman's Journal*, is supposed to be a generous man," Rob said, "but he may not have enough money."

Hays offered to take $500 on account and wait for the rest until Rob reached Canada.

Rob had most likely avoided trying to contact McMaster on purpose: it was too dangerous for both of them. But what was left? There was the knife. He had never been searched at police headquarters. He still had it, secreted now under his mattress. But that was a last resort. If McMaster didn't come through, he'd have to use it. Could the turnkey be trusted? Would McMaster help? Rob waited three days before writing, and then carefully emphasized the fact that he did not know the publisher:

> Mulberry St Prison
> Jany. 15th 1865

Mr. McMaster

Dear Sir—

My Turnkey, the bearer of this, I have bribed to release me If I can get some responsible man in the City to be my security—or guarantee that the money will be forthcoming. He says if he can get such guarantee for five hundred dollars he will get me out tonight. I have not time to explain matters or make suitable

apologies for thus addressing you—an entire stranger. Question
him as regards my condition &c. Do not promise him any money
in advance, for I believe him to be a scoundrel. Any arrangements you may make to effect my release will entitle you to my
eternal gratitude. I can refund any sum under $1500 as soon as I
reach Canada. Burn this—stationery is dangerous—

> Respectfully yrs
> Robt. C. Kennedy
> Capt 1st La Infty C.S.A.[11]

"Tell McMaster anything to persuade him that I was one of those
who took part in the fires, that I've been identified," Rob said, turning
the letter over to the turnkey. "And tell him I'm doomed unless I can
get some money, that I'm in my enemies' hands and need help.
Sweeten him good."

"Were you really concerned with the fires?"

Perhaps it didn't matter any more. Hays was in it, too, if he
helped him to escape.

"Yes."

"What part of the city—upper or lower?"

"Lower."

"What hotels did you set fire to?"

Rob grew apprehensive. What was Hays after? He asked too many
questions.

"What do you want to ask such a question as that for?"

The turnkey tried to allay Rob's suspicions. He was just curious,
he said.

Superintendent Kennedy again went to General Dix's office, a
few blocks from police headquarters, to discuss what to do about Rob's
latest letter. Inasmuch as Rob had said in it that he and McMaster
were strangers, they decided to pass it along to McMaster and to gauge
his reaction. Hays was not to say a word about the fires; it would be
wiser to let the publisher make that connection. However, the turnkey
was to try to get some reply in writing from McMaster if he showed
any interest. The superintendent was apparently concerned that the
case against Rob was weak without any corroborating evidence. Although Rob's beard was slowly growing, no one had yet been able to

positively identify him. Dix, however, was anxious to press the matter: he wanted Rob brought to trial soon. The Army, in fact, was about to publish charges on the basis of what Price had divulged.

Hooper, Dix's aide, was off duty, so Kennedy took the letter back with him to police headquarters to have one of his own men make a copy. The copy would go to McMaster, the original would be kept for the trial. If Rob and McMaster were indeed strangers, the publisher would have no reason to question the handwriting. If they *had* known each other, then it was a gamble—but, perhaps, McMaster would still not be familiar with Rob's writing.

Hays waited in the outer office of *The Freeman's Journal* half an hour before McMaster found time to see him. Their talk lasted an-other half hour. The turnkey left after scheduling another appoint-ment with the publisher later in the afternoon. It was late when he finally returned to police headquarters to report to Superintendent Kennedy, and he did not get to see Rob until the next day, Tuesday, January 17.

On Tuesday morning, Dix's Special Orders No. 14 were issued, setting up a military commission that would meet in three days to begin Beall's trial and then go on to Rob's.[12] Although Rob doubted that the authorities had any incriminating evidence against him, he did not doubt that they believed he had been involved in the plot and would convict him nonetheless.

Hays, meanwhile, reported to Rob that McMaster was willing to help but did not have the money. The publisher, he said, had pledged his word that Hays would be paid if he went to Canada, but the turnkey wanted some guarantee—in cash.

Rob could not afford to let his hope of escape pass, although he didn't trust Hays. So he prepared a second letter to McMaster:

Mulberry St Prison
N York Jan. 18

Dear Sir

The bearer Hays says he is not willing to effect my release unless he has other assurance than your mere word that the money will be paid him. Give him *no hold* on you—but if you can, satisfy the scamp that all will be right. I would not involve others in my misfortunes. There is no reliance to be placed on this man except in case it is evidently to his interest to act in good faith. You know how I am situated—must risk treachery & foul play—but think there is no danger unless you commit yourself in writing.

I submit this business to you. If you can aid me without injuring yourself I ask you to do it—but if you have to place yourself in the hands of any *son of a bitch* Why? refuse altogether and leave me to my fate.

Truly yours,
Robt. C. Kennedy

To convince McMaster, Rob decided to risk identifying himself. (Did it matter, now, anyway?)

P.S. You remember Stanton do you not?[13]

Rob saw McGee, the alternate turnkey, at his cell door. Two detectives stood beside him. Rob was ordered out of the cell: the Army wanted to see him.

Rob groped under his mattress with his hand, hidden from the turnkey's view, as McGee told him to hurry up. One of the detectives brushed past McGee and entered. He grabbed Rob's wrists and slapped a pair of handcuffs on them. Ordering Rob to stand up, he searched Rob's clothing.

The other detective waited until Rob was outside in the passageway, then entered the cell, too, and began searching the sparse furnishings. The detective lifted up the mattress, uncovering the penknife.

Hays appeared after the detective showed the knife to his colleague and pocketed it. The turnkey's eyes widened with surprise when told about the knife. What was Rob doing with it?

Maybe I could've gotten away, Rob said, only McGee hadn't given him a chance to slip it up his sleeve. He was keeping it back to use on Hays, Rob said, in case the trial went badly. The turnkey was an easy mark.

Major John Augustus Bolles, a man in his mid-fifties, had been a prominent lawyer and then Massachusetts Secretary of State. Dix's brother-in-law, he served as the general's aide de camp. It was Bolles who would prosecute both Rob and Beall as Judge Advocate of the military commission Dix had convened. It was his task to inform Rob of the charges, and to offer the appointment of a defending counsel.

Rob would be tried as a spy, arrested within Union lines in civilian clothes. The Army knew he had been in New York last November using an alias, "Stanton." Bolles had already talked to Frank Clark, and detectives had traced Rob to the boarding house on Prince Street. The Army was prepared to prove that Rob had had a hand in setting the fires in New York. Rob's fate was in his own hands. Bolles was available for help any time Rob needed him, and Rob could always have counsel of his own. However, a statement from Rob about his part in the fires and the names of the other conspirators would undoubtedly incline the court to leniency.

Rob considered the offer. Yes, he would make a statement—if it were entered at the trial.

Bolles assented and called a stenographer to take down Rob's words:

> My name is Robt. Cobb Kennedy.
>
> I have been & am in the Confed. Military Service, Capt. 1st La. infy—enlisted men's.
>
> I was in N.Y. city last Nov. at Belmont Hotel—came here from Toronto—on the hotel books as Mr. Stanton. I brought to Mr. Clarke [sic] a letter of introduction from Mr. W. L. McDonald. I came to spend a few weeks, have some fun, & run the blockade to Wilmington. I had been confined at Johnson's I. & escaped. Was in N.Y. a few weeks. Left N.Y. in Nov. Did not leave N.Y. when I left the Belmont. When I left N.Y. I was boarding at 89 Prince St.—Mrs. Oatman's. To her I paid my bills—did not go off in her debt. I left by the Hudson river R.R. by night—I think about 6 on a P.M. I took the car at the 30th St. depot—& returned to Toronto next day—I can't fix the day of the week. I was in citizen's dress. I decline to state whether I had any errand in N.Y. other than I have stated. I went back to Toronto because I found I could not get from here to Wilmington via Bermuda or Nassau. I made inquiries if there were any vessels

running the blockade from N.Y. & found there were not. I de-
cline stating whether anything had occurred that induced me to
leave N.Y. when I did.

I remained in Toronto & C.W. until Dec. 28. Came to Detroit Dec. 29 & was there arrested that day. I was on my way to
the Southern Confederacy—in the suit I now have on.

The reason I did not go from Toronto to Halifax & thence to
Wilmington via Bermuda in Dec. was that I heard that the Federal fleet were investing Wilmington.[14]

After Rob was taken back to his cell, Bolles reported to Dix. The
general said he would get out a wire to Johnson's Island. It would not
prove anything, however: Rob's escape was hardly proof of innocence
or guilt.

With only two days to prepare his defense, Beall went before the
military commission on Friday, January 20, at Fort Lafayette. The trial
was a short one. The chief witnesses against him included the part-
owner and clerk of the *Philo Parsons;* Hays, who told of the bribe offer;
and the Confederate arrested with him, Anderson, who implicated
Beall in the attempted train derailment—a "crime," said Judge Advocate General Joseph Holt in Washington, that "seems to assume that
fiendish enormity which cries loudly for vengeance of the outraged
law. So dark a picture of guilt is revolting to all the instincts of hu-
manity."[15]

The letters Beall had given to Hays to mail—two to Richmond
and one to Thompson in Canada, asking for certificates to prove he
was acting under Confederate authority and orders—had never been
posted.

Hays returned from delivering Rob's second letter to McMaster
with discouraging news. The publisher would not agree to deposit any
money in a bank in Hays's name or, as Hays also suggested, in the
name of his sister. If Hays ran the risk of freeing Rob and going to
Canada himself, McMaster would see to it that the turnkey was re-
paid. Hays, however, had no intention of doing that. He told both
McMaster and Rob as much. Rob's only hope rested in maintaining
his innocence. He had to stick by his statement to Bolles, no matter

what. No one, after all, had identified him, and the papers taken from him at his arrest proved only that he was trying to return home.

As he waited for his trial to begin, Rob struck up a friendship with the least likely of comrades, the Negro in the cell next to his, Charles Smith, a sailor from the island of St. Helena, where Napoleon had died in exile. Rob found Smith receptive to his complaints about Hays. Smith had some complaints of his own—about Hays and about the police. He'd been arrested for drunkenness and was still awaiting trial after three weeks in the dungeon.

On Tuesday, January 31, as the House of Representatives prepared to vote on the Thirteenth Amendment to abolish slavery—the Wood brothers, both lame-duck Congressmen, would vote against it that day—an armed escort of soldiers appeared at police headquarters to take Rob to the Department of the East's headquarters on Bleecker Street, a short walk away, for the start of his trial.

chapter 19

ob sat by himself at a small desk. Another small desk, for Bolles, was to his side. In front of him was a long table with six chairs behind it. A lone chair and small stand for a stenographer stood to one side. On the other side was another lone chair, for witnesses. A flag trimmed with gold tassels stood in the corner of the otherwise undecorated room. Except for the guards, there were no spectators.

The door opened and six Federal officers in parade uniforms entered in single file. Leading them was forty-eight-year-old Brigadier General Fitz-Henry Warren, United States Volunteers. Warren, a former journalist and politician from Massachusetts, was president of the court.

Warren took his place in the middle of the table, facing Rob, while the others found their places to his left and right: Brigadier General William Hopkins Morris, United States Volunteers, West Point '51, a former assistant editor of the *New York Home Journal* and inventor of a conical repeating carbine (and wounded at Spotsylvania); Colonel M. S. Howe, Third United States Cavalry; Colonel H. Day, United States Army; Brevet Lieutenant Colonel R. F. O'Bierne, Fourteenth United States Infantry; and Major George W. Wallace, Sixth United States Infantry. They were the same officers who were sitting in judgment on Beall.[1]

Warren asked Rob whether he objected to any officer on the court.[2]

No.

Warren then asked Bolles to swear in the commission. When he had finished, Warren in turn swore in Bolles as Judge Advocate. Bolles, finally, swore in the court stenographer.

Was the accused ready to plead to the charges and specifications? Yes.

Warren had the charges read aloud:

CHARGE I: Acting as a spy.

Specification 1.—In this, that Robert C. Kennedy, a captain in the military service of the insurgent States, was found acting as a spy in the city of New York, in the State of New York, on or about the 1st day of November, 1864.

Specification 2.—In this, that Robert C. Kennedy, a captain in the military service of the insurgent States, was found acting as a spy in the city of Detroit, in the State of Michigan, on or about the 29th day of December, 1864.

CHARGE II: Violation of the laws of war.

Specification.—In this, that Robert C. Kennedy, a captain in the military service of the insurgent States, undertook to carry on irregular and unlawful warfare in the city and State of New York by setting fire thereto. All this in said city of New York on or about the 25th day of November, 1864.

How did the accused plead?

Not guilty to all the charges.

Was he ready to proceed to trial?

Rob answered in the affirmative. He had apparently decided to defend himself—a decision he was soon to regret.[3]

Bolles got to his feet, a paper in his hands. He had a statement made by Rob and wanted him to acknowledge his signature on it. Bolles read the statement Rob had made in his presence twelve days earlier and showed it to Rob. Was this his signature?

It was.

Bolles turned to the court. He handed the paper to Warren, who passed it on to the stenographer: Exhibit Number One. Bolles waited until the stenographer marked the paper, then called his first witness for the prosecution—the turnkey, Edward Hays.

Bolles opened the questioning by asking him his occupation and whether or not he knew Rob.

"State if any and what communications have passed between you and him in regard to getting him out, as in regard to your taking letters, or in regard to what he has done at any time in New York."

The details of the whole sordid tale slowly unfolded, including Hays's account of his visits to Cranston, Wood, and McMaster. Hays traced his deception in detail, explaining what he had done with the letters.

"Did he at that time make any statement as to whether he was or was not concerned in the burning?" Bolles asked.

"He told me at that time," Hays said, "that he was concerned in the burning."

"What did he say?"

"He told me to state to Mr. McMaster that he was here the night of the fire—that he was one of the party and that he was recognized as one—and I asked him if it was in the upper part or lower part of the city that he was, that he set fire to the hotels, and he told me in the lower part. And I asked him which one of the hotels did he set fire to and he said to me, 'What do you want to ask such a question as that for?' I did not go any further . . . ."

Hays then related how the knife had been found in Rob's cell.

Bolles turned to the court: No further questions.

It was Rob's turn to cross-examine, if he wished to. He began by questioning Hays about the knife, trying to shake the turnkey's story but only making matters worse.

"Did the accused," Rob asked, referring to himself, "state that he intended using the knife the day he was brought over?"

"Yes."

"Not that he intended to use it, but he intended to take it so that if a chance occurred he might use it?"

"That is the statement he made. . . . He said he did not like to do it so soon. He said he was keeping it back, making it a last resort . . . He meant by that that if it came to the worst, he would wait until he would see how his trial would go and then take my life because he said I was the easiest to be got at with the knife."

Rob tried another tack:

"Did you ever receive any money from the prisoner—the accused?"

"Not for any purpose except to bring him things. I have received money to bring in things."

"Did you not receive $15 in gold from the accused?"

"No, sir."

Rob gave up. He had no more questions.

Hays started to get up from the witness chair, but Warren stopped him. The president of the court thought Bolles had been lax in examining his own witness. He wanted the trial record to be clear. He asked the turnkey which letters had been delivered and what the various recipients had said.

Rob suddenly remembered something. He asked Warren's permission to question Hays again. Permission was granted, and Rob once again confronted the turnkey.

"You state," he reminded the turnkey, "that the accused made admission that he had been engaged in firing hotels. Did not he in conversation with you tell you to tell McMaster anything you chose, instead of making admissions—that he, the accused, considered himself in the hands of his enemies and wished to be relieved?"

Hays remained steadfast.

"The accused told me that he was engaged in firing the hotels. He told me to sweeten McMaster good, to talk to him pretty good in order to get the money. This was after he told me he was engaged in firing the hotels."

"He made a statement to you for your information that he was actually engaged in firing hotels downtown, independently of what he told you to tell McMaster?"

"No," Hays conceded. "He told me to tell McMaster that he was firing the hotels downtown, and after that he told me to tell McMaster pretty good so McMaster would give the money."

Rob pressed the point.

"Did the accused tell you that he was concerned in it or did he tell you to tell McMaster that he was concerned in it?"

"He told me to tell McMaster so."

Rob was no sooner through questioning than Bolles quickly asked Hays a question.

"Did he or did he not, except for the purpose of telling you what to say to McMaster, ever tell you whether he was concerned in it or not?"

"Yes, sir, he told me he was concerned in the firing. I asked him whether he was or was not. He said, 'Yes.' I said, 'What part of the city were you in—up or down town?' He said downtown. I asked what hotels he set fire to and he then asked why I asked that question."

Bolles's second witness was Superintendent of Police John A. Kennedy. His testimony was brief. The letters Rob had sent to Cranston and McMaster were introduced into evidence as Exhibits 2, 3, and 4, along with an envelope addressed to "Mr. McMasters/Office Freeman's Journal/N York." The police official described how they were intercepted and copies made.

Bolles had one final question:

"Do you know anything from the statements of the accused, Captain Kennedy, in regard to a knife being found in his cell?"

"Not from him. I have not seen the prisoner until this morning."

Rob took his turn at questioning.

"Did the doorkeeper Edward Hays tell you that the accused had admitted to him that he was concerned in the burning of the hotels of New York?"

The superintendent affirmed this.

"Would you believe the statement of Mr. Hays under oath?"

"Most certainly I would."

Rob retired, and Bolles was on his feet again. He had forgotten to establish that the fires had been set. He asked the superintendent to relate the events of November 25 and then excused him.

The next witness, Captain Edward W. Hooper, confirmed making the copy of the letter to Benjamin Wood and presented it. It was marked Exhibit 5. Neither Rob nor the court had any questions. Bolles then called his last witness.

Rob turned, surprised, to see John M. Price enter the room with a guard. Without thinking, he took Price's offered hand and shook it.

"State your name, age, occupation and residence."

"My name is John M. Price. I am twenty-one years old. I have no occupation. My residence is Virginia."

"I noticed," Bolles said, "that as you came into Court you shook hands with the accused. Do you know him?"

"Yes, sir."

"Whence did you last meet him before this?"

"I met him in Canada."

"Do you know anything from his own statements of his being in New York City last November?"

Price turned to the court members.

"Am I compelled to answer these questions?"

"You need not answer any question to incriminate yourself," Warren declared. "Otherwise, you must answer."

Bolles had the question repeated: "Do you know anything from his own statements of his being in New York City last November?"

"I do not remember the time," Price answered. "He said he had been in New York. The date I do not remember."

"Did he state, and if so, what did he say was his errand in New York?"

"I met him and several others at St. Catharines, Canada West. I don't remember the date. It was probably a month before last Christmas. I think it was the early part of December. We were all in a room together and Captain Kennedy mentioned what he was doing here in New York. He said he came here with other parties to fire these hotels, that he fired the museum and a hotel. I don't remember the name of it."

"What museum?"

"Barnum's Museum, I believe it is called."

"Was the hotel the Belmont House?"

"I don't remember, it is so long ago and I have not thought of the matter since. I never supposed I would have to relate the conversation."

"Did he state the particulars in regard to his firing either the hotel or the museum? How he did it, or where he did it?"

"I think he said he fired it under the steps of the building, I am not certain, and that he attempted to do it somewhere else and failed. That was the museum."

"Had you yourself been in New York City at the time of the conversation, and if so, when?"

"I had been here before the conversation—I don't remember the date exactly."

"How long ago?"

"It was probably a month or six weeks before the fire."

"Had you any agency or concern in the plans for the fire?"

"No, sir, I had not," Price lied. "I knew there was a party coming to New York and I was asked to come along. I did not know what the purpose was. I could not go. I went somewhere else. I knew what the object was after the party left."

"Did you know at that time," Bolles continued, "that the accused was one of the party or that he was to be one?"

Price hedged.

"I think I did—I think I heard him say he was going."

"Do you know under what name he was here, by his own statement or otherwise?"

"Only from what I have seen in the papers. I never heard him say what name he assumed here. I don't think I ever heard him say so."

Bolles was through with his questions. It was now Rob's turn. If Rob wanted to, he could easily implicate Price; however, that would prove his own guilt. He must have wondered what hold the Union authorities had over him.

"On what charges were you arrested?" Rob asked Price.

"I have not heard of any charges being preferred against me, unless that I am a Confederate officer."

"Have any inducements been held out to you to give evidence against the accused?"

"No, sir."

"Do you still consider yourself an officer of the Confederate Army?"

"I suppose I would be if I returned there."

"What is your rank?"

"I was never commissioned. I was acting ordnance officer. I was sergeant of a battery assigned to duty in the Ordnance Department."

Hadn't Price sworn at an extradition trial in Toronto that he was a lieutenant?

"No, sir, I did not, no question was asked me in regard to my rank."

Rob had no more questions. When Bolles said the prosecution had no further witnesses to call, Rob could only ask for a delay until the following Friday to work on his defense. The request was granted. The commission adjourned to meet the next day at Fort Lafayette, where Beall was being tried. It would continue Rob's case on February 3.

Before Rob was taken away, Bolles offered his assistance to him. He was available at headquarters any afternoon after four, and would be willing to confer with Rob.

Back in his cell, Rob had no idea of what to do next, beyond appealing to Thompson and the other Confederates in Toronto for depositions to prove he was not a spy. He sent off the appropriate letters. Several times he asked Hays to see Bolles, but the turnkey only scoffed at him.

When the military commission reconvened on Friday, February 3, Rob said he was not ready to proceed because he had been unable to see Bolles. Bolles confirmed making the offer to Rob. Warren asked Rob what he proposed to do. Rob said he wanted further time to send letters to Canada and receive their answers—and he would like to acquire counsel. He told the court that he understood that a class-mate of his at West Point was now a lawyer in New York. He would like to try to get his services.

The request was granted. Warren ordered Rob's trial postponed until Thursday, February 9, at eleven o'clock—the day after the military commission was scheduled to hand down its verdict in Beall's case.

chapter 20

dwin H. Stoughton, although slightly younger than the man he was about to defend, appeared much older. He had a long moustache and dressed foppishly, paying minute attention to every detail of his clothing—as though that could hide his wounded pride.

After graduating from West Point in 1859, Stoughton served two years of garrison duty in the Army before resigning to become a scout in the West. When the war broke out, he joined the Fourth Vermont Brigade as a colonel and served gallantly in the Peninsular Campaign. By November of 1862, he was a brigadier general in the United States Volunteers. On a peaceful night in March of the following year, however, he was sleeping soundly after a party for guests at his headquarters in Fairfax Court House, Virginia, when John Singleton Mosby and twenty-nine of his Partisan Rangers stole into town on an audacious horse-hunting raid. Mosby found Stoughton asleep in his bed. He pulled off the blanket, hoping to waken Stoughton, but the general slept on, snoring loudly. Mosby, in a hurry to leave the town before the Federal troops there could regroup, pulled up Stoughton's nightshirt and slapped him on the behind. This time, Stoughton woke with a start to find himself staring into Mosby's eyes. "General, did you ever hear of Mosby?" the raider asked coyly. "Yes, have you caught him?" "No," the Virginian answered, "I am Mosby—he has caught you."[1]

Stoughton was incarcerated in the notorious Libby Prison in Richmond, and when released, his commission having expired, he gave up any attempt to resume his Army career. To add to the indignity of his capture—the ludicrous details were the source of many

177

bawdy jokes—it was said that Lincoln was more annoyed by the loss of
the horses Mosby had stolen than by Stoughton's capture.

The emotional wounds that Stoughton suffered as a result may
have clouded his approach to Rob's case. It is apparent, though, that
the general-turned-lawyer never doubted Rob's insistence that he was
an innocent victim of circumstances. Thus Stoughton's defense was a
simple one: the Government's evidence was all circumstantial; it
would only be necessary, therefore, to demonstrate that Rob was an
escaped prisoner trying to return home. Accordingly, the first
charge—that Rob had been a spy while in New York and later when
caught in Detroit—did not trouble Stoughton. Both of these
accusations could be refuted by proving that Rob's words and deeds
stemmed from his desire to get back to the South, that he was no
more than an escaped prisoner of war passing through enemy territory
in disguise. To support this point, Ann Cullen, the chambermaid, and
Mrs. Carrie Owens, the widow Oatman's daughter, could testify to
Rob's innocuous behavior while lodged in New York. Frank Clark
could testify along similar lines, and also to the fact that he'd last
seen Rob on November 21, several days before the attempt to burn
New York had been made. Moreover, one of the detectives who'd
captured Rob in Detroit could verify that Rob had had no time for
spying while in that city, and could also attest to the proof of
citizenship and pledge of conduct that Rob carried on his
person—further evidence of Rob's motive for turning up in either city.

It was therefore on the second charge—that Rob had participated
in the effort to burn New York—that the outcome of the trial would
rest. Here, then, Stoughton would have to break the testimony of
Hays and Price, the only prosecution witnesses to connect Rob with
the conspiracy. There was no one to call upon to rebut Price: his
testimony would have to be attacked in the defense summation as an
attempt to save his own skin now that he was in Union hands himself.
To refute Hays, it would be necessary to show that he was a liar in
unscrupulous pursuit of the reward money. Charles Smith, the Negro
seaman in the cell next to Rob's, could call into question Hays's
credibility by showing how the turnkey took advantage of the
prisoners under his charge. And McMaster, the publisher, could
further discredit Hays; his social prestige would add invaluable weight
to the defense case. There was some doubt, however, whether
McMaster could be persuaded to appear willingly to dispute a witness

who linked him to the Confederates in Canada. Rob had written him—or at least so he apparently informed Stoughton—because he'd once heard the publisher's name mentioned among a list of other Copperheads, along with Benjamin Wood and Hiram Cranston; Rob knew nothing of them except that they were supposedly Southern sympathizers. He'd written them blindly in the hope of enlisting their aid.

There was one more avenue to try: Canada. Rob had already written to Thompson for help, asking for money and for documents that would prove his innocence. However, he still hadn't received any response. Would Stoughton write, too? "I know the papers paint me a devil," Rob said, but he wanted to pay Stoughton for his services if possible. The lawyer shrugged off the remark: he would defend Rob, no matter what. In the meantime, however, he would also write to Thompson.

So Stoughton set about preparing his defense in complete ignorance both of Rob's complicity and of most of the relevant facts of the case. He had not seen any of the trial transcripts—a copy was not ready yet—and had to rely at first on Rob to provide the salient portions. He had not read the letters Rob wrote from prison. Nor did he know that Bolles had questioned Frank Clark prior to the trial, or that Clark was in any way connected with Jacob Thompson and Larry McDonald in Canada. He didn't know what Rob had said to the detectives in Detroit, or that Rob had actually met McMaster. Ann Cullen, Mrs. Owens, Smith the sailor—they could testify only to character, not facts. The defense case, though Stoughton didn't realize it, was on shaky ground.

Stoughton won a day's delay until Friday, February 10, in which to find the witnesses he was looking for. When the military commission resumed Rob's case at noon that day, he'd been able to locate three of them. The first was the chambermaid, Ann Cullen.

"Where were you employed during October and November, 1864?" Stoughton began.

"With Mrs. Oatman, 89 Prince Street, New York."

"Do you recognize the accused?"

"Yes, sir."

"Where have you seen him?"

"At Mrs. Oatman's."

"Did he have rooms at Mrs. Oatman's and for how long?"

"He had rooms in Mrs. Oatman's house—I cannot say whether it was two or three weeks during the time I was there—it was certainly two weeks at the time I left."

"About when did he come there?"

"I don't know whether it was in September or November—it was either the last of September or about the first of November. I can't say which."

Stoughton had apparently expected the girl to be more definite about the time.

"Was he not with her [Mrs. Oatman] during the latter part of October?"

"I think he was, but I cannot be certain about it—but I would know if I looked over the date I have on my books, because I marked down all the times. I let the rooms and I know when I let them."

Stoughton decided on a different approach, hoping perhaps that the chambermaid might establish an alibi for Rob if she admitted to romantic liaisons at times when the conspirators would have been meeting.

"In what capacity were you with Mrs. Oatman?"

"I was chambermaid and I attended the door."

"During the time the accused had rooms there, were most of his evenings spent in the house?"

Bolles interrupted.

"That is irrelevant."

Stoughton said he simply wanted to prove that Kennedy's habits while at the boarding house were those of an innocent person, not those of a spy.

Warren questioned the other members of the court. They agreed to allow the question.

"Most generally when I went up to his room in the evening I found him there, and I always found his door locked when I went up at ten o'clock to my room," the chambermaid said. "I used not to go there every evening, but as a general thing when I did I saw him in his room."

Bolles approached the witness chair. He had only two questions.

"What name did he go by there?"

"Mr. Stanton."

"Was he boarding there when you left?"

"Yes, sir—rooming there."

Stoughton next called Charles Smith, the Negro sailor who was imprisoned near Rob's own cell. Smith testified to Hays's venality:

"Mr. Hays," Smith said, "fooled me out of a pair of gloves, a penknife and a razor. I was in the cell next to the accused and he took me across on the other side into the coldest cell—this side was warmest. I asked him what the reason was. He said, 'I don't want you to talk there so much—to make a noise and be talking with people.' Of course, in that cold cell I had no blanket or nothing, so I gave him my gloves to take me back to my warm cell and he brought me back again . . . ."

"From what you know of him," Stoughton asked, "would you believe him under oath?"

"No, sir, I would not believe him."

Bolles quickly attempted to dispose of the Negro sailor's credibility in cross-examination.

"What were you there for?"

"I was carried there. There were five or six of us seafaring men on a spree and a party of men took us—the men showed their shields and took us and locked us up."

"What were you doing when you were arrested?"

"We came out of a grocery drunk—five or six of us—we were arrested on the sidewalk."

Bolles, apparently satisfied, said he had no more questions.

Stoughton's third witness was Frank Clark, Larry McDonald's one-time employee and friend. Clark, as his testimony unfolded, turned out—to Rob's detriment—to be an easily rattled witness.

"Do you recognize the accused," Stoughton began, "and if so when did you meet him and what were the circumstances?"

"I do recognize him as Mr. Stanton—that is according to the letter of introduction I received from him—I don't know that it was exactly according to the letter of introduction—it was according to the name I heard him called by, I believe the letter of introduction hadn't any name in it."

"What was the general contents of the letter?"

"A few lines—'Allow me to introduce you to one of our college boys, about spending his vacation in the city. Of course, any favors or attention you can show him, do so and oblige &c.' I believe that was the sum and substance of it. Of course, I cannot recollect the exact wording."

"About what time did you first meet Stanton?"

"I cannot recollect that. I suppose it must be three months ago—two months ago maybe—two or three."

"How often did you see him?"

"I never saw him but two or three times."

"Had he a letter of introduction to anybody else in the city?"

"Not that I am aware of."

"Was his conduct at any time such as to arouse your suspicion in the slightest degree?"

"No, sir."

"You say you saw him several times—upon what did you converse?"

"Ordinary pleasantries of the day—fine weather or something of that kind. I don't recollect anything else that passed between us."

"About what day did you last see him?"

"It is a long while ago—I don't suppose I ever saw anything of Mr. Stanton within possibly three weeks after he was here. I guess the last time I met him I met him on the street—it might have been three or four weeks—somewheres in that neighborhood."

Stoughton had one last question.

"Did you see him after the twenty-first day of November, 1864?"

"No, sir."

Bolles was suspicious. He began his cross-examination by asking Clark whether he'd seen Rob on November 21.

"No, sir."

"Why do you mention the 21st as not having seen him after that?"

"Because I could not have seen him on the 21st day of November. Because it was prior to that that I saw him last."

"Did you see him in November at all?"

"Possibly I might."

"What month was it that he brought you that letter?"

"That is more than I can tell you. I have a very vivid recollection of the 21st of November, about that time, so I can calculate on it—possibly it might have been in October when I saw him."

Bolles pressed the witness.

"Did you see him in November at all?"

"I may and I may not. If I did it must have been in the very early part."

"Did you see him in November at all?"

"I cannot state."

"Who was that letter of introduction from?"

"William L. McDonald."

"A man known as Larry McDonald?"

"Yes, sir."

"Did McDonald keep a carriage depot here which he called the 'Southern Carriage Depot'?"

Stoughton protested: "Irrelevant, irrelevant."

"Overruled."

Clark answered: "That was the sign on the door."

"At that time you were in his employ?" asked Bolles, again pressing Clark.

"Yes, sir."

"When did he give up that depot?"

"Somewheres in the neighborhood of 1861 or 1862."

"After the war broke out?"

"Yes, sir."

"What became of him?"

"At one time I heard he was a sutler in a New Jersey regiment."

"What became of him in the service?"

"So far as my knowledge is concerned I know nothing—but I have heard reports."

"Where did you hear from him next?"

"I never heard from him. His residence was in Westchester County."

"How long was he in the service?"

"That is more than I can say."

"At what time do you know he ceased to be in the service?"

"That is more than I can tell."

"Where was the letter from?"

"The letter was from Toronto."

"How long has he been in Toronto?"

"That is more than I can tell."

"How long since you have known him to be in Toronto by the receipt of letters or messages from him? When was the first time you heard from him there?"

"Something like eighteen months ago."

"You know by letter from him that he was there a year and a half ago?"

"Yes, sir."

"Do you know that Larry McDonald was ever a member of any college?"

Stoughton, undoubtedly wanting to take the pressure off Clark, rose to object.

Bolles insisted: "I propose to show that neither McDonald nor the witness were ever members of any college and the phrase—'one of our college boys'—was not used in the ordinary meaning of the term."

Warren consulted with the others on the court panel. Stoughton's objection was sustained.

Bolles tried another tack.

"Did Stanton ever tell you what he came to New York for?"

"No, sir."

"Was anybody else introduced to you by Larry McDonald by letter of introduction about this time?"

"Yes, sir, a man of the name Chenault."

"What became of Stanton after he delivered to you his letter of introduction?"

"I took him to the Belmont Hotel directly opposite my place, and introduced him to the bookkeeper as a gentleman that wished to obtain a room there."

"Not mentioning any name?"

"No, sir, I did not know his name then."

"Hadn't you asked him his name?"

"No, sir."

"How long after receiving him and the letter of introduction did you find out what name he went by at the hotel?"

"I saw him write his name."

"Didn't you tell me," Bolles asserted, "it was three weeks after he arrived in the city before he stated his name?"

"I object," Stoughton said.

"Overruled."

Bolles waited for Clark's answer.

"I don't recollect that I did make any statement of that kind," Clark finally said. "I recollect you asked me something that had a bearing on three weeks, but it was not in reference to Stanton's name—if I did you misunderstood me. You have got the two mixed together. I recollect saying that my memory was not particularly good, that I do not recollect a man's name—something to that effect, when you were taking my statement. If I did say that, it was a mistake—I don't see how I could have made such a mistake."

"Did you take Chenault to the Belmont House also?"

"I did."

"How often did you see him?"

"Half a dozen times I suppose."

"Did you see him and Stanton together after he came to town?"

"Yes, sir, once or twice. Once at the hotel when I introduced them, and once I met him on the street, I think, I am not sure."

"Were they ever in your place together?"

"Not to my recollection."

"Did you ever hear any conversation between them?"

"Never anything more than 'How do you do,' something of that kind—nothing of any moment."

"Do you know why McDonald went to Canada?"

"Of my own knowledge, I do not."

Stoughton interrupted again.

"This line of questioning is hearsay," he said to Warren. "You cannot allow it."

"It is legitimate," Bolles insisted.

Warren leaned back. The court would be cleared to discuss it.

Stoughton might well have wondered what had ever led Rob to Clark: Bolles was making him sound like a Southern agent. Stoughton decided to fight for more time. His defense, obviously, was going badly.

The court reconvened, but before its decision could be announced, Bolles advised that no ruling would be necessary: he had no more questions to ask Clark. Stoughton, surely relieved, immediately asked for more time to import witnesses from Johnson's Island to prove that Rob had been a prisoner there and escaped—and was then trying to run the blockade to get back South.

When Bolles said he would concede that Rob had been a prisoner there, Stoughton requested a delay to produce two other witnesses who had been unable to appear that day. He could, however, have them before the court the next morning.

Warren assented. The trial was adjourned until the next day,

Saturday, February 11. The court had no other business before it. It had completed Beall's case. He had been found guilty. The court had sentenced him to be hanged.

"Mrs. Carrie Owens."

Mrs. Owens was the daughter of Mrs. Oatman, the widow who ran the boarding house on Prince Street. She confirmed Rob's presence in the city until November 21, four days before the fires.

"What do you know of his habits while so staying at your mother's house?" asked Stoughton, determined to prove that Rob's stay in New York was innocent.

"He was in the house nearly all the time—he acted very much like a gentleman while there. I know nothing against him."

"What did the accused say about leaving the city when he left your mother's house?"

"He merely said he was going to leave the house. I don't know that he said the house—he said he was going to leave."

Stoughton was finished, and Bolles declined to cross-examine, so Stoughton called his next witness: Detective James P. Bennett. Stoughton had but one point in mind to make: that Rob had been arrested before he could possibly have committed any act of espionage.

"Were you one of the party that arrested him in Detroit?" the lawyer began.

"Yes, sir—Mr. McDougall and I."

"Please state the circumstances of the arrest."

"We took the cars at the junction, some three miles from Detroit, where we had been watching for several days. We saw the accused in the cars, and when he got out of the cars at the depot in Detroit we waited until he got some seventy-five or a hundred feet from the depot and we there arrested him in the street."

Once Bennett's brief report was completed, Stoughton handed the detective over to Bolles for questioning. The Judge Advocate proceeded, in effect, to turn the defense witness into a prosecution witness.

"How was the accused dressed when you arrested him?" Bolles began.

"He had on a dark overcoat and dark pants over that suit he has on now."

"This gray suit was concealed by a dark suit outside?"

"Yes, sir."

"Who and what did he tell you that he was?"

"Mr. McDougall was talking to him and asked if he had a passport. He had a pass. He asked him what was the name. He said Richard Cobb. And while he was talking and had the pass, Mr. McDougall said, 'Your name is Stanton.' The arrest was then made. The name Richard Cobb was on the passport."

"Do you know from any statements that you have heard whether he was concerned in the New York fires?"

Disturbed by the direction the questioning was taking, Stoughton broke in at this point. The question, he said, did not refer to any matter that the witness had been examined upon in direct questioning.

"Sustained."

Bolles tried again:

"Among the circumstances of the arrest, which continued from the time you took him until you delivered him over, were there any statements made by him in regard to his connection with the New York fires?"

Stoughton again objected:

"The arrest and testimony of the witness regarding it extend only up to the time the detectives put their hands on him, not to the time of his delivery in New York City or before the court."

"Sustained."

Bolles attempted a new maneuver.

"Among the circumstances attending the arrest, before he went to the Biddle House, were there any statements made by him or to him in regard to his connection with the New York fires?"

"I object!"

Bolles again withdrew the question.

"Have you stated, and if you have not, please state all the circumstances attending his arrest."

Bennett explained the details of the arrest, including how Rob had "made a move" to get his pistol.

". . . and then we closed in and grabbed him. He was taken to the Biddle House and after I returned we searched him. I had his overcoat, searching it, and McDougall searched his other clothes and found a paper and a twenty dollar Confederate note stitched into the coat."

Stoughton was again on his feet.

"I ask the court that the papers alluded to be brought into court so that I might ask some questions with regard to it."

Warren conferred with his officers on the court. The commission decided to adjourn for three days, until Tuesday, February 14, at eleven o'clock, unless there were any objections.

The next session was a brief one. Bolles, at Stoughton's request, introduced into evidence the pistol Rob had carried, the passport made out to "Richard Cobb," Rob's paymaster's receipt with his name and rank on it, and the $20 Confederate bill. Rob was upset that the certificates Thompson had given him were not included, but Stoughton planned to continue pushing for them.

Stoughton again sought a delay: Rob had written five letters to Southern officers in Canada to obtain evidence, but as yet had not received an answer. The lawyer also asked for a copy of the testimony to date.

Bolles, however, opposed any further delay, insisting that any reply from Canada could not be introduced as evidence anyway. Warren cleared the court, but—instead of conferring with his fellow officers on the commission—he went down the hall to see General Dix. On returning, he announced that Dix had agreed to the postponement and to the defense's receiving a copy of the testimony, but on the condition that the accused provide his argument in writing. The trial was delayed still another day when Dix ordered the commission diverted to other business.

Stoughton, meanwhile, persuaded James A. McMaster to testify, to disprove the turnkey's testimony. Although reluctant to do so, McMaster may have believed that his refusal to testify would be taken as a sign of guilt. Besides, his name had already been brought up at the trial and he stood to gain by refuting what had been said.

Rob, for his part, apparently felt certain McMaster would confine himself to Hays's visits, and not mention—let alone acknowledge—his part in the plot to burn New York. That McMaster would testify was encouraging in itself. There was good news, too, about Beall, who had been moved from Fort Lafayette to Fort Columbus on Governor's Island, waiting to be hanged. Beall had won a postponement. He was to have been hanged on Saturday, February 18, but a new date had been set: the following Friday, February 24. In the meantime, Beall's mother had been allowed to visit him, and an immense outpouring of popular opinion was clamoring for his pardon. A group that included eighty-five members of the House, six Senators, the Librarian of Congress, and other leading citizens had appealed to Lincoln to cancel the execution outright. The President, it was said, had never been so pressed.

It was a clear day—a little warmer—when Rob's trial resumed on Tuesday, February 21. McMaster was Stoughton's sixth and final witness. His newspaper, after its initial condemnation of the fires, had fallen strangely silent on the subject and there had been no mention in the paper of Rob's capture or trial.

Stoughton took pains to treat the publisher with great respect, apparently hoping his attitude would be reflected in the military commission's reaction to McMaster's testimony.

"Do you know the accused?" Stoughton began.

"I do not."

"Do you know the turnkey Hays of the police headquarters?"

"I do not know him of my own knowledge any such person," McMaster said, beginning his explanation of his interviews with Hays. "There was a young man who told me his name was Hays—his first name I do not know—and that he was doorkeeper in the Mulberry Street Headquarters. I met him twice or three times at my office . . . It was then that I continued, 'If this letter comes from a commissioned officer of the Confederate Army, and he is afraid of nothing but the accusation of hotel-burning he may put his mind at ease.' I then said, which I must now under oath qualify to show that I was not saying what I did not know—I then said positively, 'Those burnings, or that affair, was the work of no such man.' I recollect he made some remark about the bungling affair. I said, 'It was rather the work of some half crazy women, or non-combatants'—and I had in my mind that no man engaged in fighting, much less a commissioned officer, would have attempted to burn down the city of New York, and attack it in its strongest points instead of the weakest and do so little damage—that is why I made the remark so positive. If I had been exact at the time I should have said, I thought so . . ."

Stoughton had obviously hoped for a simple, straightforward account—a forceful denial of Hays's testimony, with the sharp dramatic effect that would have emanated from a person of

McMaster's standing. Instead, the publisher was deep into a rambling, long-winded, torturous rationalization of his confrontations with Hays.

". . . he said, 'Can I not get the money?' or 'Are you not going to give me the money?' I said to him, 'No, sir, if there is a Captain Kennedy of the Confederate service in New York, who has come from Canada, he probably knows some of those hirelings of the Confederate Government on whom Colonel Thompson is said to have been spending some millions in gold.' He asked who I meant. I said, 'Thank God, I don't know, and don't wish to know. I am not one of them, and I am sorry that any man should have suspected me as one to apply to for such an act as this—to do such a thing as this . . .' "

McMaster droned on for nearly twenty minutes. At last, when the publisher had completed his remarks—a defense of his own acts, contrived and devious in its details—Stoughton, hoping to recoup the situation, went over with McMaster, almost word by word, what Hays had testified.

"Did you ever tell Hays that you would pledge your word that he should get the money he asked if he released Kennedy?"

"No—Not a word of it . . . I never told him anything of the kind . . . Not one word of it . . . No, he did not . . ."

Stoughton walked back to his seat. He had no more questions. Had he saved the situation?

Bolles, obviously feeling there was no need to attack McMaster's recitation, declined to cross-examine.

Stoughton could not have been optimistic about Rob's chances. He had no further witnesses, and as yet had received no word from the Confederate authorities in Canada. All he could do was ask for another adjournment, until Thursday, February 23. He would need time, he said, to rearrange the defense argument to make it conform with the new evidence introduced that day.

Cannons boomed in the distance, punctuating the city's celebration of Washington's birthday, as Rob and Stoughton, in a room at police headquarters, went over the wording of the summation. They had prepared almost twenty-five pages. The certificates Bolles had promised would be attached to them later.

The situation was now discouraging. Beall was to be hanged in two days at Fort Columbus. Lincoln was leaving it to Dix to dispose of the case as he saw fit; the president wouldn't interfere. The general, on the other hand, had declared that the possibility of a pardon rested with the president—that as far as he, Dix, was concerned, there was no such option.

As for the letters Rob and Stoughton had sent to Canada, not a single one had been answered. Rumor, in fact, had it that the Confederate commissioners there were taking to the woods. Jeff Davis had issued a proclamation to save Bennet Burley from extradition, saying the seizure of the *Philo Parsons* had been a legitimate belligerent operation ordered by Richmond.[2] But it hadn't helped at all.

There was, however, a bit of news that would prove of interest to Rob. Another Confederate who spelled his name like Beall was in New York—a general, William N.R. Beall, who had been a prisoner at Johnson's Island when Rob was there. Beall had been made a Confederate agent to handle the sale of cotton from the South, brought to New York aboard a Federal ship. The proceeds were to go to buy clothing and food for Rebel prisoners. Grant had approved the arrangements and allowed Beall to be paroled to supervise the sale.

"Mr. President and Gentlemen of the Court. May it please the Court . . ."

Stoughton read aloud the summation, which was written in the first person, as though Rob himself were speaking.

"I am arraigned on charges known to the court—and will therefore not repeat, but propose to take them up in the order in which they are alleged . . ."

Stoughton's defense rested on the prosecution's failure to make any direct connection between Rob and the fires in New York. But even if he had been a spy, the lawyer continued, there was a distinction between a spy caught in the act and one who had subsequently escaped beyond the jurisdiction of the "offended belligerent." Such a person, when later arrested, "is not subject to punishment for his acts as a spy on any previous occasion."

Stoughton then proceeded to impugn the testimony of the prosecution's chief witnesses. Price, he said, "sees a possible avenue of escape from ignominious incarceration or death . . . Knowing his own desperate condition, he seeks to draw vengeance . . ." Hays, who accepted bribes for favors, "is so anxious, greedy, that he resorts to the meanest shifts." With the possibility of a $20,000 reward "floating before his vision, he almost feels money tickling his palm . . . .

"Thus stands my case. Nothing to prove the charge save the testimony of these two deeply interested men Price and Hays, the one struggling, by heaping charges upon me—and by accusing me of confessing crimes of the most revolting nature—to earn a pardon for his own offenses—the other eagerly striving by lending himself to all sorts of deception and fraud to get the sum of $20,000 which he understands to be the reward for conviction of his victim. Both realize how utterly helpless I am . . ."

At Fort Columbus on Governors Island on the next afternoon, Friday, February 24, John Yates Beall turned to face the South and whispered a prayer as a black hood was drawn over his eyes. "Let those of us who must die for the right side," the *World* commented, "do so as well as he who died for the wrong side." Beall was the first person to be hanged in the military district as a spy since Major John André, involved in Benedict Arnold's treasonous attempt to surrender West Point to the British, was hanged on October 2, 1780, at Tappan, New York. "The case of Beall on the Lakes," declared Lincoln with a heavy heart, "there had to be an example . . . I had to stand firm . . . I can't get the distress out of my mind yet."[3]

The military commission that had convicted Beall and was trying Rob reconvened on Monday, February 27, at eleven o'clock. Bolles's address was lengthy—longer than Stoughton's had been. It had been written over the weekend, with the shadow of Beall's death hovering above his pen.

"More than three weeks have now elapsed, may it please the Court, since this trial began," Bolles declared. "Every request made, every delay asked for, by the accused, has been granted. He has had a full, fair and patient trial . . ."

Slowly, deliberately, the Judge Advocate retraced the prosecution's evidence, dismissing immediately the point raised by Stoughton that the trial itself was illegal. That issue, he said, had already been decided in the case of Beall. Bolles insisted that Rob's admission of being both in New York and Detroit in civilian clothes was *prima facie* evidence of his being a spy. Such evidence might be rebutted by proof, "but, unfortunately for the accused, no rebutting evidence is produced by him. The two papers attached to his address are not evidence, not offered as such, nor admitted as such. . . .

"No sane man," Bolles went on, "under like circumstances, would have gone to New York to have a gay time, feeling every hour, as he must have felt, the pressure of the halter about his neck."

Bolles dismissed the evidence of all of Rob's witnesses as irrelevant to his innocence. Indeed, Clark's testimony proved "the accused came from a suspicious quarter, Toronto, the rendezvous of those rebel emissaries." Similarly, Detective Bennett's recitation had "strengthened the prosecution's case."

The prosecution, Bolles noted, "has offered proof of the prisoner's own confessions—confessions made to his brother officers in Canada—confessions repeated to one of his doorkeepers in New York—confessions contained in the letters of the accused, and implied in his acts of bribery, and in his procurement, and concealment, and threats of using, or attempting to use, deadly weapons, the knife in New York and the pistol in Detroit, to effect his escape." Bolles pointed out that although written on the same day, the letters to Cranston and Wood were contradictory: in one, Rob wrote that he had not been informed of the charges against him; in the other, that he was to be tried for attempting to fire the city. "This contradiction as to the sources of his knowledge, or opinion, is remarkable. If he had not been told what were the charges against him, must not his opinion have been the deduction of his own mind from his own knowledge of his complicity in the plan of universal incendiarism, which was attempted on that night of horrors, the 25th of Nov., 1864? What means the offer of $1500 in gold for his escape? It cannot be reasonably regarded as the measure of his desire to escape from confinement as a mere prisoner of war. Had he so dreaded detention as a prisoner of war, would he have loitered week after week in New York in October and November while the memory of Johnson's Island was fresh in his mind? If that offer of $1500 means anything, it means, as he says in those letters, that his life was in danger . . . .

"No words of mine are needed, or none would be adequate, to describe the enormity of such a crime," Bolles concluded, tears welling in his eyes.[4] "The law of Congress declares that a convicted spy must be sentenced to death. The law of war declares that the mode of death must be ignominious. If a spy be thus doomed, what penalty does he deserve who has abandoned the field of legitimate and honorable war, stolen in disguise into his enemy's country, and there attempted to set fire and destroy in the nighttime a great and populous city?"

Bolles walked over to Rob, extended his hand, and spoke his regrets. Rob was then led out and taken back to his cell at police headquarters.

The military commission deliberated for only a short time before reaching its verdict.

In Hell, March 2, 1865

Having slept the greater portion of the day, I cannot sleep to-night, and as I have the conveniences at hand, propose committing some of my thoughts to paper. In thinking all over the circumstances of my trial, I must believe the verdict of my judges will be Not Guilty. But thinking also that I am a captive in the hands of enemies, who regard it a crime worthy of death to be an officer of the Confederate States Army, I am doubtful of their verdict . . .

I do not believe that a member of the commission, or Major Bolles, the Judge-Advocate, believes me to have acted as a spy or guerrilla, but I may be pronounced guilty of both charges. If I am executed, it will be nothing less than judicial, brutal, cowardly murder.[5]

The decision now rested with Dix. It was not a difficult one for him to make; still, he had hoped that in the days following the end of the trial Rob would break down and divulge the details of the conspiracy, implicating others. The news from police headquarters, where Rob was still being detained, must have distressed the puritanical general. The prisoner was drinking heavily—the whiskey apparently being smuggled in by his lawyer—and cursing, shamelessly and continuously.

It was probably Sergeant Young who talked Dix out of stopping the whiskey smuggling: Rob seemed to talk more freely when drinking. There was still a possibility he might at last confess to his part of the scheme, and implicate the other conspirators.

Reluctantly, Dix agreed, although he was afraid the whiskey would make Rob all the more dangerous. To deter any chance of his escaping, he decided to transfer him to a Federal prison. Young could question him there. But Dix took extraordinary precautions to make sure Rob didn't escape:

> Headquarters Department of the East,
> New York City, March 3d, 1865

Mr. Kennedy, Supt of Metropolitan Police
New York City.

   Will deliver to the order of Lieut. Col. Martin Burke USA. Comd. Fort Lafayette New York Harbor the person of Robert C. Kennedy now in confinement at Police HdQts. NY City.

> By Command of Maj. Gen. Dix
> D.T. Van Buren
> Col & AAG

NB. Before delivering Mr. Kennedy to Col Burke he will be thoroughly searched for concealed papers, particularly the lining of his clothes & the soles & lining of his boots.[6]

A special escort would be provided, too, to prevent any attempt to escape:

> Headquarters Department of the East,
> New York City, March 3d, 1865

Lt. Col. Martin Burke USA.
Comd. Fort Lafayette
N.Y. Harbour

   The Major Genl. commanding the Dpt directs that you send an officer & two guard[s] to NY City for the purpose of conducting to Fort Lafayette one Robt. C. Kennedy, who is now confined at Police Headquarters, Mulberry St NY City.

   The said Robt. C. Kennedy will be carefully guarded. He is reported as a very desperate man.

part 7

FORT LAFAYETTE

If I wuz you, I'd stop right here an' pray;
If I wuz you, I'd stop right here an' pray;
If I wuz you, I'd stop right here an' pray;
O, my Lord, O, my Lord, what shall I do?

O run, sinner, run, an' hunt you a hidin' place;
O run, sinner, run, an' hunt you a hidin' place;
O run, sinner, run, an' hunt you a hidin' place;
O, my Lord, O, my Lord, what shall I do?

O what you gwinter do when death comes a-creepin' in de room?
O what you gwinter do when death comes a-creepin' in de room?
O what you gwinter do when death comes a-creepin' in de room?
O, my Lord, O, my Lord, what shall I do?

Chris' tol' Nicodemus dat he mus' be born agin;
Chris' tol' Nicodemus dat he mus' be born agin;
Chris' tol' Nicodemus dat he mus' be born agin;
O, my Lord, O, my Lord, what shall I do?

chapter 21

ohn D. Allison—shorn of his mutton chops, but still with goatee and moustache—was now waiting to be freed, but he still kept up his diary. He was on the list for exchange, which Grant had reinstituted now that the end of the war was in sight. Allison was back at Fort Lafayette, sharing a cell with a gruff-looking Irishman named Henry Mulrennon. Suddenly, one afternoon, they were joined by a reeling man, his hair unkempt, the gray suit he wore dirty and rumpled. It was Rob, his hands in chains.

> [March] 4th . . . Late today, 3 p.m. a stranger "fresh fish" was
> ushered into our cell. He had drunk deep of that which "a man
> puts into his mouth to take away his brain" . . .[1]

Although the walls and domed ceiling were whitewashed, the cell was so dark that a candle had to be used in midday.[2] There were two narrow barred and glassed "loopholes" at the end of the room, flanking a hearth where a coal fire burned quietly, but little of the gray winter sunlight penetrated the room. Four iron bedsteads lined the walls. The shelves above them held an assortment of books, wicker baskets, and clothes that had been tossed haphazardly on top. Another small barred window was by the door.

From the loopholes, less than one hundred yards away across the white-capped waves of the Narrows, could be seen the Grecian portal and walls of Fort Hamilton. A steam barge—the very one that had carried Rob across the water—was returning to a dock thrust out into the bay from the wide walk in front of the fort. A sentry on the wall

The Narrows and New York Harbor, looking north from Fort Hamilton, Brooklyn, a watercolor by Frances Flora Palmer. A few hundred feet offshore is Fort Lafayette, site of Robert Cobb Kennedy's execution. The fort was razed in the 1960s and the reef on which it stood became the foundation for one of the two towers of the Verrazano Narrows Bridge. Courtesy of The New-York Historical Society.

paced leisurely. To the north of Fort Hamilton, a road through a forest of naked trees led to the heart of Brooklyn.

Rob's cell in Fort Lafayette faced east and was next to the guardhouse by the sallyport. Across the choppy Narrows to the west, which he could not see, was Fort Richmond, sister guardian of the entrance to New York Harbor. Fort Lafayette was situated on Hendrick's Reef, a two-acre jumble of boulders that had been smoothed over when construction on the fort was started in 1812 at the time of the war with Britain. It had not been ready for use, however, until 1822. Because of its shape, it had originally been called Fort Diamond, but was renamed in honor of the Marquis de Lafayette during his visit to New York in 1824. The fort's walls were of brownstone ten feet thick and were high enough for two tiers of emplacements for nearly 100 cannon. Most of the guns were positioned to sweep the approaches to the harbor. Inside the walls was a parade ground of about a quarter of an acre.

Although Allison was cheerful, Mulrennon constantly worried about whether "the man in the long overcoat" would show up: the sutler, who dispensed perishables and nonperishables, including whiskey, if one had the cash. The guards sneaked in other extras, too, for money. Mulrennon was used to a warmer climate. He had served five years in the Regular Army, and on his discharge married and settled in Key West, Florida, remaining, as he put it, "as quiet as an Irishman could well be."[3] With the outbreak of the war he was the first in Key West to hoist a Confederate flag. He organized a unit known as the Key West Avengers, and was abruptly run out of the city by Unionists. He spent the next years as a blockade runner, operating out of Havana, until his capture. His wife had died the previous December after a visit to the fort, and Mulrennon was even now appealing to Federal authorities to be allowed to return home to care for his children.

Mulrennon and Allison had shared for a while this same cell with John Yates Beall before Beall had been taken to Fort Columbus to be hanged. In fact, Allison had a lock of Beall's hair. It had been given to him by "the Commodore"—Admiral Franklin Buchanan, commander of the *Virginia,* the ironclad more popularly known as the *Merrimack.* (Farragut had defeated him at Mobile.) Beall had given Buchanan the lock of hair before being transferred to Governor's Island to be hanged. Buchanan, in turn, had given it to Allison.

As yet, Rob had not been informed of the verdict in his own case. He proved to be a temperamental cellmate, brooding at times, but more often than not laughing and joking—"putting up a front." And sometimes he would suddenly lash out against the North. His moods varied from optimism about his fate to certainty and dread of his future:

March 4.

This is a gala day for my enemies. They will do their best to honor Abraham, and celebrate the recent Union victories. The Federals have obtained possession of Charleston, Wilmington, and other places along our seaboard, but not by valor. Circumstances—military necessity—caused the Confederates to evacuate them. The dogs ought to remember that they did not take Charleston by open warfare, that Gillmore & Co. have hammered in vain long at her gates and the "nest of secession" only succumbed when there was an army in its rear. They swear that Charleston made no resistance, without considering that her sons are in the peerless band of Lee. G——d——n them, let them subjugate the South and then triumph.[4]

Three men visited Rob the next day: Detectives Young, Bennett and McDougall.[5]

"What the hell do you want?"

He and his men were only doing their job, Young explained. They'd come to see if Rob needed anything.

"I need my freedom."

A sentry appeared, to take Allison and Mulrennon outside. This was a treat: they were never allowed out for fresh air.

It was cold in the cell, Young observed. Didn't Rob mind?

"I get a little Bourbon with the rations to keep warm," Rob replied.

Young offered to get him more. Was there anything else Rob wanted?

Yes, there was. He'd like to see General William N. R. Beall if he was still in New York. Could Young arrange it?

If Rob wrote an official request, for the record, Young said, he'd take it to General Dix.

"I need more stationery and things, but Beall could get them for me."

Perhaps Rob would like to make a statement?

"I've told you I have nothing to say—I'm innocent."

Did Rob mean that after all that was said at the trial he still insisted he hadn't set the fires?

"What was said was a lie. Hays tricked me and distorted what I said. As for Price—" Rob spat on the floor—"he's trying to save his own skin. He turned against his flag and his brother to send a fellow-comrade to the scaffold."

Then Rob hadn't set the fires? Young asked again.

"I'd do it now—gladly," Rob said, with sudden vehemence. "If I had the chance, if I had my way, I'd burn and cut up every place and person in the city—burn the museum—burn this fort!"

The detectives said they would return again. Perhaps Rob would feel like talking at another time.

This time it was Rob who had a question: Was the verdict in yet?
No. Bolles was due back from Boston that day, Young explained.
General Dix was awaiting his return.
How did Young think it would go? Rob asked.
Young gestured with his thumb downward.
"Against you."

March 5.

. . . The conduct of Gen. Stoughton has been most noble;
he came to my assistance when I was utterly friendless . . . His
conduct has almost disarmed me of any malice toward the Yankees, although they have made the fairest portion of my country
a desert. Stoughton knows that when at West Point I was not
sectional in my feelings or associations; that gentlemen were always welcome to my room, whether born in Maine or Louisiana.
He knows that I think myself right in my present position. If I
had been the scoundrel that some New York journals represent
me, would he have so promptly tendered his services as counsel,
without expecting a reward? I have no doubt he believed me
unable to remunerate him in any manner, and undertook my
defense merely through remembrance of "old times." I believe my
cause to be a just one—that it will ultimately succeed I have no
doubt. If there is a just God he must favor those who most deserve it. Some detectives came to see me to-night. When asked
their opinion of the result of my trial, they replied, "We think it
will go against you." As every one knows who happened to know
me, their opinion has no effect on me. It is to their interest to
convict me. They get a considerable reward in that case.
    I wrote to Chief Detective Young to-night to procure an in-
terview between myself and Gen. Beall, C.S.A. I hope the Yankee authorities will grant it. I am much in need of articles Beall
could furnish me. The d——d vermin are so numerous that I am
almost in the condition of Lee's veteran who wanted a pound of
mercurial ointment. Like him I am afraid to sneeze for fear the
d——d lice would regard it a gong for dinner, and eat me up.

> Oh, never, never, never, will a true Confederate soldier
> Forsake his friends or fear his foes;
> For while our Lord's Cross proudly floats defiance,
> I don't care a damn how the wind blows.

What was up? Allison wondered as he packed his Bible and other belongings into a canvas bag. Why were he and Mulrennon being moved to another cell?

The guard shifted his rifle to his left shoulder. They want you two prisoners transferred to Battery 5, he said—with the bounty jumpers. More than 170 bounty jumpers and bounty brokers—pariahs in the eyes of the Confederate prisoners—had arrived the day before.

Rob, the sentry said, was to have the cell all to himself from now on. And he had a visitor, too—waiting in the commandant's office.

Allison eyed Rob's hair and beard one last time. He'd given Rob a "barbering," trimming the unruly hair—the first time he'd ever given anyone a "hair cutting." He and Mulrennon waved to Rob as they left.

The guard returned five minutes later to take Rob up to the commandant's office.

The officer in the freshly ironed uniform introduced himself: Captain Von Eickstedt of General Dix's staff. He'd been asked to read a communication to Rob. Von Eickstedt unfolded a paper. It was dated two days earlier, the twelfth of March, 1865, and addressed to Lieutenant Colonel M. Burke, commander, Fort Lafayette:

> Colonel:
>
> Please inform Robert C. Kennedy, by reading to him this letter, that he has been condemned to death and that the sentence has been approved. The time for his execution has not been fixed, but it will probably not be later than the last of next week. He will have a previous notice of four or five days.
>
> In the meantime if he desires to make any communications to his friends, they will be promptly forwarded. You will please say to him also that any request he may make will be cheerfully granted, if consistent with the performance of the painful duty devolved on me.
>
> I am, respectfully yours,
> John A. Dix,
> Maj. Gnl.[6]

"Condemned to death." Rob gaped in wonder, incredulous of the words.

Dear father

. . . I have no time to enter into particulars; suffice to say I have been condemned to die either as a spy or guerilla, or perhaps as both. It is not necessary to make excuses to you. You know I am incapable of being either. You know that I would do nothing unbecoming a Confederate officer, and I consider those characters suited only to a mercenary wretch, or one too cowardly to meet his enemy in open and honorable combat.

Although I receive an ignominious death, I have been guilty of no act that should cause you, mother, or any of the children to blush for their son or brother. I am simply in the hands of my enemies and I am to die. I can die but once and the only disgrace in the matter lies on those who condemned me to death merely on the evidence of perjured witnesses. I do not fear death but would so like to see you all again. May God bless you and may every true Southerner resign his life as cheerfully as I do mine.[7]

On the same day, Stoughton wrote Lincoln with a new legal argument: Congress, the lawyer pointed out, had stipulated that the tribunal in a case like Rob's should consist of thirteen officers. Anything less, he said, quoting former Attorney General William Wirt, would not be " '& lawful court, and an execution under their sentence would be murder.' "[8] Stoughton again attacked the testimony of Price and Hays, although incorrectly identifying Price as the Confederate informer in Beall's trial, too. Hays, he repeated, "reports patented confessions with a large pecuniary reward before his eyes."

That done, Stoughton helped Rob compose a personal plea to Lincoln. Rob wrote the letter with great care. His handwriting exhibited a restraint that is not apparent in his other letters. He underlined certain words to stress his points. He slipped, however, in writing that "It was shown that I was ever in the City of New York after the 21st of Nov." He hastily inserted a "not":

TO

His Excellency Abraham Lincoln
President of the United States

Sir

I have been arraigned before a Military Commission, charged with having acted the spy and guerilla,—tried, found guilty, and sentenced to receive an ignominious death. I respectfully *request* you to review the proceedings of the Commission in my case, and give your attention to the following statement . . .

. . . Please consider the *character* of the witnesses produced against me. It was not shown that I was ever in the City of New York after the 21st of Nov, four days previous to the occurrence of the fires which I am condemned to die for kindling. Do not understand me as casting any improper reflection on the members of the Commission. I suppose they did their duty as conscientious men, perfectly aware of the responsibility of condemning a human being to death.

Granting the evidence adduced sufficient for convicting me of this last charge, is not the penalty too severe for the offense? Arson is not punishable with *death*. An example is not needed for one has just been made in the person of Capt Beall. He was convicted of conducting unlawful warfare and was executed. Is not his fate a sufficient warning to offenders? My blood is not necessary to the welfare of this country. I feel that I do not deserve death. If I have ever taken the life of a human being it was done on the field of battle—not in unlawful warfare. I have been an enemy of your Government since the outbreak of the present unhappy war, but I have been an open, and honorable one. I am not a spy, or guerilla—holding each character in abhorrence—The first as a mercenary wretch and the last, as one who strikes for plunder and too cowardly to meet his enemy in open combat. In conclusion, allow me to say that if my sentence is carried out my life will be *unnecessarily* sacrificed. The nation of which you are Chief Magistrate, is certainly powerful enough to be generous, to protect itself without resorting to *unnecessarily severe* measures towards those so unfortunate as to fall into the hands of its authorities. There are ties which bind me to life and render it dear to me.

I throw myself entirely on your clemency and respectfully ask, at least a commutation of my sentence.

> I have the honor to be
> Very respectfully
> Your ob'dt serv't
> Robert C. Kennedy
> Capt. C.S.A.
> Prisoner under sentence of death

Fort Lafayette
Mar. 14th 1865⁹

chapter 22

oseph Howard, Jr., adjusted the pince-nez on his nose.[1] Two drunken sailors in the front of the streetcar, he noted, were laughing boisterously. Across the aisle, chatting together, sat several market women, their large baskets at their feet. A lame peddler, the only other passenger, dozed in the rear, his head tossing jerkily as the streetcar headed down the long country road that led from the Fulton Ferry slip to Fort Hamilton.

In his mid-thirties, Howard was baldish, slim, and wore a moustache and pointed beard. He always dressed in black, including a broad-brimmed black slouch hat. He was probably the best known newspaper correspondent of his time, and without doubt the most controversial. He seemed everything a good newspaperman should and shouldn't be: aggressive, ingenious, a colorful writer; but egotistical, a creator of hoaxes, a panderer of falsehood. He was the apple of Henry J. Raymond's eye and one of the first reporters on Raymond's pro-Lincoln *New-York Times* to earn a regular byline. (Even when his articles appeared in other journals they were signed, "Howard of the Times.") His father had been a deacon of Henry Ward Beecher's church, and young Howard himself had served as the famed preacher's secretary until he turned to journalism for a career. Once on the *Times*, he saw to it that Beecher's sermons were amply covered.

It was Howard's cockiness that endeared him to Raymond. For example, when he was barred with other reporters from covering Major General Philip Kearny's funeral in September 1862, Howard held open the wires to his paper by having the telegrapher transmit the genealogy of Jesus while the reporter slipped into the funeral procession wearing a surplice and carrying a prayer book.

Howard's critics were legion. Some charged that he had "covered" the daily doings of the Prince of Wales on his tour in 1860 while a day's ride behind. Others said Howard's coverage of the battle at Balls Bluff, Virginia, the following fall was gleaned from what the stage-driver of a rival reporter had told him over a few drinks at a Maryland bar. Cartoonists had a field day when Howard distorted the old over-coat and felt hat Lincoln donned to slip into Washington for his first inauguration into a "long military cloak and Scotch plaid cap."

His crowning hoax created a minor national crisis. It occurred while he was city editor of *The Brooklyn Daily Eagle*—a job he had taken after a dispute with Raymond. In mid-May of 1864, in conniv-ance with another *Eagle* reporter, Howard drew up a fake presidential proclamation. In it, "Lincoln" called for a draft of 400,000 men and set aside May 26 as a day of fasting, humiliation, and prayer—clearly defeatist talk. Howard and his colleague hoped to make a killing on the gold market when the proclamation was published. The faked Associated Press "flimsies" were delivered to New York papers, but all but two newspapers became suspicious and destroyed their editions. The two papers that printed the proclamation, the *World* and the *Journal of Commerce*, were immediately shut down by Dix, who—acting on orders from Secretary of War Stanton approved by Lincoln—arrested their editors as well. Governor Seymour, alarmed at the spectre of a police state, reacted by ordering Dix and four of his aides arrested. Lincoln countered by telling Dix to use the Army and the Navy, if need be, to resist being jailed. The incident finally simmered down when Howard confessed. The two papers were allowed to resume operations after two days. Howard and his accomplice, however, were thrown into prison for several months.

Howard's fraud did not faze Raymond. He gave "Bogus Joe" a job again on the *Times*, and provided him with juicy assignments. On Thursday, March 16, 1865, the journalist, with a pass wangled from Dix—he was back in officialdom's good graces again for his efforts in trying to rescue Superintendent Kennedy from the hands of a Draft Riots mob—was on his way to interview Rob in the prison where he himself had once been held.

Howard waited at Fort Hamilton for the barge to take him across to Fort Lafayette—"a low, diamond-shaped structure, sitting squat upon a pile of rocks, a few hundred feet from the shore, unattractive, dismal and gloomy with no redemptive sign, save the beautiful flag

which floats over, from sunrise to sunset." It was a misleading exterior,
Howard acknowledged. "The universal testimony of those who have
been there," he wrote, "is that for comfort, cleanliness, and systematic
regularity, it is unsurpassed."

The barge trip was short, but the water cold and the current swift
("no swimmer would care to brave it"). Small boats that hazarded
within a hundred yards of the fort faced the danger of being fired
upon. Howard landed at the foot of a stairway, where he was chal-
lenged by a sentry and his pass examined by a sergeant. He was left
standing outside the sallyport while the sergeant took the pass inside.
At last the Officer of the Day, First Lieutenant Samuel W. Black,
appeared with an armed sentry to lead the reporter inside and up a
long, freshly whitewashed, spiral stairway. On reaching the top, Howard found himself on a balcony of the second tier, looking down
onto the parade ground with its shot furnaces, magazines, and pyra-
mids of cannonballs, all painted black. A solitary sentry paced with
monotony in front of three broad casement doors that were padlocked
and chained. Off the second-tier balcony where Howard stood were
the officers' and soldiers' quarters.

At the call of his escorting sentry, Howard was ushered into one of
the rooms to meet the commandant. Lieutenant Colonel Martin
Burke, a tall, lean, keen-eyed veteran of the regular army, was in his
mid-sixties. He'd first been commissioned in 1820, and had been
cited three times for gallantry during the Mexican War. He was a fussy
old man who liked to keep his fort spanking clean. Burke disdained
the social whirl of New York and had not set foot in the city for four
years; in that time, he had gone ashore from the fort only twice.
Instead, for company, he had had a notable array of Southern officers
and citizens: the Maryland legislators whose friends donated the iron
bedsteads in Rob's cell; former Minister to Spain Pierre Soulé of New
Orleans; Lee's chief intelligence officer, Brigadier General Roger A.
Pryor; George W. Lamb Bickley, head of the subversive Knights of the
Golden Cross; and, until three days before, Brigadier General Richard
Lucien Page, who was captured after the fall of Mobile. The predomi-
nance of Confederate luminaries and Copperheads had earned for the
fort the nickname "The American Bastille." To its inmates, however,
it was known as "The Hotel de Burke." They even had a newspaper,
The Right Flanker, which they believed the colonel didn't know about.
As Howard, once a "guest himself," said, "They would a thousand

times prefer old Martin Burke, with all his eccentricities, querilities, and sternness of discipline, to some holiday Gigadier-Brindle who would pay less attention to the solid comfort and more to the dress parades of his command."

Howard found the colonel in a grumbling mood. Burke was ordinarily a "jolly and sui generis commandant," accustomed to smoking his pipe on his porch in conversation with one of his illustrious prisoners. However, the recent influx of motley, swindling bounty jumpers and brokers had dampened his humor.[2] After forty-six Southern soldiers and political prisoners were transferred on March 13, a total of 175 jumpers and brokers had been shunted to the fort. There were now 191 prisoners—the most the fort had ever held. To make room for the new arrivals, the partitions between the batteries had been removed. The prisoners slept chained together between the 100-pounders. A coarse lot, they jeered at their guards constantly.

"Ah, yes," Burke signed, "no one ever knows what they came here for. This is a Temple of Innocence."[3]

After listening to the colonel's complaints, Howard was led by Lieutenant Robert P. Wilson to Rob's cell. He found Rob standing by the coal fire. Rob courteously acknowledged his salutation, shook hands with both the reporter and Wilson, and asked them to take a seat. (Howard thought Rob looked "thin and old and nervous . . . a changed man.")

Rob listened quietly while Howard explained that his readers, indeed the entire nation, were interested in his case.

"I would like to deny," Rob stated, "that I ever set fire to Barnum's Museum. I understand one newspaper said I told Bolles that."

That was a sharp practice, wasn't it? Howard asked. Had Rob lied, then, when he said he hadn't taken part in the plot?

"Lied? Who lied?" Rob said. "Price lied. I thought the court was made up of high-toned, honorable men, but their verdict belies their appearance. They were hard on me because of Bolles. My evidence was not allowed to be entered." Rob stared down at the handcuffs on his wrists. "I've never known a court martial to end in acquittal. They're organized solely for conviction."

Howard said he understood that Rob had written the president.

"Yes, the other day. I asked for clemency . . . Mr. Lincoln is a good-hearted sort. Anyway, it can do no harm."

Was Rob comfortable?

Cell No. 2, Fort Lafayette, where first John Yates Beall and later Robert Cobb Kennedy were held prior to their being hanged. From *Harper's Weekly*, April 15, 1865. Courtesy of The New-York Historical Society.

"I'm all right. The officers furnish me with a little tobacco and some Bourbon—the same ration they get. But I can't seem to eat much, I've no appetite, and I toss about all night without sleeping. That damn Price—saving his own neck by perjury and lying."

The reporter said he'd heard that the chaplain was seeing Rob regularly. It must be a great comfort.

Rob didn't answer immediately. The Reverend John Burke, post chaplain at Fort Hamilton, first dropped by after Rob had been informed of the verdict.[4]

"The parson is a devilish good fellow and it does me good to hear him talk, but that's about it."

Didn't Rob believe there was a chance of God's mercy?

"My father was a good straightforward man and my mother a Methodist and I always said my prayers and all that, but what does it amount to?" Rob shrugged his shoulders. "If I die I don't know where I shall go or what will be done with me . . . I know all about the doctrine, and I suppose I ought to be a Christian, but damn it all, I can't—no, I can't." Rob lowered his voice. "Captain [John Yates] Beall said that he found great consolation in the Christian faith. He rested confidingly upon the arm of the Saviour who died for him and for all sinners. Now I have a high regard and esteem for him—more, indeed, than for any other Confederate in Canada, but in this he seems to labor under an hallucination. My mature judgment is that this is all nonsense. If there were any efficacy in it, the prayers of my pious old mother would have kept me out of this trouble and saved me, perhaps, an ignominious death."

Was that how Rob felt about his fate? Howard asked.

"I don't know—no, I don't feel that way. Like Beall I don't think there is any ignominy about it. It would be undeserved and unfair but I think I shall survive it. I wouldn't care so much if it weren't for my little sisters who need my protection. I haven't heard from my parents since Vicksburg fell. They're both old—the family is utterly broken by the war."

Lieutenant Wilson motioned to Howard that it was time to leave. Howard got up, pocketing his notes. If there was anything he could do . . . ?

No, there wasn't. "This fort is the only place where I have been treated decently by Federal officers. I've been in a half a dozen prisons but have never been comfortable until now."

Rob picked up an envelope from the table. He handed it to Wilson. If the lieutenant would post it for him, he would be grateful. It was an embittered note to a Confederate he had befriended in Toronto:

Fort Lafayette
March 16, 1865

S.V. Mitchell
71 Bay Street
Toronto, C.W.

Dear Judge —

Col. Thompson has treated me most shamefully in not even answering the letter my counsel, General Stoughton, wrote, ask-

ing if he would defray my legal expenses. It is well for him, if he
has acted as I suspect, that I can never see him again . . .[5]

Stoughton's arguments to Lincoln were rebutted by Bolles in a
letter to Dix, which the general then forwarded to Judge Advocate
General Joseph Holt in Washington. Stoughton's point about the
makeup of the court, Bolles said, "would have been well taken" had
Rob been tried by court martial instead of by a military commission.
As for the testimony of Price and Hays, Price was not the witness who
appeared against Beall—and, moreover, to make a distinction
Stoughton had overlooked, Price was "a rebel *officer*, not soldier"—
and Hays was not acting under the inducement of any reward.[6] To
further underline this point, Dix, in his covering letter to Holt, said
the reward offered by the Common Council "was intended to be paid
on conviction by a civil court . . . The case having been taken out of
the hands of the civil authorities by the U.S. the reward cannot be
paid to any one." Apparently the hotelkeepers, following suit, re-
tracted their offer. So that settled the argument that the turnkey Hays
had testified to get the rewards. Price, in addition, "was in the rebel
service, but has abandoned it in disgust."
    Rob's appeal to the President was sent to the White House
through Holt, along with a note from Dix. In effect, the general
sealed Rob's fate:

> I enclose a letter from Kennedy to the President. I have
> thought it best to send it to you, instead of forwarding it directly
> to him.
>   You will see that Kennedy does not deny that he set fire to
> Barnum's Museum, and I have some reason to think he will con-
> fess his guilt before his execution.[7]

The next day—Sunday, March 19—Dix, without a hint of what
he had reported, wrote Burke:

> Please advise Robt. C. Kennedy that I shall issue tomorrow
> the order for his execution on Saturday, the 25th inst.
>   His letter to the President asking for a commutation of his
> sentence has been forwarded. I desire him to understand that I
> have not said, and shall not say, anything to the President in
> opposition to such an exercise of mercy; but that I consider it at

least very improbable, and that it would be far better for him to
prepare for his end than to indulge in expectations of relief,
which may prove illusive.

It is my wish that the execution take place at Fort Lafayette;
and I shall so direct, unless there is some grave objection.

Please repeat to Kennedy the assurance given in my letter
announcing to him the sentence of the Court, that any indul-
gence he may ask will be cheerfully granted, if consistent with
the performance of my duty.[8]

Stoughton and Lieutenant Wilson visited Rob to inform him of
Dix's order. Afterward, Allison and Mulrennon were allowed to visit
him. Rob had asked to see them a few days earlier, expecting that he
would be transferred to Fort Columbus as Beall had been. Allison
found him

laughing & in fact just as formerly . . . Seems to have made no
preparation for that gloomy fate that awaits us all . . . Says he
will meet his fate as a Confederate soldier should—but protests
that the execution will be murder.

The visit was cut short when Wilson reappeared with Colonel
Burke and Chaplain Burke. The two men were not related. Rob asked
the commandant whether the execution order had arrived yet. No, it
hadn't, the colonel told him. Burke had, in fact, been worried by the
likelihood of Rob's being hanged at Fort Lafayette, because there had
never been an execution under his command there before. He'd asked
Dix to send both a gallows and someone to operate it.

Rob had one more request. Could he have a photograph taken to
send back to his parents and friends? The colonel said he would pass
on the request to Dix.

Rob held the poker between his handcuffed hands and pressed the
foot of his good leg on its hooked end with all his strength.[9] It gave
way slightly. Rob pressed again, pulling the poker in the opposite
direction. Suddenly, there was a sound outside. Rob went to the small
window by the cell door. The post adjutant, Colonel Burke's nephew,
Captain Thomas H. French, was coming across the parade ground on

his rounds. Rob slipped the poker under his mattress as French entered. He extended his wrists to the officer. French checked the handcuffs, looked about casually, and left.

Rob remained still until French's footsteps retreated. Then, he took the poker from the mattress and began to bend it again, until he had succeeded in straightening the hook. He put the poker in the coal fire and waited for it to heat. Outside, on the parade ground, a sentry paced back and forth with regularity. Next door was the guardhouse, cut off from view by a small meat-storage bin. He would have to slip past the guardhouse, however, to get to the sallyport. Two more sentries patrolled outside . . . and then there were the icy waters of the Narrows. The best chance would be to knock out the sentry on the parade ground and take his uniform. Wearing it, he could at least get to the sallyport and perhaps beyond before an alarm was raised. There was only a token of moonlight—not enough for accurate marksmanship once he got into the water.

Rob drew the poker from the fire. Its tip glowed red. He pressed the tip into the hard oak around the staple that held the hasp on the outer side of the door. The wood turned black as the tip hissed into it, but it was hardly damaged. Rob returned to the fireplace to reheat the poker.

He had started three holes when he heard footsteps coming toward the cell. Rob darted from the door, thrust the poker at the hearth, and dropped onto his bed. Colonel Burke entered. Behind him, Rob could see Allison, Mulrennon, and a soldier carrying a lamp. Burke sniffed the burnt wood and quickly discovered the holes in the door. He was outraged.

Rob was left with his arms pinned behind him by a double set of manacles. Chains were attached to his ankles. Burke ordered another lock added in the morning, and a guard stationed outside the door day and night from then on.

chapter 23

The weather changed suddenly. Tuesday, March 21, was a bright, bland day, with a light breeze that carried the first soft scent of spring. On battlefields throughout the South, Union armies prepared for their final thrust against the enfeebled forces of the Confederacy. Sheridan now completely controlled the Shenandoah Valley, after annihilating Jubal Early in a succession of clashes. Grant, with more than 110,000 troops, edged closer to Richmond and Petersburg, tracking Lee relentlessly, while Sherman, with 60,000 men, asserted his mastery of the Carolinas.

Those who had endured hardships with Rob would scarcely have recognized him. To Headley, he had been "sincere, true, intelligent and absolutely fearless."[1] Fell, who had known him at Johnson's Island, had called him "a perfect daredevil, and no situation, however perilous, seemed to daunt his courage."[2] Jackson, his roommate in Toronto, had described him as "the boldest of men."[3]

Rob was continually drinking now, and was often drunk. To his captors, Rob evinced "the cunning and the enthusiasm of a fanatic, with the lack of moral principle characteristic of many of the Southern Hotspurs."[4] Von Eickstedt, who'd informed him of the military commission's decision, attributed Rob's astonishment on hearing the verdict partly to his "peculiar temperament, and partially to the singular deficiency in his logical power. Although born of a good family, Kennedy is almost stupid." A visitor to the fort said, "His curses and imprecations are terrible; his profanity most offensive, and his indecency of language almost inconceivable." Rob, the visitor added, "was not conducting himself with dignity, the manliness or courage, which

217

one would expect." Howard perhaps came closest in describing Rob as displaying "nervous insanity."

The findings of the military commission were published in the newspapers of March 21 as General Orders No. 24 from Dix's office:

Finding

Of specification 1, charge I, guilty.
Of specification 2, charge I, guilty.
Of charge I, guilty.
Of specification, charge II, guilty.
Of charge II, guilty.[5]

The judgment was harsh:

The attempt to set fire to the city of New York is one of the greatest atrocities of the age. There is nothing in the annals of barbarism which evinces greater vindictiveness. It was not a mere attempt to destroy the city, but to set fire to crowded hotels and places of public resort, in order to secure the greatest possible destruction of human life . . . In all the buildings fired, not only non-combatant men, but women and children, were congregated in great numbers, and nothing but the most diabolical spirit of revenge could have impelled the incendiaries to act so revoltingly.

The participation of the accused in this inhuman enterprise is a crime, which follows him, and his liability to answer for it is not to be cast off by withdrawing for a time from the jurisdiction within which it was committed. He has not only been guilty of carrying on irregular warfare, in violation of the usages of civilized States in the conduct of war. Crimes which outrage and shock the moral sense by perpetrators must not only be deprived of the power of repeating them, but the sternest condemnation of the law must be presented to others to deter them from the commission of similar enormities.

Robert C. Kennedy will be hanged by the neck till he is dead at Fort Lafayette, New York Harbor, on Saturday, the 25th day of March, instant, between the hours of 12 noon and 2 in the afternoon.

To further explain the severity of the punishment, Judge Advocate General Joseph Holt returned Stoughton's appeal to Lincoln to the White House with the letters of Bolles and Dix, adding, for the president's benefit:

> In view of the unparalleled atrocity of the crimes committed, the rigid enforcement, as ordered by Gen. Dix, of the death penalty, awarded by the Court, seems demanded by every consideration looking to the safety of society and the vindication of military laws.[6]

Rob still held out hope for a reprieve. On Wednesday, the twenty-second—only three days before the execution was scheduled to take place—he had five visitors. First, Allison and Mulrennon were allowed to see him briefly. To them he exhibited bravado:

> We found him in his usual good spirits. poor fellow it almost made me weep to see how he was shackled and ironed . . .

Allison gave him a pair of socks and a shirt before leaving. On the way back to his cell, the young Kentuckian saw the gallows being carried into the fort.

The next visitor was Gus McDonald's widowed mother, who appealed to Rob to help free her son from city prison. Then, two photographers from Clarke's Union Photographic Gallery appeared.[7] Rob was escorted outside under the fort's gallery where the light was better. He was unchained and posed in a wooden armchair.

The next day, the twenty-third, Young arrived with U.S. Marshal Robert Murray.[8] Murray, charged by Dix with supervising the execution, went off to confer with Colonel Burke. Young, still hoping to wrest a confession from Rob that might include a clue to the other participants in the plot, failed to achieve his purpose. He came away instead with Rob's signature on a paper that removed the last shred of doubt still existing about Allison's innocence and also completely exonerated Gus McDonald.

Before he left, Rob sought Young's opinion about the possibility of a pardon from Lincoln. It was doubtful, the detective answered candidly, inasmuch as the president was leaving Washington that day to visit Grant at the front in Virginia. When Rob then asked a favor, Young agreed to do what he could:

> Detective Office
> 300 Mulberry St.
> March 24th 1865
>
> Lieut Co'l Martin Burke
> Com'd'g Fort Lafayette
>
> Dr Sir
>
> during my interview with Robert C. Kennedy yesterday he requested me to send him a bottle of whiskey. I promised to do so provided it was approved of by Gen'l Dix and yourself. the General desires me to say to you that he approves of it.
> Yours respectfully
> John S. Young
> Chief of Detective Police[9]

Allison said good-bye. He was being set free after taking the oath of allegiance.

Chaplain Burke appeared. He'd come to read some prayers with Rob, he said.

"I'm not a bad man," Rob insisted.

He'd have to believe in God's mercy, Parson Burke said. He must prepare himself.

Could the chaplain arrange for him to see General William N.R. Beall? He hadn't been able to get permission from the Army.[10]

The clergyman promised to write a note immediately.

When Colonel Burke and Howard of the *Times* came by later in the evening, they found Rob at the little pine table, smoking furiously. A bottle stood at his elbow. The table was littered with paper and envelopes.

> My personal acquaintances at Johnsons Island
> My dear fellows
>
> I leave this world in a few hours, and write merely to bid you adieu. You, my former roommates and fellow prisoners will have some curiosity to know my feelings on this trying occasion. Know that I am just as when I left you. Would avoid my fate if possible,

but as I cannot, will try to bear it with becoming fortitude. It is a sad reflection that I am never again to mount a horse or fire a pistol. Your friend has been most unlucky in the game of life since he left you, but no matter what, as Genl. Cheatham observed at Murfreesboro "whether we die today or tomorrow." In regard to the future it is but a leap in the dark, I can only hope for the best. There are too many to mention by name but I wish the most humble my protege "Turk." Goodbye. Be true to your cause and country. I have been so.

> Your unfortunate friend
> RC Kennedy[11]

There was one for his family, too, Rob said. Would the colonel see to it that it got through the lines? It was a letter he had spent hours in writing, trying so hard to battle his own fears. He wanted his mother, his father, the family, to believe he had died with dignity. He also wanted to believe that he would die that way. Face turned to the South, like John Yates Beall:

My Dear Mother:

Your eldest son dies tomorrow . . . This is sad news to you, but you must bear it in a becoming manner.

Let it be a comfort to you under this grievous affliction that I feel that I can meet that death if not with resignation, at least with calmness. Although I die as a felon I do not feel like or consider myself one. These things will occur as long as the world exists, regard them merely as the fortunes of war.

I would like to live to see and be with you again, but Fate has ordained otherwise and it is needless to murmur at what is inevitable. You are growing old and must in a few years pay the "debt of nature."

This will be a terrible blow but let us hope that we may soon meet in another and better world. My mind was prepared for this as soon as I was captured the last time. I knew what was in store for me when I learnt the charges against me, death or almost endless captivity. That and the belief that I was utterly friendless, rendered me somewhat reckless . . . I was imprudent and defiant, and doubtless created much of the prejudice which now exists against me. Capt. Beall, of whom you will hear in time, was executed here a short time since under circumstances similar to these in which I am placed.

I regret it was not my fortune to be tried and executed first, for then he would have been spared . . . I am to be buried at Fort Hamilton. I saw them building the scaffold this afternoon for my execution, which is to take place here . . .

It is now nearly two years since any communication has passed between us. What changes may not, in the meantime, have taken place in our little family circle?

In regard to preparation for a future state, I can only say I have not, as yet, felt any fears on the subject. I have not been a bad man, nor can I claim to myself any particular merit. My general course through life was upright and honorable: and although I can recall many irregularities that I would wish blotted out from the "book of my remembrances," still I cannot feel any of that remorse men usually express under similar circumstances.

I do not like to die, life possesses for me many attractions and I feel on contemplating the scene that is to come off tomorrow, very much as I did on going into the first general engagement in which I participated; my greatest dread being that I will exhibit fear. There may come an overwhelming sense of the awful scene, in which I am to be the principal actor; I hope there will not. It is my misfortune if I do not realize my true condition. I am condemned as a spy and for violation of the laws of war . . . I ought to have written all the particulars, but efforts have been made to obtain a reprieve or commutation of the sentence and I was not without a hope of success until to-day and I deferred writing until too late. You will learn all. Be assured that I feel a consciousness of having done all right or at least that the act was justifiable. Think of me as if I had fallen in battle. How I would like to see and embrace you and the other loved ones again; my love to them all, also to all kindred and friends.

Think not of my faults, think not of my weaknesses but remember me only as your loving and unfortunate son.

Robt. Cobb Kennedy[12]

There was no hope, the colonel said. Knowing that, Burke continued, would Rob like to make a statement? Speak his mind?

Rob said, no, he wouldn't inform on anyone.

That wasn't his purpose in asking, the colonel explained, that, he'd leave to the detectives. But Rob had read the commission's findings. How could he justify his actions?

It was true. His story hadn't been told. This was a chance to vindicate himself in the eyes of all. He'd make a statement but, Rob said, pointing to Howard, he wanted the reporter to print it and some other things he'd written. Would Howard do so? Howard promised he would.

Rob then asked Burke to promise that he would not make any use of what he said if a chance for a reprieve occurred. The colonel agreed.

Rob dictated the confession:

> After my escape from Johnson's Island I went to Canada, where I met a number of Confederates. They asked me if I was willing to go on an expedition . . .
>
> I wish to say that killing women & children was the last thought. We wanted to let the people of the North understand that there are two sides to this war, & that they cant be rolling in wealth & comfort, while we at the South are bearing all the hardship & privations. In retaliation for Sheridan's atrocities in the Shenandoah Valley we desired to destroy property, not the lives of women & children although that would of course have followed in its train.
>
> Done in the presence of Lt. Col. Martin Burke
J Howard Jr
March 24th, 10 1/2 P.M.[13]

Would the colonel tell Dix that Rob would tell all he know— provide names—if the general delayed the execution?

It was too late, the colonel replied. No one would believe him now.[14]

chapter 24

The sun rose at 5:56. About an hour later, a guard appeared outside Rob's cell with another soldier, who was carrying a tray. On it were mugs of tea and coffee, a platter holding a steak, another with a mackerel, and some bread. Rob, who had gotten only two hours' sleep, ate the meat and fish ravenously. He spiked the tea and coffee with whiskey before downing the contents of both mugs. The guard unlocked his handcuffs so that he could wash and dress. He donned his gray suit, trying to smooth out its wrinkles.

Howard found him subdued, leafing through a prayer book, when he came by at nine. Although the weather was balmy, a fire burned in the fireplace. Rob tossed the book on his rumpled bed. He wanted to talk with someone. He gestured toward the book: "I don't care for it."[1]

Stoughton was at the fort, Howard reported, and he'd brought General William N.R. Beall.

Where were they? Rob asked, suddenly excited.

With Colonel Burke. They'd be down soon, Howard said.

Rob sat down at the table. Howard began to edge toward the door.

Don't go, Rob implored. He just had a note to write. It was a curious thank-you for a bottle of whiskey.

Ft. Lafayette, March 25th, 1865

J.S. Young:

Dear Sir—I am much obliged by the sending of that article.

In answer to your desire to ascertain the present state of my feelings towards you and associates, I can only say I bear you no malice. You did your duty as detectives, with, perhaps, as much

225

kindness to me any others would under similar circumstances. Our professions have been different; what appeared right and proper to you seemed unfair and dishonorable to me; for example, the manner in which Hays was instructed or allowed to act in order to obtain evidence against me.

Be assured I appreciate the many little acts of kindness extended by you and others to

Respectfully yours,
R.C. Kennedy.[2]

As he finished, Stoughton and Beall were allowed into the cell. The forty-year-old Confederate general was dressed in civilian clothes.

He had some things to send home, Rob said; if they could locate a pair of scissors, he'd like to send locks of hair to his family. While they were gotten, Rob began to cry.

"Captain," Beall said, "you must die like a soldier—like a Southern officer."

"It's a hard thing to die on a day like this," Rob answered. "The damn Yankees."

Rob quieted down when the scissors were brought. He sat down on the edge of his bed and snipped several locks of his hair and put them into envelopes that were lying on the table, already addressed.

Marshal Murray came in and handed Rob a set of photographs. Rob glanced briefly at his own likeness and began placing them in the envelopes, too, as Chaplain Burke joined the others at the far end of the room. When Rob finished sealing the envelopes, the minister stepped forward: it would be good to read together now. The two sat by each other on the bed, reciting from the "Book of Common Prayer."

The landing outside Fort Hamilton was thronged. Wives and friends of officers formed little groups, gossiping with one another as they waited for the barge to take them across to Fort Lafayette. Captain Wright Rives went from group to group, checking passes, trying to weed out the invited from the merely curious—a number of whom had paid $50 for a pass.

A small steamer in the Narrows blew her whistle. It carried members of General Dix's staff from Manhattan. The steamer drew close to the shore, slowing to allow the barge to reach the landing first. On the barge was a lone passenger, Patrick Kiernan, a bounty broker who was being freed. He jumped onto the landing before the barge had tied up and disappeared into the crowd.

Shortly before noon, Marshal Murray and General Beall returned to Rob's cell with Lieutenant Wilson and a stranger dressed in black, George Isaacs, the official executioner.[3] Rob sat at his table, arranging his letters. Chaplain Burke was reading aloud from the Bible.

"Are you the unhappy man who is in trouble?" Isaacs asked in a friendly way.

Rob shrugged.

"Oh, yes, you are the man," Isaacs continued, cheerfully. "What do you weigh?"

Rob didn't answer.

"You must weigh 170 pounds."

"170 hell!"

"Then your weight is about 140. What is your height?"

Rob remained silent. Isaacs measured him with his eyes, and then left the cell.

Rob then asked to see Howard, and the reporter was summoned. Howard, Rob reminded him, had promised to see that his confession was printed—with nothing stricken.

"I want the people of the North to know that I'm no fiend and did not wage war on women and children except as a matter of necessity and retaliation."

After Howard repeated his promise to print his statement, Rob picked up his pipe. Would Howard see that his mother got it? He handed it to the reporter.

Isaacs returned as one o'clock drew near. Seeing him, Rob screamed, "I don't know who the hell you are!"

"There is no need for that language, captain," General Beall interjected. "These men are not your enemies."

"All right, I am prepared for this thing. Bind my arms."

Isaacs moved in front of Rob. Rob extended his hands, then drew them back hurriedly. "Wait a minute." He shook hands with Howard,

Wilson, Stoughton, then Beall. "This is a cowardly murder," he said to the Confederate general.

Isaacs pinioned Rob's arms in front of him. He fitted a noose around his neck, then took a black hood from his pocket and started to put it on Rob's head.

"Am I to wear this to the gallows?"

It was necessary, Marshal Murray explained. It was meant to save Rob anguish.

Rob acquiesced, finally, as Isaacs slipped the hood on his head. It was left rolled up, like a turban, so that Rob could see to walk to the gallows.

Rob began to cry again. Beall held him in his arms, pressing Rob's head to his shoulder. "Oh, this is hard of the damned Yankees to treat me in this way," Rob sobbed. "I have been a regular soldier and should not have been treated so."

Beall dabbed Rob's eyes with his handkerchief.

"May I keep it?"

The general stuffed the hankie into Rob's breast pocket. Come, he'd go with him, the general said. Beall led Rob slowly from the cell and stood with his arm around Rob's shoulders as the others formed a line.

"Can't they shoot me? Must I hang?"

Lieutenant Black, the Officer of the Day, led the procession. Behind him came Chaplain Burke, then Rob and General Beall. Colonel Burke, Marshal Murray, and a deputy followed. Stoughton and Howard brought up the rear. They marched slowly into the sunlit parade ground to the accompaniment of a slow drum roll.

The fort's garrison was lined up on the west and east sides of the yard—sixty men on each side under the command of a lieutenant, standing stiffly at attention. The nearly 200 bounty jumpers and brokers, unwilling witnesses, were ranged in lines behind the troops, chained together. Above, on the balcony girding the second tier, the clusters of women under parasols grew silent as the procession headed for the center of the yard.

The gallows was not the usual trap-door type but operated instead by pulling the body upward into the air with a swift jerk. It consisted of two upright, buttressed beams across which, at a height of about twenty feet, a third beam crossed. One of the beams had several notches on it. A "gift" from The Tombs in New York, it was the same gallows on which a Negro seaman who'd murdered his captain; a pirate; and, most recently, John Yates Beall, had been hanged. A thin rope threaded through pulleys on the cross-beam fed into a small wooden shanty on the side. In the shed, out of sight, a deserter from Maine who'd been promised a pardon in return for the task watched through a peephole, his hand on an axe, ready to chop the rope that would release a system of weights. A stained pine box lay on the ground in the shadow of the shed. A flooring of planks was under the gallows. A stool was positioned directly under the other end of the rope, which dangled about four feet off the ground, a hook on its tip.

Rob limped unsteadily in the procession, his eyes fastened on the ground, avoiding the gallows. He was trembling violently. Isaacs waited to lead him up onto the planks. Rob sat down on the stool as Captain French, the post adjutant, began to read General Orders No. 24:

"Before a Military Commission, which convened at . . ."

Rob jumped to his feet. He tore the hood from his head with his bound hands, and tossed it to the ground. Isaacs bent and picked it up as French continued.

"Specification First—In this, that Robert C. Kennedy, a Captain in the military service of the insurgent States—"

"I'm no traitor!" Rob shouted.

". . . on or about the 1st day of November, 1864 . . ."

Rob sneered.

". . . attempted to burn and destroy said City of New–York, by setting fire thereto—"

"Well, is that a crime?" Rob shouted again.

". . . crimes, which outrage and shock the moral sense by their atrocity—"

"That's a lie!" Rob stamped his foot several times, weaved slightly, and began muttering to himself. "A damned lie, a damned lie."

He beckoned to Murray. The marshal stepped onto the planks and pulled Beall's handkerchief from Rob's pocket. He wiped Rob's nose with it.

". . . By command of Major-General Dix." French completed the reading.

"Gentlemen, this is murder! I warn you, Jeff Davis will retaliate!" Rob turned to Colonel Burke. "Come here if you please."

Murray stopped the colonel with his hand. The marshal stepped up to Rob instead. "One moment," he said. Chaplain Burke advanced onto the planking. All heads but Rob's bowed as the chaplain started reading from the Episcopal service for the condemned.

"Dearly beloved, it hath pleased Almighty God, in His justice, to bring you under the sentence and condemnation of the law. You are shortly to suffer death in such a manner that others, warned by your example, may be the more afraid to offend . . ."

The rope, as a reporter from the Herald noted, was swaying gently in the wind. A sudden gust blew it against Rob's back. He turned, thinking someone had tapped him to get his attention. Terror filled his face when he saw it was the rope. Rob shrank from it as it rocked back and forth, toward him and away, toward him and away.

". . . So may you cast yourself with an entire dependence upon the mercies of God, through the merits of our Saviour and Redeemer, Jesus Christ."

The chaplain knelt and took Rob's hands in his.

"May you die like a man and a Christian. May God have mercy on your soul."

"Colonel," Rob said, ignoring the chaplain, "wait a minute. I want to make a statement to these gentlemen." He began to shout. "I consider this a judicial, brutal, cowardly murder! There was no occasion for the United States Government to condemn me!" He turned to General Beall. "Tell my friends—." A spasm in his throat cut off his words in mid-sentence. Rob gagged, tried to clear his throat. Isaacs came up from behind and hooked the noose to the end of the gallows rope, leaving a curl of slack.

"I say, colonel," Rob pleaded, regaining his voice, "can't you give me a drink before I swing off?"

Burke turned away. Isaacs placed the hood back over Rob's head. Rob reached out to take Beall's hands in his as the hood was lowered over his eyes. Isaacs stepped back and nodded to French. It was 1:16 P.M. The captain drew his saber. Then, suddenly, Rob began to sing:

> "Trust to luck, trust to luck,
> Stare Fate in the face,
> For your heart will be easy
> If it's in the right place—"

The clang of the falling weights echoed throughout the yard. Rob's body shot six feet into the air, twitching, until—after a minute or so—it hung limp. The body swayed slightly, circling slowly, for twenty minutes, the time prescribed by law, after which it was low-ered. Dr. Kendall, the post surgeon at Fort Hamilton, bent over the body and removed the hood from Rob's head. His face was pale. He suffered little pain, the doctor said to Isaacs; the neck was broken.[4]

Two soldiers grabbed Rob's arms and legs and lifted him into the pine box. The lid was put on top and hammered in place. Two more soldiers appeared to help. Together, the four men carried the box through the sallyport and to the barge. The ranks of the garrison troops opened as they passed through.

A horse-drawn cart carried the box to the Soldier's Burying Ground outside Fort Hamilton. The box was lifted from the cart and slid into a six-foot hole, which two soldiers immediately began to fill with dirt. They left the little mound, with a wooden marker stuck into the ground at its head:

> R.C. Kennedy
> Rebel spy
> executed
> Mar. 25, 1865

General George G. Meade pointed with his finger, sketching for Lincoln the action of that morning's battle for Fort Stedman. The two sat on horses atop a high slope overlooking the point where Union countercharges had routed the Confederate forces. It was the first time the president had visited a battlefield in the immediate wake of the fighting. The dead, Northern and Southern, lay in silence. Burial squads were already at work. The wounded groaned in pain as surgeons moved from one fallen soldier to another. Lincoln's horse picked its way across the scene. The president looked "worn and hag-gard," Captain John S. Barnes, who was accompanying him, recalled. "He remarked that he had seen enough of the horrors of war, that he hoped this was the beginning of the end, and that there would be no more bloodshed."[5]

Fifteen days later, Lee surrendered. Lincoln himself lay dead from an assassin's bullet on a Saturday twenty-one days afterward. The last Southern troops—those of General E. Kirby Smith—laid down their arms on May 26.

Robert Cobb Kennedy was the last Confederate soldier executed by the Federal government in the Civil War.[6]

part 8

AFTERMATH

Go tell Aunt Gracie,
Go tell Aunt Gracie,
Go tell Aunt Gracie,
The old grey goose is dead.

The one she was savin'
The one she was savin'
The one she was savin'
To make a feather bed.

She died early this mo'nin'
She died early this mo'nin'
She died early this mo'nin,
Under the old green apple tree.

She left two little goslin's
She left two little goslin's
She left two little goslin's
One for you an' one for me.

chapter 25

Hugh Shaw lay on his cot resting, unable to see the two men playing cribbage on the table pushed against the head of the bunk. He could tell who they were, however, by their distinctive accents. One was a Federal private like himself—a twenty-five-year-old Englishman who'd joined the New York Islanders, a Scottish regiment, nearly two years ago. The other man wore a blue officer's overcoat and spoke with a drawl. He was telling the Englishman about his exploits during the war. Despite the overcoat he wore, he was a Confederate. He'd been with Jefferson Davis, trying to reach Mexico, until a few hours before Davis's capture in Georgia by Union cavalry. He'd served with Morgan, too, and not only knew John Wilkes Booth but had even taken part in an earlier plot to assassinate Lincoln. The man went into particulars in describing an expedition he had led in New York. He'd gone by two names on that occasion—"Colonel Maxwell" and "Drake"—and outwitted the city's chief of detectives, "Old" Young.

Shaw, who was being held in the military prison at Louisville, Kentucky, on a charge of disobeying orders, repeated what he overheard to the prison commander the next day. The Englishman, Alfred W. Wheels, who was waiting to be sentenced on the same charge, was ushered into the commander's office afterward. He confirmed Shaw's story. Both men signed depositions.[1]

Within a short time Robert Maxwell Martin was in Fort Lafayette, facing the possibility of being tried by a military commission on charges of being a spy. Police Superintendent John A. Kennedy assured the Army that both Martin and John W. Headley could be identified as participants in the attempt to burn New York City.[2] The superintendent said "the same witnesses" who had appeared against Robert Cobb Kennedy could be assembled to testify against them.

The trial never took place. Judge William H. Leonard of the New York State Supreme Court ruled that with the end of the war the writ of habeas corpus had been restored and civil law again made paramount to military law. Martin was turned over to New York authorities for trial on civil charges of arson. However, the Circuit Court for the Southern District of New York found that, although the evidence showed that Martin was indeed in the city at the time of the attempt to burn it and had known certain suspected Southern agents, these facts only raised "the general suspicion that the prisoner was here for no good purpose."[3] There was not enough proof, the court said, to warrant the charge of arson. The charges were dismissed.

On February 19, 1866, after nearly seven months in prisons, Martin was freed. He received an unconditional pardon from President Andrew Johnson that summer. Headley also received a pardon from Johnson, although the president's Amnesty Proclamation had specifically exempted "all persons who have made raids into the United States from Canada."[4]

Martin settled in Evansville, Indiana, where he ran a tobacco warehouse. He moved to New York City in 1874, where he worked as an inspector of a tobacco company's warehouses in Brooklyn. In 1887, he returned to Louisville as a tobacco broker. When the old war wound in his right lung began hemorrhaging, Martin went back to New York for treatment. He died there on January 9, 1900, and was buried in Greenwood Cemetery, Brooklyn—the same cemetery where John Yates Beall had been interred before his family claimed his body for reburial in Virginia.

Headley lived for two years after the war at Nebo, Kentucky. He joined Martin in Evansville after that, remaining sixteen years in Indiana before returning to Louisville in the 1880s. He was Secretary of State of Kentucky from September 1, 1891, to January 1, 1896. At the turn of the century, nearing sixty, he began to write his memoirs.

As for the other Confederate officers who took part in the plot to burn New York City, the information is scanty. Harrington became a lawyer for the Southern Pacific Railroad, and was living in Los Angeles in 1896. Ashbrook was an insurance broker in Cynthiana,

Kentucky, in 1905. What happened to Chenault is unknown. The same is true of Price, the turncoat who testified against Rob.

Two days after Kennedy's execution, Gus McDonald was freed. Larry McDonald returned from Canada and lived in New York after the war. Jacob Thompson fled to England, but returned to settle in Memphis, Tennessee, with a good deal of his private fortune still intact. Clement C. Clay was imprisoned with Jefferson Davis in Fort Monroe for a year without trial before being allowed to return to Huntsville, Alabama. He died in 1882. James P. Holcombe, the third Confederate commissioner in Canada, was principal of Bellevue High School, Nelson County, Virginia, at the time of his death in 1897. Dr. Luke F. Blackburn, who had suggested to Martin that they poison the New York water system, went into farming in Arkansas but soon returned to Kentucky. He helped to fight an outbreak of yellow fever in the state in 1878, and the next year was elected governor.

Cleary, Thompson's secretary, practiced law in Covington, Kentucky, until his death in 1897. Hines, military commander for the Confederate commission in Canada, became chief justice of Kentucky, dying in 1898. Bennett S. Young, leader of the raid on St. Albans, was president of a number of railroads and of a bridge company in Indiana. He was invited by the state of Vermont to take part in a reenactment of the raid on its fortieth anniversary in 1904, but the Grand Army of the Republic protested that his appearance would commercialize the pageantry, so Young himself cancelled his acceptance. He dedicated the Confederate Monument in Arlington Cemetery in 1914, and when he died three years later received a hero's burial.

Burley, second in command to John Yates Beall during the *Philo Parsons* episode on the Great Lakes, was extradited to the United States from Canada. He was tried for the theft of forty dollars from the clerk of the steamer. The trial ended in a hung jury, and while awaiting a new trial he escaped. Burley returned to England and became an author and prominent war correspondent, covering, among other conflicts, the Russo-Japanese War. He died on the eve of World War I.

Charles H. Cole, who was supposed to get the officers of the *Michigan* drunk so that Beall and his men aboard the *Philo Parsons* could board and seize the warship, turned state's evidence to testify against the others. He was developing mining interests in Texas when last heard of in 1869. Anderson, who turned informer at Beall's trial, was released from federal custody on March 27, 1865, two days after Kennedy's execution. What happened to him is unknown. Little is known also about the fate of Sanders. His name last appeared in newspapers during Grant's campaign for the presidency four years after the war. Hyams slipped out of history after appearing briefly to incriminate Clay and Davis in Lincoln's assassination. He had approached the United States consul in Toronto in April 1865, to sell information about the operation of the Confederate commission in Canada. On the basis of what he divulged, Thompson, Clay, Larry McDonald, and Cleary were indicted by a Canadian jury for breaches of neutrality, but all escaped imprisonment.

Both of the Wood brothers returned to Congress. Fernando took a trip to Europe as the war drew to a close. He was defeated as a candidate for mayor in 1867, but was elected to the 40th Congress and to seven succeeding terms, dying in 1881 just before the opening of the 47th Congress. His brother Benjamin served as a state senator in 1866—67 and was elected to the 47th Congress, serving until 1883. He died in New York in 1900. Horatio Seymour ran for President against Grant in 1868 and lost. He died in Utica in 1886.

John A. Dix left the Army after the war and was appointed Minister to France, serving until 1869. As a Republican, he was elected governor of New York in 1872, but was defeated for reelection two years later. He ran for mayor of New York in 1876, but was also defeated for that office. He died in 1879 at the age of eighty and was interred in Trinity Cemetery, Riverside Drive and 153d Street, New York City. Lieutenant Colonel Burke, commander of Fort Lafayette, was breveted a brigadier general for his services during the war, dying in 1882, about eighty years old. Joe Howard, Jr., continued to work for newspapers and was president of the New York Press Club for a time. His "Howard's Column" was widely syndicated in 1886. He died in 1908, in his mid-seventies.

John A. Kennedy resigned as police superintendent in 1870 to become president of a streetcar company. Two years later he became collector of assessments for the city, a post he held until his death in 1873 two months short of his seventieth birthday. Chief Engineer John Decker of the Fire Department led the last big fire fought by the New York volunteer companies when Barnum's Museum burned down on July 13, 1865. Only a few persons were in the building, since it was a hot day. No one was killed or even seriously injured, although some animals perished. It was believed that Southern sympathizers, irate over a wax figure in the museum showing Jefferson Davis in his wife's petticoats trying to escape capture, had set the blaze. Before it was brought under control, the fire spread to seventeen nearby buildings, fourteen of which were totally destroyed.

Amos C. "Turk" Smith was still in close confinement and on a restricted diet (because of his part in Kennedy's escape) in mid-January of 1865; however, he survived his imprisonment at Johnson's Island. Lieutenant T. E. Fell, another inmate, was still alive in 1891, when he wrote his brief account of Kennedy's escape. Edward A. Jackson, Kennedy's roommate in Toronto, wrote a brief account of Kennedy's military career for *Confederate Veteran* in July 1908. Following his release from Fort Lafayette, John D. Allison returned to his wife in Canada and went to work there. Mulrennon was freed from the fort six days after Kennedy's execution.

General William N. R. Beall became a general commission merchant in St. Louis. He died in 1883, just before his sixtieth birthday. General Joe Wheeler survived an attack by two Federal officers after the war—one of them claimed to have once been his prisoner—to become a commission merchant and Congressman, and—in the Spanish-American War—a major general. He fought at San Juan Hill and in the Philippines. The former Confederate cavalry leader died in New York in 1906 at the age of sixty-nine.

Kennedy's other friends at West Point died early in life. Edwin H. Stoughton passed away in Boston on Christmas Day, 1868, at the age of thirty, after having left his New York law practice because of failing health. Stephen De Witt Clinton Beekman never survived the war. At the outset he volunteered in Edward D. Baker's "First California" Regiment, a Pennsylvania unit made up mostly of Philadelphians. Beekman, a first lieutenant, fought at Balls Bluff and throughout the Peninsular Campaign, but did not get along with the Philadelphians, who, he contended, were prejudiced against him. He tried to resign in March 1862, when he got bronchitis, but was turned down. A second such appeal in June of that year was accepted, as his company was about to be merged with another. Beekman hoped to get a commission with a New York volunteer unit, but suffered a recurrence of the diarrhea that he had first contracted on the banks of the Chickahominy River. Recovering, he enlisted in January 1864, as a private in the mounted infantry and sought out classmates from West Point for references in order to get a commission. He was made a second lieutenant in March of that year, but was soon hospitalized with phlegmonour erysipelas—a disease of the liver or kidney usually aggra-vated by alcohol. He died of it on July 7, 1864, in Virginia, at the age of twenty-eight.

Beekman sounded almost paranoid about his early experiences in the war. In tendering his resignation from the 71st Regiment (named the "First California" in honor of Baker, a good friend of Lincoln who had become a lawyer in San Francisco), Beekman said he had been "unjustly dealt with" because "I am a *New Yorker*, among comparative strangers who are *Philadelphians* and strongly prejudiced against me. I know that my resignation would be pleasing to the majority of the regiment." He lied in applying for a commission on January 25, 1864: "I was for over two years at the United States Military Academy at West Point and resigned during Jefferson Davis' administration as Sec-retary of War." Not only was his "resignation" a lie, but phrasing it in such a way as to imply that he did so because of Davis compounded his duplicity. Beekman acknowledged in his plea for support of his application on March 3, 1864, that "I find the service quite hard—of course, not what I have been accustomed to at any time in my life."[5]

The American consul in Toronto, D. Thurston, wrote Seward on April 7, 1865, that a person named Hyams, "intimately associated with Rebels here," had approached him with "important information." Hyams told Thurston "that he had been connected with the Rebels for several years—& that all their schemes and plots were well known to him—which he was desirous of communicating to me if I would first remunerate him for doing so." Thurston told Hyams he would first have to submit the information to Washington before he could agree to any payment. Hyams accepted the arrangement and divulged a number of Confederate plans, including one then current to attack Federal shipping on the Lakes with a steamer called the *Georgianna*. He also gave the names of several Southern officers being commanded by "Col. Martin alias Maxwell" who were planning to devastate the Maine countryside. He gave the address where Larry McDonald was manufacturing torpedoes and combustibles to use on the *Georgianna*. Thurston had the house searched and found the torpedoes coated with a mixture of broken coal and pitch to look innocently like fuel so that they would be thrown into ship furnaces unawares.[6]

Thurston informed Washington on May 1 that same year that a Canadian grand jury had returned true bills against Clay, Thompson, Cleary, and McDonald. "These bills," he was advised by attorneys, "were found principally on the evidence of Godfrey J. Hyams but we would not deem it safe to proceed to trial without strong corroborative evidence."[7]

Even before Rob's last letter to his family reached Homer, Federal steamboats were plying the Ouachita under flags of truce with trade permits and Confederate guards. Farmers from miles around rushed to meet them to barter their cotton for scarce commodities: flour, meat, axes and other tools, medicine. The war, for Claiborne Parish, was all but over, and its economy was a total wreck. Four years of conflict had cost Louisiana half of its livestock, two-thirds of its farm equipment, and the third of its total wealth represented by the $170 million invested in slaves. In addition, nearly 12,000 of her sons would never return.

Although never occupied by Federal forces during the war, the parish was soon swamped by carpetbaggers after the war ended. Taxes were pushed up to force out secessionist landowners. "Too proud to stay where his neighbors could see his poverty," Rob's father, Dr. John Bailey Kennedy, sold out his land in December of 1865 and moved downstate to Vermillionville, a small Cajun village west of Baton Rouge that, by coincidence, was later renamed Lafayette.[8] A loyal former slave, Moses Portlock, went with him. Dr. Kennedy was able to purchase several hundred acres and a house built of cypress and twelve-inch-thick walls of moss and plaster. He tried to return to farming—rice and sugar cane this time—but found it difficult without slave labor. Portlock settled nearby with his wife Winnie and four children on land that would later be known as the Portlock Addition. The Reconstruction Era, recalled Rob's brother-in-law, Dr. Thomas Battle Hopkins, was "too dark for me even to look on." A yellow fever epidemic swept through Vermillionville in 1867. Cliff, nineteen years old, and Kate, twelve, caught the disease. Dr. Kennedy volunteered to fight the outbreak. His two children recovered, but he was infected.

Dr. Kennedy died on October 7, 1867, at the age of sixty-two. He left a meager estate, worth only $2,000 in 1870.[9]

Rob's mother, Eliza Lydia Cobb Kennedy, lived on until January 23, 1891, dying at the age of seventy-five—"miserable" after the loss of two sons in the war. Until the end, she answered the knock of every stranger at her door, hoping it would be Johnny, but her twenty-three-year-old son, wounded and missing after the battle of Ezra Church outside Atlanta in 1864, never returned. Hyder Ali, however, recovered from his wound, received in the same battle. He stayed on in Homer for two years, serving as Clerk of Court there until 1868, when he joined his family in Vermillionville. Hyder married Elizabeth Richardson in 1869 and lived until he was sixty-three, dying in New Orleans where he had become a customs collector. Dr. Hopkins returned from the war a father: his son Frank had been born in January of 1865. His wife, Mary Willis Kennedy, gave birth to a second child, Eliza Cobb Hopkins, on December 15, 1866, but it was a difficult labor and she took ill and died on March 23, 1867, two weeks shy of her twenty-ninth birthday. Her sister, Susanna, then almost fifteen, took over the care of Mary's two youngsters, as was the custom. Dr. Hopkins fell in love with the young girl, and two years later wed her. Susanna died on August 16, 1903, two weeks before her fifty-first birthday. Dr. Hopkins lived until he was eighty-nine, dying on October 15, 1922.[10]

Cliff Kennedy married Mary Ellen Black, the daughter of a widower, Captain L.A. Black of Mississippi, in the early 1870s. The couple had two children in Lafayette, the first of whom was named for Rob, before moving to Lufkin, Texas, where Cliff became a jeweler. He died on September 1, 1922, seventy-six years old. Kate, the youngest of the Kennedy children, outlived all her brothers and sisters. She went to live with Susanna in Dr. Hopkins's household in her early teens and there met Alexander A. Morgan, the stepson of Captain Black by a second marriage, whom she married in 1875. Kate died on May 18, 1931, seventy-five years old.

Descendants of Dr. Kennedy still lived along the same street in Lafayette up until 1980 in old, white, wood-frame houses with airy screen porches and tiny lawns.[11] Some of the streets nearby, where his farm once stood, bear the first names of his grandchildren, and there are streets named Hopkins, Morgan, and Portlock although none named Kennedy. About thirty-five acres of the old land that was left was leased to a cotton farmer.

The Kennedy farm in Homer no longer exists. Mary Jane, the Negro seamstress, was given the dogtrot house when the family moved, but it, along with other homes in the area, was burned down when the Federal government took over the land and seeded it with pine trees. The Caney Division of the Kisatchie National Forest now encompasses the area. Thick undergrowth covers the earth between the tall pines. Dirt roads cut through the forest, leading past small graveyards whose stones are broken in two or are too weathered to read. Hawks crisscross the sky and small game scampers through the woods, but otherwise there is no sign of life.

In 1872, Edward A. Jackson, who had roomed with Rob in Toronto, visited his grave at Fort Hamilton, 200 yards back of the fort. As Jackson sat on a bench in the graveyard, an Army officer strolled by. "Do you know that young man?" he asked Jackson, pointing to Rob's grave. It turned out he was a West Point classmate of Rob's, but Jackson did not catch the name. The officer told Jackson about Rob's "last hour" and took him on a tour of the fort. "All his courtesies were meant as honor to Kennedy, and by me so taken," Jackson later wrote in *The Confederate Veteran*. His article, entitled "A Forgotten Hero—R.C. Kennedy," told about the visit to the gravesite, and appended to it was a poem written by a fellow Confederate soldier, R.B. Mayes, who, like Jackson, was from Yazoo City, Mississippi.

KENNEDY'S DEATH SONG

Trust to luck, trust to luck, stare Fate in the face;
Your heart will be easy if it's in the right place.

Though Luck may betray, though Fate may destroy,
Be faithful to Duty, and she'll give you joy.

O, had I a score of lives, I would give
One and all to my Southland; I'm hers, die or live.

Though life it is sweet, though earth it is dear,
To die for my country brings heaven more near.

Take away your black cap; I'll look in your eye.
No, don't turn it from me; see a Southerner die.

Turn my face to the South; it follows my heart.
I'm ready, crack your whip, sir, and on with your cart![12]

Rob's body did not rest at Fort Hamilton for many more years. In January of 1885, because the Army needed room to expand the fort, his and ninety-seven other graves were opened and the remains transported ten miles east.[13]

By then the wooden marker over Rob's grave had disintegrated, and the bones inside what was left of the pine box had crumbled into dust. The remains were taken to a private burial ground, Cypress Hill Cemetery, on the border between Brooklyn and Queens and down the street from Cypress Hills National Cemetery. There, a number of Union and Confederate soldiers, many known, some unknown, were reinterred in a corner of a tree-shaded slope. Interspersed between the headstones of men from Massachusetts, New York, Ohio, and other states of the Union rest more than a score of men—Rob among them—under identical stones that read:

"Unknown Confederate Soldier"

Gather the sacred dust
Of the warriors tried and true,
Who bore the flag of nation's trust
And fell in a cause as great as just,
And died for me and you.

Gather them, each and all,
From the private to the chief,
Come they from cabin or lordly hall;
Over their dust let the fresh tears fall
Of a nation's holy grief.

No matter whence they came,
Dear is their lifeless clay;
Whether unknown or known to fame,
Their cause and country were the same—
They died—and they wore the gray.[1]

notes

The following abbreviations are used on second reference to citations in the footnotes:

AGO	Adjutant General's Office
CR	Confederate Records
JAG	Office of the Judge Advocate General
LPMC	Lafayette Prison, Miscellaneous Correspondence
MM-3513	Military proceedings in the case of John Yates Beall
MM-3729	Military proceedings in the case of Robert Cobb Kennedy
N.A., RG	National Archives, Record Group
OR	*War of the Rebellion, a Compilation of Official Records of the Union and Confederate Armies*
PMFPR	Union Provost Marshal's File, Prison Records 1862–65
USACC	U.S. Army Continental Commands
USMA	U.S. Military Academy

ACKNOWLEDGMENTS

1. Fitzhugh Lee, Calendar memorial (Des Moines, Iowa: Kenyon Co., 1910). The poem, entitled "They Should Not Rest Apart," is attributed to a Father Ryan and is included with other Confederate poems and songs on the back of the memorial.

247

PROLOGUE

1. *Frank Leslie's Illustrated Newspaper,* Dec. 17, 1864.
2. Allan Nevins and Milton Halsey Thomas, eds., *The Diary of George Templeton Strong,* Vol. 3 (New York: Macmillan Co., 1952), p. 521. Strong quotes a friend on the increase of "harlotry" in the city due to the influx of Southern women who had to choose between prostitution and starvation. His diary is the source of many of the details in this book regarding the city, including daily weather conditions. Strong was at a meeting of the U.S. Sanitary Commission on the night of Nov. 25, 1864, when he heard "the melancholy bell of Calvary Church tolling the alarm again and again at short intervals."

CHAPTER 1

1. See notes for Chapters 2, 11, 12 and 13.
2. An exhibition of Edwin Booth's Shakespearan roles, held at the New York Public Library at Lincoln Center in the summer of 1981, included a photograph of the three Booth brothers in costume for "Julius Caesar." It was the only time that the three ever did appear together.

CHAPTER 2

1. The following newspapers and periodicals were used to recreate the events of and surrounding Nov. 25, 1864: *Brooklyn Daily Eagle, Brooklyn Standard, Frank Leslie's Illustrated Newspaper, Harper's Weekly* and *New Monthly Magazines, New York Daily News, New York Daily Tribune* and *Weekly Tribune, New York Evening Post, New York Freeman's Journal and Catholic Register, New York Herald, New York Journal of Commerce, New York Leader, New-York Times, New York Weekly Day-Book,* and *New York World.* In addition, the following other sources were employed: Journal of Chief Engineer John Decker; Alfred E. Baker, "Fire Marshal's Report to the Mayor/June 1–Nov. 30, 1864," (New York: Holman, 1865); John W. Headley, *Confederate Operations in Canada and New York* (New York and Washington: Neale Publishing Co., 1906); National Archives, Record Group 153, "Office of Judge Advocate General," Military Proceedings in the case of Robert C. Kennedy (MM-3729). Although all the sources agree that the first alarm was sounded from the St. James Hotel, there is some difference as to the number of fires and their sequence. Decker's Journal lists the St. Nicholas, Barnum's, the Lafarge, the Metropolitan, and the Belmont as sites of the other fires, in that order. Baker lists, in order, Barnum's, a

dock, the Howard, the Fifth-Avenue, a barge, and a lumberyard. At Robert Cobb Kennedy's trial, Superintendent Kennedy listed the order as the St. James, the Lafarge, the St. Nicholas, Barnum's, the Belmont, the United States, the Tammany, Lovejoy's, the Metropolitan, the Astor, the Fifth-Avenue, a lumberyard, and the docks. The sequence followed throughout the text is based on compiled newspaper accounts and on Headley's movements as he recounted them, with one major exception: *Frank Leslie's Illustrated Newspaper* ran a sketch of the International Hotel on Dec. 17, 1864, as part of a series depicting the hotels that had been the sites of fires. There was, however, no attempt to set the International on fire on the night of Nov. 25. Instead, there was a fire at the hotel three nights later when a lighted match was thrown on bedding in a storeroom adjoining some water closets. As noted in Chapter 15, this fire was also blamed on rebel incendiaries and perhaps explains Leslie's mistaken use of the sketch. For further details, see notes for Chapters 11, 12, and 13.

2. J. Frank Kernan, *Reminiscences of the Old Fire Laddies* (New York: M. Crane, 1885), pp. 193–94, is one of the few eye-witness accounts in existence. Kernan recalls "with particular vividness" being at the Winter Garden ("The house was crowded to its utmost capacity") when the alarm was given. He says "the wildest confusion, amounting to a panic, pervaded the vast audience."

3. *New York Daily News*, Nov. 28, 1864.

4. N.A., RG 109, "Confederate Records." Martin's chance encounter with Sergeant Young is related in depositions given by Hugh Shaw (Union Provost Marshal's File, Prison Records 1862–65) and Alfred Wheels (Lafayette Prison, Miscellaneous Correspondence), who heard Martin brag about it when they were in prison together after the war in Louisville, Kentucky.

CHAPTER 3

1. Newspapers of the day often referred to city detectives as "Kennedy's spies."

2. *New-York Times*, Nov. 27, 1864. Dix's announced pledge to find and prosecute the perpetrators was issued on Nov. 26 as General Orders No. 92; his renewal of the drive to register Southerners in the city as General Orders No. 93. (Both were carried by other local newspapers in addition to the *Times*.)

CHAPTER 4

1. N.A., RG 94, "Adjutant General's Office," Military Academy Application 122–1854. The physical description of Kennedy is based on newspaper accounts following his capture in Detroit (Isaacs the executioner drew out of him his height and weight) and his photograph, taken three days before he was executed. The photograph was discovered and identified by me. It was among other photos in the family album in possession of his great-grandniece, Mrs. W. A. LaFleur.

Contemporary newspapers, official records of Fort Lafayette, and John D. Allison (in his diary) all mention that Kennedy was photographed in prison, the newspapers identifying the photographer as one Clarke. On the back of the photograph, which is a little larger than wallet size, is the identification "Clarke's Union Photographic Gallery, 643 Broadway corner of Bleecker Street, N.Y." The likeness conforms to written descriptions. The family was unaware that it was a photograph of Kennedy, although it had been kept along with those of Kennedy's father, brothers, and sister Susanna. In addition to their descriptions from the photographs, Mary's is taken from a letter Dr. Hopkins wrote on Feb. 5, 1908, entitled "Pictures." Then seventy-five, Dr. Hopkins recalled a number of incidents in his life. He and Mary were wed on Sept. 15, 1859, in a double ceremony with Julia C. Thompson and Edmund D. Bugg, a cousin. According to a letter among the Kennedy family papers, Dr. Hopkins was a graduate of the Pennsylvania Medical School.

2. Morris Schaff, *The Spirit of Old West Point, 1858–1862* (Boston: Houghton, Mifflin, 1907), p. 77.

3. Ibid., p. 67.

4. Jones's endorsement was perfunctory: "The within applicant is a permanent resident of the Parish of Claiborne in the 4th Cong Dist of Louisiana & I hereby recommend him for the appointment of cadet in the Military Academy at West Point." (N.A. RG 94, AGO, Military Academy application 122–1854.)

5. RG 404, U.S. Military Academy Archives. All materials concerning Kennedy and his classmates at West Point are located under a variety of documents: Superintendent's Letter Book, No. 3; Register of Delinquencies No. 7; Military Academy Order No. 11 (July 7, 1856); and Adjutant's Letter Book (October 31, 1845, to March 8, 1858), as well as progress reports and general merit rolls.

6. Stoughton's name is sometimes misspelled. It appears as Staughton, for example, in the West Point records of cadet admissions.

7. *Regulations for the United States Military Academy at West Point, New-York* (New-York: John F. Trow, 1853), p. 36.

8. RG 404, USMA Archives, Barnard to Gen. Joseph G. Totten, Army Chief Engineer, June 28, 1856.

9. N.A., RG 94, AGO, USMA, Extracts from proceedings of the Academic Board. Kennedy and Beekman were among thirteen found deficient in the annual examinations of June, 1856, and among seventeen that the Academic Board recommended "ought not to be permitted to return." The additional four cadets included three who were court-martialed and one who resigned.

CHAPTER 5

1. *New York Herald*, Oct. 30, 1860. Moore's remarks were made in a letter to *The New Orleans Delta* in response to questions raised by prominent citizens as to what Louisiana should do if Lincoln were elected. the *Herald* reprinted the reply. Moore, a Democrat, said that "if we cannot win the Presidential victory, that [sic] we can at least present to the enemy an unbroken column and a united defiance."

2. *New-York Times*, July 20, 1860. The eclipse, which began at 7:10 A.M. and lasted until 9:11 A.M. on the morning of July 18, was observed at New York University and Harvard.

3. An account of Beekman's visit, including the dance, was related to the late Mrs. Margaret Moore Vail by the Negro valet who accompanied Kennedy to war.

4. Ibid. The former slave told her that he was sitting outside the open window of the Kennedy library on the morning in question (July 18, 1860), and overheard the conversation.

5. J.W. Dorr, "A Tourist Description of Louisiana in 1860," *Louisiana Historical Quarterly* 21, No. 8 (October, 1938): p. 1183. Dorr's account of his visit to Homer is dated July 18, 1860.

6. Ibid.

7. Ibid.

8. Details of the Kennedy and Cobb lineage and history are from genealogical papers and from a number of short, typed family histories, several unsigned, in the possession of Mrs. W. A. LaFleur. Among them are "Dr. John Bailey Kennedy/1805–1867"; "Kennedy History," with the ending notation "compiled on July 8, 1938 from information supplied by Miss Eliza Cobb Hopkins and A.A. Morgan, Sr. and added to later by Mrs. B.A. Kennedy and from information in the Battle Book"; a copy of the will of James Kennedy, Jr., filed apparently on March 18, 1822, in Chester County, South Carolina; and "The Kennedy Family," by Miss Hopkins, dated Dec. 7, 1947, and, by the same author, and bearing the same date, "A Few Little Happenings in the Cobb Family and From the Bugg Family." Miss Hopkins was the second daughter of Mary Willis Kennedy and Dr. Thomas Battle Hopkins. A spinster, she died on March 12, 1959, at the age of ninety-two. Her writings are the source of such facts and incidents as, for example, the seamstress Mary Jane, The Story Teller, the "tanery" and sewing machine, Eliza Cobb Kennedy's religious bent, the gift of spoons from "Cousin" Howell, the horn Henry Willis Cobb kept to call his young slaves to dance for guests, and the peculiarities of Charles Bugg.

There is some confusion as to the day of Dr. Kennedy's birth. The tombstone over his grave in the Protestant Cemetery, Lafayette, La., reads March 5, 1805. However, the photostat of the family Bible in Mrs. LaFleur's possession gives the date as March 4, 1805. (The Bible was lost to the family for some time.)

The Kennedy name is misspelled in both the volumes of white inhabitants and slave inhabitants in the Census of 1860. In the former, the name is spelled "Kenada," while Hyder's name is given as "Hiderelle." On the slave list, the Kennedy name comes out "Kenedy." The registers were written by different recorders, although certified by the same census taker. Apparently they were semiliterate.

Newspapers at the time of Kennedy's capture and trial identified him variously as Howell Cobb Kennedy and Howell Cobb Stanton, and reported that he was a relative, possibly a nephew, of Howell Cobb.

Coincidentally, sometime in the week of Nov. 20, 1864—perhaps only a day or two before the fires in New York—William Tecumseh Sherman was spending the night on a plantation in Georgia as his army paused briefly in its historic march. Upon learning that the plantation belonged to Howell Cobb, Sherman ordered it burned to the ground ("Spare nothing"), according to James Ford Rhodes, *History of the United States*, Vol. 5 (Port Washington, N.Y.: Kennikat Press, 1967, copyright 1892–1919), p. 22.

Clyde Kennedy, a North Louisiana farmer unrelated to the Kennedys of Homer, is the source of some of the observations about that part of the state, including farm life, weather, crops, and the like. His ancestor, W. R. Kennedy, was one of the first settlers in the area. Other sources heavily relied on include the following articles: "Claiborne History" by Herbert Ford and "The Court House" by W. M. Shaw in *Claiborne Parish Sketches* (Homer, La.: Claiborne Parish Historical Association, 1956); "Early Transport Service and an Old Cemetery" by Gilbert C. Ownes and "Shotgun and Dogtrot" by Ted 'Larry Pebworth in *Historic Claiborne* (Homer, La.: Claiborne Parish Historical Association, 1962); "Brief Memories of the Civil War of 1862–64," from an unsigned, handwritten manuscript on file at the Ford Museum, Homer; "Claiborne Parish," a reprint from *The Claiborne Guardian* of June 8, 1881, edited by Jack Smith, "Culture of the Indians of North Louisiana" by G. W. McGinty, and "The Military Road Across Claiborne Parish and the Village of Old Haynesville" by Mabel McEachern Stewart, all in *Historic Claiborne '65* (Homer, La.: Claiborne Parish Historical Association, 1965); "Boom or Bust—Louisiana's Economy During the 1830's" by Merl Reed, "Impact of Epidemic Yellow Fever on Life in Louisiana" by Jo Ann Carrigan, and "Vignettes" from *Louisiana History* IV, No. 1 (Winter 1963); "A French Traveler's View of Ante-Bellum New Orleans" by Henry B. Hill and Larry Gara, "Gloom Envelops New Orleans" by James O. Lang, "The Physiognomy of Rural Louisiana" by Fred Kniffen, and "Some Irish Foot Prints Among the Tall Pines" by Garnie W. McGinty, *Louisiana History* IV, No. 4 (Fall 1963).

9. Eliza Cobb Hopkins, "A Few Little Happenings in the Cobb Family and From the Bugg Family."

10. Frank Vaughn, editor of *The Claiborne Advocate*, named the parish seat. Claiborne had originally been part of Natchitoches Parish. From Claiborne were carved the parishes of Bossier (1843), Jackson (1845), Bienville (1848), Webster (1871), and Lincoln (1873). Today, Claiborne Parish covers 778 square miles.

11. James W. Nicholson, *Stories of Dixie*, rev. ed. (Baton Rouge: Claitor's Book Store, 1966), p. 6.

12. Ibid., p. 104. Nicholson describes the traveler as a scholar "who has read much and traveled more, and who knew that section of the state intimately as it was before the Civil War."

13. From writings of Miss Eliza Cobb Hopkins, Kennedy family papers. The process of making a powder horn was described in a letter by Clyde Kennedy of Bernice, La.

14. *The Claiborne Advocate* of March 28, 1855, noted that there were 980 planters in the area of Homer, most of whom averaged only fifteen bales of cotton yearly. The total crop for the entire parish is given as 14,700 bales "or 6.5 million pounds."

15. Because of a courthouse fire in the former parish seat of Athens in 1849, no records of land transactions are available for the years before then. The first

recorded transaction involving Dr. Kennedy is dated July 26, 1851 (although some of the homestead grants were predated to 1850). They usually involved forty-acre parcels, but some were larger. (The largest was for 121 acres in mid-September of 1854.) Typical of the bonus grants that were exchanged was Dr. Kennedy's purchase on July 20, 1853, of forty acres from Charles Francis C. Jumonvile, a private in Captain Ducrois's Company, First Regiment, Louisiana Militia, War of 1812. Dr. Kennedy was joined in some of the transactions by his wife, indicating that some of his sales were of land either inherited by her or given to them jointly.

According to the Census of 1860, RG 29, there were other farmers in the Homer area with more property than Dr. Kennedy—values reaching $100,000 in one case, $60,000 in another, and a merchant with $75,000—but most residents averaged between $30,000 and $40,000 worth of property. Of Dr. Kennedy's forty-nine slaves, three females were mulattoes and all but seven of the twenty-three female slaves were more than eleven years old—the age when slave children were put into the fields to work. Of the total of twenty-six male slaves, all but eleven were more than ten years old. The oldest female slave was forty-five (there were two that age), and the oldest male thirty-eight. Most of the others, male and female, were in their twenties or thirties—the most valuable ages from a work standpoint.

CHAPTER 6

1. The movements and battle accounts involving the First Louisiana Infantry, Regulars, as well as references to Kennedy in battle reports, are taken from *War of the Rebellion, a Compilation of Official Records of the Union and Confederate Armies* (Washington: Government Printing Office, 1880–1901), as well as narratives given in the Bibliography (which see). The First Louisiana, which became known as Strawbridge's Infantry, should not be confused with the First Special Battalion, Louisiana Infantry, commanded by Major C. R. (Bob) Wheat until his death in 1862. The latter was called the Louisiana Tigers (a name adopted by the brigade of which it was a part), and fought with the Army of Northern Virginia at Bull Run and in the Peninsular Campaign.

Kennedy's application for a commission, N.A., RG 109, CR, Secretary of War, Letters Received, is dated June 14, 1861, "Warrington, Fla." It is to L. Pope Walker, then Confederate Secretary of War, and reads in part: "I am now a Lieutenant in the Regular Regt. La. Infantry. Was appointed as Cadet in the Army of the United States & served at Military Academy, West Point from June 1854 to July 1856." Kennedy's signature appears on a number of muster rolls, and as many as ninety-two times as witness to the payroll covering Aug. 30–Oct. 31, 1861. (N.A., RG 109, CR, Rolls, Co. G, 1st La. Inf.)

2. The name of the Negro valet who accompanied Kennedy to war is unknown. A Moses Portlock, a former slave, followed Kennedy's father to Lafayette, La., after the war. Portlock was about Kennedy's age, according to the Census of 1870 in Lafayette Parish. It is possible that he was the one who, in the custom of the time, went off with Kennedy to tend his horse, fix his meals, launder his uniforms, and so forth. Mrs. Vail said that, according to Mrs. Roberta Cobb Kennedy Girard, the valet

referred to Kennedy as "Mister Robert." She herself called him "Robert," but "Rob" appears to be what he was generally called by his contemporaries.

3. OR, Series I, Vol. VI, p. 836.

4. OR, Series I, Vol. VI, p. 798.

5. OR, Series I, Vol. X, Part 1, pp. 536–539. Details of the First Louisiana's action on the first day of Shiloh, including Gladden's death, are taken from reports filed by Adams and by his successor after Adams was wounded—Col. Z.C. Deas of the 22d Alabama.

6. Lloyd Lewis, "Shiloh, Bloody Shiloh," in Ernest Hemingway, ed., Men at War (New York: Crown, 1942), p. 233.

7. New Orleans Picayune, April 8, 1862.

8. Ned Bradford, ed., Battles and Leaders of the Civil War (New York: Appleton-Crofts, 1956). Grant's quotations are from his account of Shiloh: "Southern dash" (p. 87); "severest" (p. 91); "complete conquest" and "material influence" (p. 94).

CHAPTER 7

1. N.A., RG 109, CR, La. Quarterly Return of Deceased Soldiers of 1st La. Regt. The First Louisiana lost fifty-one men at Shiloh, and eight more died before the following July of wounds received in the engagement. Company G's losses were six killed and eighteen wounded; only eighty men remained as April ended. Gladden's Brigade, of which the First Louisiana was part, suffered a total of 129 killed, 597 wounded, and 103 missing. Of the total division—the 2d, under Brigadier General J. M. Withers—the aggregate loss was 1,918 out of a total of 6,482 troops. The total strength of Withers's division going into the battle of Murfreesboro was 7,774, his losses due to casualties 2,519.

2. OR, Series I, Vol. XX, Part 1, p. 686.

3. N.A., RG 109, CR Special orders dated Nov. 15, 1862.

4. Wheeler, in reporting on the expedition on Oct. 30, 1863, mentioned Kennedy along with thirteen other officers of his staff "for their gallantry and good conduct" (OR, Series I, Vol. XXX, Part 2, p. 725). Part 4, p. 741, ibid., has the following Special Orders, No. 79, dated Oct. 12 and signed by an aide of Wheeler:

"I. Capt. R.C. Kennedy will proceed to Chattanooga on business connected with this corps. He will instruct Maj. O.P. Chaffie to procure at least 16,000 horseshoes, 2,000 pounds of nails, for which application has been made to army headquarters. He will also instruct Captain Jones to use every exertion to procure the ammunition for which application has been made to army headquarters. These things will be forwarded here as quickly as possible.

"II. Captain Kennedy is authorized to impress horses on the route for himself and courier, to be returned by him on their return to this headquarters."

5. Kennedy's capture is mentioned in a number of Union dispatches. The substance of the messages he carried was of some importance, since Wheeler not only disclosed his losses but also his immediate plans. OR, Series I, Vol. XXX, Part 2, p. 665, and Part 4, pp. 436–437, 445, 463.

6. Brigadier General Meriwether Jeff Thompson, "Diary of Prisoner on Johnson's Island—1863," United Daughters of the Confederacy Magazine XVII, No. 9 (September, 1954): pp. 30–31. Thompson also claimed credit for the song that follows, which he entitled "Damn It! Let It Rip."

7. James D. Horan, Confederate Agent: A Discovery in History (New York: Crown, 1954), p. 36. The poem was written by one of General John Hunt Morgan's men during the incarceration of Morgan and a number of his officers at Johnson's Island before their transfer to the penitentiary at Columbus, from which they subsequently escaped.

8. T.E. Fell, "Escape of Prisoners From Johnson's Island," Southern Historical Society Papers XVIII (January–December, 1890): pp. 429–430. Included with Fell's statement was a "correction" of an account by Lieutenant J. H. Carpenter of New Orleans describing the escape on "Cold New Year's" and including Dr. Luke P. Blackburn—"chief surgeon of the division of Sterling Price, of Missouri"—among those who escaped.

8. OR, Series II, Vol. VII, pp. 995–996. Major Thomas H. Linnell, superintendent of the prison, reported Kennedy's escape on Oct. 16, 1864, identifying him as a member of the First Georgia Infantry. This mistake is sometimes repeated in other reports and, as far as I can gather (because I once made the same error), it was because of the abbreviations scrawled by clerks. "La." in hard-to-read script is easily misinterpreted as "Ga." Linnell reported that the "first intimation" he had of the escape was on the fourteenth, and that he believed, as the result of inquiries, that the escape had occurred on the fourth and that Kennedy had escaped by scaling the prison fence between the blockhouse and Block 1. Linnell placed Clark, the roll-caller, under immediate arrest and preferred charges against him for disobedience of orders. The sentinel on duty on the fourth was also arrested.

Clark and Sergeant Hewitt later explained what had happened. As Clark put it, "the fact is the prisoners in the prison deceived me by answering to his, this escaped prisoner's, name." It had resulted because "by mistake and without intention I erased the name of a prisoner who still remained in the company and who afterwards answered to the name of a prisoner who had made his escape." (N.A., RG 109, CR, PMFPR, Johnson's Island.)

"Turk" Smith (ibid.) wrote the prison superintendent that the Smith first singled out as Kennedy's helper was the wrong Smith. He gave himself up, "being unconscious of committing any offence in assisting a fellow prisoner and mess-mate to gain his liberty." His note is dated Nov. 16, 1864. An inspecting officer at Johnson's Island reported on Jan. 8, 1865, that Smith had been kept on a low diet since Nov. 17, 1864, and suggested that he be restored to his former prison status. On Jan. 18, 1865, a prisoner exchange agent made an appeal that Smith be released from close confinement or irons. (OR, Series II, Vol. VIII.)

O. Edward Cunningham, in " 'In Violation of the Laws of War': The Execution of Robert Cobb Kennedy" (*Louisiana History*, Vol. XVIII, No. 2, Spring, 1977), p. 191, says that Kennedy was one of only twelve rebels who "apparently" were able to escape from Johnson's Island.

CHAPTER 8

1. Headley, *Confederate Operations*, p. 268. Headley also later describes McDonald as "one of Colonel Thompson's closest friends." N.A., RG 94, AGO, TurnerBaker Papers, identifies McDonald as a sutler with the 26th New Jersey Regiment who was being sought for turning over his stores to Confederates and for assisting them in capturing Union horses near Culpepper Court House, Dec. 27, 1862.

2. The spy route is given in detail in a letter to Secretary of State William H. Seward from R. J. Kimball, U.S. consular agent in Toronto. (Despatches from U.S. Consuls in Toronto, 1864–1906, Public Archives of Canada.) The letter, dated Jan. 3, 1865, notes the use of microphotography and invisible ink. "This information," says Kimball, "is *reliable*, from a person who *has seen* the dispatches and has personal knowledge of the facts."

3. Jacob Thompson, "A Leaf from History" (Union Republican Congressional Committee) p. 4. Thompson's report, from Toronto on Dec. 3, 1864, also appears in OR, Series I, Vol. XLIII, Part 2, pp. 930–936.

4. Headley, *Confederate Operations*, p. 215.

5. A number of sources say Thompson used the alias of "Carson," among them the depositions of John Maughan, dated Dec. 22, 1864, and of Maurice Langhorn, dated Dec. 19, 1864, Colonial Office Papers, Public Archives of Canada.

6. *New-York Times*, Oct. 19, 1864.

7. T. E. Fell, "Escape of Prisoners," pp. 428–429. His report of Kennedy's escape route and other remarks attributed to him are all taken from this article.

8. Claiborne Parish, Office of the Secretary of Police Jury: Minutes of meetings of Police Jury, Vol. A, p. 67. According to Act No. 33, on Jan. 5, 1863, Dr. Kennedy was "hereby appointed overseer on the Homer and Eldorado road, from the ward line between 1 and 2 to the Middle Fork bottom, and that he warn [sic] and work his own hands, J. E. Birch's hands, Mrs. Jane Smith's hands, J. J. Smith's hands, and all other hands not otherwise apportioned in the bounds of said road."

9. Edward A. Jackson, "A Forgotten Hero—R. C. Kennedy," *Confederate Veteran*, XVI, No. 7, (July, 1908): p. 330. All quotes attributed to Jackson are from this article.

10. A number of depositions in OR, Series II, Vol. VIII, made after the war, when the government was trying to implicate Davis and Clay in Lincoln's assassination, credit Kennedy with being a prime mover in both the assassination plans and other activities in Canada. Judge-Advocate Holt later withdrew all the depositions after discovering that his source for them, Sanford Conover, was totally untrustworthy. (Hyams was also involved in the Davis-Clay case.)

11. N.A., RG 109, CR, PMFPR. According to Hugh Shaw's deposition, Martin said that he knew Booth well. Alfred Wheels's deposition (N.A., RG 109, CR, LPMC) is the source of Martin's comment about drinking with Booth. Interestingly, a bill of exchange on a Montreal bank dated Oct. 27, 1864, was found on Booth's corpse. Wheels's deposition also mentions the plan to poison New York's water supply, as well as details of the conspirators' activities in New York as related to him by Martin.

12. Public Archives of Canada, Foreign Office Papers, contains a letter from H.H. Emmons, apparently a United States agent, dated May 11, 1865, "London, Canada," to American authorities in which Emmons says Blackburn should be also indicted "for his infamous scheme to introduce yellow fever into our cities."

13. Thompson, "A Leaf from History," p. 8.

14. N.A., RG 109, CR, LPMC, deposition of Alfred W. Wheels.

15. Unsigned letter, dated Nov. 1, 1864, St. Catharines C.W., Public Archives of Canada, Foreign Office Papers. It is believed to have been written by Clay and was intended for Benjamin in Richmond.

16. *New York Journal of Commerce*, Jan. 10, 1861. Wood's remarks were made in an address to the Common Council on January 6.

17. *The New-York Times*, Nov. 7, 1864, stated that "Horatio Seymour in his present position has served them [the Copperheads] better as a power for mischief than all their other agencies combined," and that Seymour's record in office "plainly shows him to be an enemy to the war of the worst description."

18. Headley, *Confederate Operations*, p. 216.

19. Ibid., p. 265. The names of those who took part are given by Headley, but "Chenault" appears to be an alias. There is no record of him in the Compiled Confederate Service Records at the National Archives. Moreover, it is doubtful that he would have used his real name—and Frank Clark, testifying at Kennedy's trial (N.A., RG 153, Judge Advocate General, Military Proceedings in the case of Robert C. Kennedy, MM-3729), gives his name as Chenault. (At the same time, Kennedy was going by the name "Stanton.") The name of the eighth member of the original band, as noted in the text, is unknown. Of interest is an article that appeared in the Aug., 1954, issue of the *United Daughters of the Confederacy Magazine* (p. 7), in which the author, Jerome P. Alexander, then apparently of an advanced age, recalled a relative, "Cousin" Henry, telling him about having taken part in the plot. According to the article, "A Deed of Deering: The Confederate Attempt to Burn New York City," "Cousin" Henry was a South Carolinian who left home at the age of sixteen to join Morgan's men, and was one of those who escaped with him from the prison in Columbus. "Henry," Alexander wrote, "used to tell us youngsters about a part he took in an attempt to burn New York City. Some 'chemist' had given them 'Greek fire,' which could not be extinguished. Henry said that they had started fires in the Astor House and other hotels, but that the fires all went out. He remarked, lugubriously: 'Greek fire's a lost art.' " Who this "Cousin" Henry was is uncertain. I attempted to contact Alexander without success, and it can probably be assumed that he is dead. According to him, though, "Cousin" Henry settled in Texas after the war when carpetbaggers took over his native South Carolina.

20. Headley, *Confederate Operations*, p. 256.

21. *Quebec Morning Chronicle*, Oct. 26, 1864. Young's letter is dated Oct. 21, "Frelighsburg, C.E.," and is addressed to the editor of *The Evening Telegraph*. A clipping of the Quebec paper is in the Foreign Office Papers, Public Archives of Canada.

22. Jackson, "Forgotten Hero," p. 330.

23. The letter attributed to Clay (see note 15, above) also notes the failure of "the chemical preparations" in the St. Albans raid, which otherwise "would have succeeded." (By then, Kennedy and the other conspirators were already in New York.) Obviously, no one thought to caution them on the use of the combustible, unless the message was never received—or perhaps the failure of the chemist to arrive from Canada is the explanation. I would guess that there was simply no other means available to make the attempt—certainly none if only the handful of men were to accomplish all they set out to do. The Public Archives of Canada also has on file a letter from Bennet Burley to a Dr. S. B. Bates in Toronto dated Oct. 17, 1864, in which Burley asks whether Thompson has been able to procure "Greek fire." Of interest is his next remark: "I forgot to ask you if the composition does not require some time to saturate before it can be used."

CHAPTER 9

1. *Miller's Stranger's Guide for the City of New York* (New York: J. Miller, 1864), pp. 24–25.

2. Charles Cooper Diary, 1853. (Manuscripts and Archives Division, New York Public Library.) Cooper completed the lengthy account of his five-week visit to the city while returning to England that November aboard the *Lucy Thompson*. An earlier visitor, James Silk Buckingham, wrote after a visit in the late 1830s that Broadway was "not sufficiently ample for the due proportion of its length" and that "all is hurry and bustle." Allan Nevins, ed., *American Social History, as recorded by British Travellers* (New York: Henry Holt & Co., 1923), pp. 310, 312.

3. Cooper.

4. Ibid.

5. Charles P. Daly, "On the Origin and History of the New York Fire Department," 1871 (Charles P. Daly Papers, Manuscripts and Archives Division, New York Public Library). Daly says that with the exception of Constantinople, New York "perhaps" suffered more frequently from fires than any other city in the world. *The New York Leader*, which ran a regular column of doings in the department, complained on Nov. 19, 1864, that "To reach the fire is the last thing thought of; to save getting 'passed' or to 'pass' another company the great object of the run. When at last at the fire if there happens to be one, the great object seems to be to take care of their dignity even if a whole block should burn." *The Annual Report of the Board of Commissioners of the Metropolitan Police* (Albany: C. Wendell, 1865) complained that "New York ought to be better guarded against fire than any other city; but it is not.

The rate of insurance is the sure test of the relative safety of property in different cities. Measured by this standard, the city of New York ranks low in the scale of safety." The Board urged the adoption of the "pay system for firemen."

6. *New York Herald*, Oct. 16, 1863. The story, headlined "Opening of the Opera Season—The Age of Shoddy," was echoed by Robert Tomes in his article, "The Fortunes of War," *Harper's New Monthly Magazine*, 29 (June–November, 1864). He referred to the "suddenly enriched contractors, speculators, and stock-jobbers" as the "Sybarites of 'shoddy' " who "are spending money with a profusion never before witnessed in our country, at no time remarkable for its frugality."

7. *Harper's Weekly*, April 1, 1865.

8. New York (State) Secretary of State, *Census for the State of New York for 1865* (Albany: C. Van Benthuysen & Sons, 1867). Despite the economic boom in New York during the war, the city's population declined from a total of 813,669 in 1860 to 726,386 in 1865—a drop of about eleven percent.

9. Headley, *Confederate Operations*, p. 266. The details of this meeting and others, unless noted, are from Headley's memoirs. He provides the description of McMaster, and also recalls Martin's spotting Young in the street. The sequence of events involving the plotters follows his account, with additional matter from contemporary newspapers.

10. Carl Sandburg, *Abraham Lincoln: The War Years* (New York: Harcourt, Brace & Co., 1936), vol. 1, p. 45.

11. George Winston Smith and Charles Judah, eds., *Life in the North During the Civil War* (Albuquerque: University of New Mexico Press, 1966), pp. 7–8. Dix's remarks were made in a speech to a convention of War Democrats in Nov. 1, 1864, at Cooper Institute.

12. *New-York Times*, Oct. 30, 1864.

13. Ibid.

14. The *New York Herald* guessed, in its edition of Nov. 27, 1864, that there were 12,000 or 14,000 Southern refugees residing in the city. The next day, it upped its estimate to between 40,000 and 50,000—a large part of them women and children. (Due to the failure of the registration drive, no accurate account is available.)

15. *New-York Times*, Oct. 30, 1864.

16. McMaster's home was on what was once known as Billing's Row, a portion of West 50th Street between Eighth and Ninth avenues.

17. Headley, *Confederate Operations*, p. 267.

18. N.A., RG 153, JAG, MM-3729.

19. Headley, *Confederate Operations*, p. 268, gives the address of McDonald's piano store as 73 Franklin Avenue. It actually was on Broadway at the corner of Franklin Place. I have assumed that he and Martin used a side entrance on the latter street.

20. N.A., RG 59, "Department of State," Letters Sent 1864. George Templeton Strong wrote in his diary on the following day, Nov. 3, that "Seymour's

'friends' are ready to emerge from their tenement-houses and cellars and suburban shanties and from every gambling shop and brothel in the city whenever there shall be an opening for pillage, arson, and murder like that of July, 1863" (when the Draft Riots took place). (Nevins and Thomas, eds., *Diary of George Templeton Strong*, vol. 3, p. 508.)

21. Sandburg, *Abraham Lincoln*, vol. 1, p. 71. Sandburg says Superintendent Kennedy armed himself with a revolver and unwittingly went aboard the train to Washington that Lincoln would secretly board in Philadelphia.

22. Edward G. Longacre, "The Union Army Occupation of New York City," *New York History* 65, no. 2 (April, 1984): p. 153. Longacre notes that Butler shrewdly stationed most of his New York troops on the Jersey side of the Hudson River on Election Day.

23. Benjamin F. Butler, *Autobiography and Personal Reminiscences of Major-General Benj. F. Butler* (Boston: A. M. Thayer & Co., 1892), p. 757.

24. See notes 15 and 23, chapter 8. Charles A. Dana, in his *Recollections of the Civil War* (New York: D. Appleton & Co., 1898), never names the "young man" who became the undercover courier who carried the dispatches between Canada and Richmond. However, Philip Van Doren Stern, in *Secret Missions of the Civil War* (Chicago: Rand McNally, 1959), p. 258, identifies him as one Richard Montgomery, and says he was the one who gave Dana the information about the plot to burn New York. Stern says Montgomery was an associate of Sanford Conover, whose efforts to incriminate Davis and Clay (and, posthumously, Kennedy) in Lincoln's murder were thrown out by Holt. Stern says the American consul at Halifax forwarded word to Seward of the Election Day plans. Dana (p. 241) says that "the confidence of the Confederates in our agent and in theirs never seemed to be shaken." He then goes on to report how the courier brought a document of "extraordinary consequence." What is strange, however, is that Dana then reports that an officer was dispatched to New York and was in a room at the St. Nicholas Hotel, washing his hands before dinner, when the fire there broke out. If it is true that Dana received word of the plot that was to embrace other cities in addition to New York, then it was the plan set for Election Day, November 8; there is no satisfactory explanation of the lapse of time in getting the officer from Washington to New York. Moreover, Dana says the document said the plan envisioned a fire "particularly" in Barnum's Museum, when Headley and Kennedy are clear about the fact that none whatsoever was preplanned. The explanation behind all of this confusion may be that Dana wrote his "recollections" thirty years after the event, and may have got some of the facts mixed up.

CHAPTER 10

1. *New-York Times*, Nov. 16, 1864. The banquet in Butler's honor was held on Nov. 14.

2. *New York World*, Nov. 26, 1864. This, and a number of other rumors, some of which are mentioned in the text that follows, are from newspaper stories published immediately after the fires.

3. N.A., RG 393, "(U.S. Army Continental Commands) Department of the East," Letters Sent 1864. Dix, writing to Adjutant General Edward D. Townsend in Washington, asked that the latter "Please show this to the Scy's of War."

4. *New York Daily News*, Nov. 22, 1864. The article is headlined "Horrible."

5. Ibid., Nov. 23, 1864.

6. *New-York Times*, Nov. 6, 1864.

7. Headley, *Confederate Operations*, p. 271.

8. *Frank Leslie's Illustrated Newspaper*, Dec. 17, 1864.

9. *New-York Times*, Nov. 22, 1864. The *Times* called it the "severest and most protracted rain storm" of the season.

10. *New York Daily News*, Nov. 23, 1864.

11. Headley, *Confederate Operations*, p. 271.

12. N.A., RG 109, CR, LPMC, deposition of Alfred W. Wheels.

13. Headley, *Confederate Operations*, p. 272.

14. N.A., RG 393, USACC, Department of the East, Letters Received 1865. Kennedy refers to the test of the "Greek fire" when he says in his confession that "at one time [we] concluded to give the whole thing up." Headley's reasoning that the chemist or Longmire had pulled a fast one is usually accepted as the truth of what went wrong on the night of Nov. 25, 1864, but it is not substantiated anywhere else. In fact, Fire Marshal Baker is quite clear in his report that the chemist had done his job "sagaciously" and that the fault lay with those who set the fires.

15. Headley, *Confederate Operations*, p. 273. The idea of starting the fires early to allow the hotel occupants to escape, as Headley reports, raises the question of whether this could be another reason why the plan failed. *The New York World* of Nov. 28 noted that the early evening hour was probably the period of most activity at the hotels. *The New York Herald* of Nov. 27, speaking of the attempt at the St. James Hotel, noted: "Fortunately, the hour being early, sufficient means were on hand to subdue the flames." However, it seems naive of the Confederates to have believed that they could set the fires and not destroy lives as a result. As the *Herald* notes, most of the hotels involved, although spacious, had long, narrow hallways that would become bottlenecks of congestion in case of emergency or panic.

It is possible to retrace the routes each of the six Confederates took, although few landmarks remain to guide the way. Of the few that do, Trinity Church and St. Paul's Chapel are the probably the most prominent edifices that remain from the New York of the 1860s.

16. Ibid.

CHAPTER 11

1. Diary of a school girl in New York City (Manuscript Division, New York Historical Society). The anonymous girl wrote that November 25 was a "very pleasant day rained all morning."

2. Nevins and Halsey, eds., *Diary of George Templeton Strong,* vol. 3, pp. 565–566.

3. *New-York Times,* Nov. 25, 1864. The story about Sherman's march begins in column one, the one about Thanksgiving in column 7. Sherman's marching orders were issued by him on November 9.

4. Evacuation Day celebrations have long since gone out of style in New York City. In 1864, however, the flag abandoned at the Battery by the British on the day they left still existed. It was displayed at a lecture sponsored by the Y.M.C.A. at the Academy of Music earlier in November, according to the *Times* of Nov. 4.

5. It is not surprising that Kennedy chose the alias of "Morse." Samuel F. B. Morse, the inventor of the telegraph, lived in the city and was a well-known opponent of the war and of abolition, among other things. (He was also against women's rights, socialism, and free love.) Morse was president of the American Society for Promoting National Unity in Crisis, and helped to start an aid program for inhabitants of the Shenandoah Valley.

All the aliases and room numbers used in the text are based on newspaper reports of the fires, and of the identities given by the occupants of the various rooms. The exchanges between Martin and the staff at the St. James Hotel and French's are similarly based, even to the hesitant manner in which Martin signed the St. James register. The same is true of other incidents mentioned—Headley at the Everett House, Kennedy at the Tammany, and so forth.

The movements of the conspirators in this and the next two chapters were compiled from a study of newspaper reports, Kennedy's confessions, and Headley's memoirs. A major difficulty was encountered with regard to the latter. For example, Headley says it was arranged to meet back at the cottage on the evening after the fires, but Kennedy, in his confession only four months later, makes it quite clear that all the conspirators were at the Exchange Hotel the next morning.

Headley wrote his memoirs forty years after the events, and perhaps simply mixed up some facts. The mistake in the address of McDonald's piano store, for example, has already been noted (note 19, chapter 9). More seriously, though, Headley referred to the setting of fires at several hotels where they never occurred: the Hoffman House, St. Denis, Brandeth's, Gramercy Park, Everett House, and City. (There was no City Hotel, but he may have meant Hiram Cranston's New York Hotel). I have assumed that these hotels were probably on the incendiaries' lists, and that Headley therefore assumed that attempts were made to burn them. Also, he credits himself with setting fires at the City Hotel and Everett House, although neither was ever mentioned in any report as the site of a fire.

Where necessary, I have also drawn upon the descriptions given in the newspapers by hotel clerks, guests, and so forth, as to who was where at such and such a time. I had to do this, for example, in the case of Chenault. Kennedy in his confession (N.A., RG 393, USACC, Department of the East, Letters Received 1865) says he and a friend went to Barnum's. I have assumed that friend was Chenault, inasmuch as the two of them were close together at times in the city, as witness their checking into the Belmont Hotel on their arrival in New York, as Frank Clark testified at Kennedy's trial. The movements of Kennedy, Martin, Headley, Ashbrook, and Harrington are easier to piece together.

6. N.A., RG 393, USACC, Department of the East, Letters Received 1865. Kennedy in his confession says that he had been drinking. (See note 13, Chapter 23, for full text.) Newspaper accounts of his last days in prison bear out his tendency to turn to drink in times of stress.

7. Headley, *Confederate Operations*, p. 272.

CHAPTER 12

1. As was the case with other incidents, the exchange overheard by the merchant Ward was reported in newspaper accounts. Ward was later taken to see John D. Allison at police headquarters, but, of course, could not identify him as one of the conspirators.

2. Headley, *Confederate Operations*, p. 275.

3. N.A., RG 393, USACC, Department of the East, Letters Received 1865.

4. Headley, *Confederate Operations*, p. 276. (Headley also recounts Kennedy's actions at Barnum's.)

5. Headley, *Confederate Operations*, p. 277. Headley's surprise at the quick and orderly response of the volunteer fire units was echoed by others. The *Herald* of Nov. 27, which devoted its entire front page and two of six columns on another page to reports of the fires, declared: "No better opportunity could have afforded itself than the above occasion to assure the public of the watchful duty so willingly performed by the members of the New York Fire Department. From the first toll of the alarm of the fire bells, till near the dawn of morning, were the firemen on the constant go from one section of the city to another. The bells hardly closed on the alarm of one district when another told that their services were needed in another. In the Second, Fourth and Seventh Districts the firemen worked unceasingly, and with such a will that we doubt if any of the fires could have escaped their control."

6. *New York Herald*, Nov. 28, 1864. The newspaper carried a lengthy account of both the incident at the Tammany and Martin's difficulties at French's across the street. *Harper's Weekly* also carried a version in its issue of Dec. 17, 1864.

CHAPTER 13

1. *New-York Times* and *New York Herald*, Nov. 26, 1864.

2. N.A., RG 109, CR, depositions of Hugh Shaw (PMFPR) and Alfred Wheels (LPMC).

3. N.A., RG 393, USACC, Department of the East, Letters Received 1865.

4. Headley, *Confederate Operations*, pp. 277–280. Headley not only recounts his movements with Martin, including the incident outside McDonald's store, but also describes how Martin alerted the others on the train to be prepared to fight their way out if detected.

5. *New York Herald*, Nov. 27, 1864.

6. *New York Evening Post*, Nov. 26, 1864.

CHAPTER 14

1. *New York Herald*, Nov. 28, 1864. The account of this incident and of others that follow (such as that concerning Campbell the carpenter) are drawn from a variety of local newspapers in the period immediately following the night of the fires.

2. Alfred E. Baker, "Fire Marshal's Report to the Mayor/June 1–Nov. 30, 1864," pp. 4–5.

3. Ibid.

4. Ibid.

CHAPTER 15

1. John D. Allison, diary written "while a prisoner at Ft. Lafayette, N.Y. (New York Harbor), Nov. 14, 1864 to March 29, 1865" (The Filson Club, Louisville, Ky.). All the quotations attributed to Allison are from his diary. The boy he was confronted with may have been the employee of the Fifth-Avenue Hotel who served the floor on which a fire had been discovered and who could identify the occupant of room 148, "Mr. Hicks" (actually Martin).

2. Typical of the letters received by the Department of the East (N.A., RG 393, USACC, Department of the East, Letters Received 1865) was one from "Loyal Man" who said rebel sympathizers frequented the Belmont Hotel. Another from a Philadelphian gave an address on Irving Place as a rendezvous for spies, adding that its keeper—a female—was a secessionist.

3. *New-York Times*, Nov. 28, 1864.

4. N.A., RG 153, JAG, MM-3729. The resolution of the County Board of Supervisors reads:

"Resolved, That C. Godfrey Gunther, Esq., Mayor of the City and County of New York, be and he is hereby authorized and requested to offer a reward of five thousand dollars ($5,000), payable from the County Treasury, for the arrest and conviction of said incendiaries, or either of them,—said amount to be paid upon the certificate of the District Attorney of such arrest and conviction."

5. *The Brooklyn Eagle*, March 25, 1865, said Kennedy was found by city detectives because of his "peculiar gait." Dion Haco, in *Rob. Cobb Kennedy, the Incendiary Spy* (New York: Hurst & Co., 1866), says Kennedy was known to police "principally by his peculiar gait and long hair." The *Times*, Feb. 28, 1865, said "A clue singularly obtained was successfully followed."

6. N.A., RG 393, USACC, Department of the East, Letters Sent 1865.

CHAPTER 16

1. Thompson, "A Leaf from History," pp. 2–4. All of Thompson's remarks are taken from his report.

2. Ibid.

3. Ibid.

4. Ibid.

5. *Richmond Daily Examiner,* Nov. 30, 1864.

6. *Richmond Whig,* Dec. 2, 1864.

CHAPTER 17

1. Headley, *Confederate Operations,* pp. 284–307. (Headley is the major source of information about the conspirators' movements in Canada.)

2. N.A., RG 393, USACC, Department of the East, Letters Sent 1865.

3. Phillip R. Shriver and Donald J. Breen, *Ohio's Military Prisons in the Civil War* (Ohio State University Press for the Ohio Historical Society, 1964), p. 41. The unsigned letter was followed a week later by another that read:

"SIR if your notice marked XX which was placed upon the bulletin board this morning was meant as a reply to a communication which was in the drop letter box last Monday morning the 12th inst. and which communication related to one Mr. Kenedy [sic] late of Johnson Island, and now in Canada, I can inform you that I was the writer. I am in Block 7 mess 2 Co. 14. If your notice was not relative to the above named communication this can do no harm as I suppose you will not allow this to be exposed to any of the other prisoners, or others who might communicate it.

"Very respectfully yours,

"GEORGE WM PAUL 15th ARK INF."

Paul's motive in implicating Kennedy is unknown. Perhaps it was just a play for extra rations.

4. Details of the derailment attempt and the subsequent escape are based on Headley; testimony at Beall's trial (N.A., RG 153, JAG, Military Proceedings in the case of John Yates Beall, MM-3513); Wheels's deposition (N.A., RG 109, CR, LPMC); and newspaper accounts.

5. The activities of the New York detectives were described by newspapers following Kennedy's arrest. The *Times* of Feb. 5, 1865, reported that Young even sent Larry McDonald a note afterward to thank him for his help.

6. N.A., RG 153, JAG, MM-3729. The passport as well as the certificate of citizenship, pledge, $20 Confederate bill and quartermaster's receipt referred to in the text that follows are among the papers attached to the transcript of Kennedy's trial.

7. In James D. Horan, *Confederate Agent: A Discovery in History* (New York: Crown, 1954), p. 251, there is a description of the party, but it must be treated with caution. Two outstanding errors come to mind: Although Horan gives the correct date for the attempt to burn New York, he says it was Thanksgiving Day. Then again, although he gives the correct dates for the executions of Beall and Kennedy, he says Kennedy was hanged before Beall! In the case of the party, however, Price's testimony at Kennedy's trial (N.A., RG 153, JAG, MM-3729) bears out the fact that there was a get-together held in Canada sometime in December.

8. Headley, *Confederate Operations*, p. 323.

9. Ibid., p. 323. Headley is incorrect in saying that Ashbrook witnessed Kennedy's arrest on the train, as Detective Bennett's testimony at Kennedy's trial shows (N.A., RG 153, "Office of Judge Advocate General"). Details of the capture are based on that testimony and subsequent newspaper accounts.

10. N.A., RG 153, JAG, MM-3729.

11. Haco, *Rob. Cobb Kennedy*, p. 54. Haco's name is probably a pseudonym. He is credited on the title page as the author of "Osgood, the Demon Refugee," "Cheatham, or the Swamp Dragons," "Perdita, the Demon Refugee's Daughter," "Larry, the Army Dog Robber," "John Wilkes Booth, the Assassin" and "etc., etc., etc., etc." Haco was apparently a hack who turned out two-penny novels of intrigue. The book on Kennedy is seventy-one pages long, and is based on newspaper accounts and portions of Kennedy's trial. It is probable that Haco was a journalist who had covered the story and spoken to city detectives. However, there is much that is obvious hogwash and trumped up in his work. He invents an involved and implausible contretemps to explain why the chemist from Canada never arrived, and also says Kennedy was betrayed by a "Little Nell"—a woman with whom Kennedy became acquainted while boarding in Prince Street. (This is probably an allusion to Ann Cullen, the chambermaid.) Haco says Nell visited Kennedy in Toronto after the attempt in New York, was rebuffed, and in revenge informed on him, later identifying him to the police "in spite of the altered appearance which he presented." This is nonsense. Ann Cullen, if indeed she was the woman Haco called "Little Nell," actually testified in Kennedy's behalf at the trial. The quotation, "These are badges of honor . . ." appears to be one of several that Haco got from detectives, and conforms to newspaper accounts of Kennedy's behavior after being caught.

CHAPTER 18

1. Loosely translated, "The times are changed, and we are changed with them." Beall's usage of "mutatantur" is incorrect: there is no such form of the Latin verb "mutare." He undoubtedly meant "mutantur." According to the Donnell Foreign Language Library, the Latin phrase Beall used was first employed by Rapheal Holinshed in his *Chronicles of England*, 1577, and later, 1661, by Cellarius in *Harmonica Macrocosmica: Preface*. A somewhat similar expression—"Omnia mutantur non et mutamur in illis" or "All things are changed, with them we, too, change"—was written by Lotharius I, Emperor of Germany, 795–855, and is found in Matthias Borbonius's *Delicial Poetarum Germanorum*, Vol. 1.

2. N.A., RG 153, JAG, MM-3513. Beall's diary is attached to the transcript of his trial. He probably did not know of Kennedy's capture, since the news of it was not made public until Feb. 5, by which time Beall was in Fort Lafayette, where his own trial had started on Jan. 20. He had been transferred to the fort on Jan. 2.

3. Ibid.

4. Ibid. The fact that Beall pronounced his name as "Bell" as well as incidents regarding the bribe offer are from the trial record. The amount of the bribe was substantial. According to *Manual of the Corporation of the City of New York* (New York: D.T. Valentine, 1865), doormen such as Hays earned only $600 a year. Other salaries given are $786 for patrolmen, $900 for detectives, and $1,200 for police captains. Inspectors Dilks and Leonard each received $2,000 annually, Superintendent Kennedy and Chief Engineer Decker $5,000.

5. Ibid.

6. Ibid.

7. Ibid. The description of the cell is based on Beall's diary. The substance of the scenes between Kennedy and Hays, Superintendent Kennedy and Bolles, et al., is based on testimony offered at Kennedy's own trial and the piecing together of newspaper accounts. McMaster testified that Hays told him that Kennedy swore "at a terrible rate." The letters Kennedy wrote, whether in the original form or a copy, are attached to the transcript as exhibits, as is his statement to Bolles.

8. That Kennedy was not informed of the charges was not unusual. Lincoln had first suspended and then modified the privilege of the writ of habeas corpus. Congress enacted a law on March 3, 1863, that tried to force the government to modify secret and arbitrary arrests; still, martial law prevailed.

9. N.A., RG 153, JAG, MM-3729.

10. Ibid.

11. Ibid.

12. N.A., RG 393, USACC, Department of the East, Letters Sent 1865. Dix informed Secretary of War Stanton on Jan. 17 that Beall was being given two days to prepare for his trial.

13. N.A., RG 153, JAG, MM-3729.

14. Ibid.

15. N.A., RG 153, JAG, MM-3513. Holt's judgment of the train episode is attached to the transcript of Beall's trial.

CHAPTER 19

1. Several newspapers later reported that Kennedy's trial, like that of Beall's, was held at Fort Lafayette. This was incorrect. The trial was held at the headquarters of the Department of the East, 49 Bleecker Street.

2. N.A., RG 153, JAG, MM-3729. All the questions, testimony, objections raised by Stoughton and Bolles, requests, etc., quoted at the trial in this and the next chapter are from the stenographer's hand-written transcript. Only minor changes

have been made. For example, McMaster is incorrectly identified throughout, except when he himself takes the stand, as McMasters. (Headley, incidentally and oddly, makes the same mistake.) In addition, certain phrases were changed for grammatical or stylistic purposes. For example, the stenographer, quoting a witness, often wrote, "Said he . . ." I have changed this to, "He said . . . ."

It is my opinion that Kennedy was railroaded. There was never any direct evidence linking him to the fires, nor any identification by anyone directly involved. The evidence against him was purely circumstantial and based on hearsay. How much such evidence is worth may be adduced by the result of attempts after the war to bring Martin to trial using the same witnesses. The efforts were thrown out by civilian courts for lack of evidence. Undoubtedly the strain of four years of war and the closeness in time between the attempt on New York and Kennedy's trial, together with his behavior and the bribe offer, contributed significantly to the verdict.

3. The *New-York Times* of March 26, 1865, reported that Kennedy wrote on March 2 that he had looked to Bolles to offer assistance but that Bolles had scoffed at his rebuttal evidence. The newspaper account went on to say that it was only after he, Kennedy, was convinced that he would get no aid that he finally asked for a delay in order to acquire counsel.

CHAPTER 20

1. James J. Williamson, *Mosby's Rangers* (New York: Sturgis & Walton, 1909), p. 40.

2. Public Archives of Canada, Foreign Office Papers. Davis issued a proclamation to protect Burley, saying that the *Philo Parsons* episode was a "legitimate belligerent operation . . . ordered, directed, and sustained by the authority of the Government of the Confederate States of America against the United States of America."

3. Sandburg, *Lincoln*, Vol. IV, pp. 132–133.

4. *New-York Times*, March 26, 1865. According to what Kennedy wrote on March 2, Bolles had actually shed tears after the summation. He also shook his hand, and asked Kennedy to pity him.

5. Kennedy's letter was carried by several newspapers as a part of their report of his execution.

6. N.A., RG 109, CR, PMFPR, Lafayette Prison. The letter that follows is from the same source. (The *Times* of March 6, 1865, incorrectly reported that Kennedy was taken there by Young, Bennett, and McDougall.)

CHAPTER 21

1. Allison, *Diary*. Allison, in one of the few eye-witness accounts of Kennedy's last days, mentions him nine times. Incidentals include his having been given a lock of Beall's hair, and the haircut he gave Kennedy. Allison's observations and

those of newsmen who visited Kennedy or interviewed those who did are combined in the text to present a chronology and description of Kennedy's stay in Fort Lafayette.

2. *Frank Leslie's Illustrated Newspaper,* April 15, 1865, carries an illustration of the cell. Joseph Howard, Jr., also describes it after his visit on March 15 (*New-York Times,* March 17, 1865). Earlier, in January, General Beall was briefly placed in the cell, and he commented: "The commanding officer, Col. M. Burke, and the other officers of the fort are kind and courteous, but the quarters are small and crowded and are so dark that it is difficult to read or write without the aid of a candle or lamp" (*OR,* Series II, Vol. VIII, p. 40). *Right Flanker,* the magazine put out by earlier prisoners, noted that an attempt had been made to saw through the bars.

3. N.A., RG 109, CR, PMFPR, Lafayette Prison. Mulrennon's remark was made in a letter, dated Dec. 12, 1864, that was not posted by prison authorities. His name is sometimes misspelled in records as "Mulrennal," "Mulrennan," or other variations of both.

4. *New-York Times,* March 26, 1865. Kennedy's letter was also carried by other local newspapers. Kennedy wrote a great deal while at the fort, according to the *Times,* but ordered most of his writings destroyed. However, Captain Robert P. Wilson, post quartermaster, made copies of some of his dated letters. Those of March 4 and March 5 are among those Wilson later made public. The "In Hell" letter of March 2 was presumably carried to the fort by Kennedy from police headquarters, and similarly found its way into the newspapers.

5. The exchange between Kennedy and Young is based on Kennedy's letter of March 5 (reproduced in part on p. 203) and subsequent reports in newspapers.

6. N.A., RG 109, CR, PMFPR, Lafayette Prison.

7. Mrs. Hyder A. Kennedy, *History of the Execution of Robert Cobb Kennedy* (Kennedy family papers: privately published, 1915). Mrs. Kennedy's account was written in response to T. E. Fell's article in the *Newnan* (Ga.) *Herald,* a reprint of which she had seen in *The Atlanta Constitution.* Fell urged that a more complete history of Kennedy's "life and tragic death" be furnished by his friends and family. Mrs. Kennedy said her work was based on information provided by Kennedy's mother and his brother, Hyder, both dead at the time of her writing. The eight-page pamphlet also quotes Fell, and Kennedy's confession. It includes not only Kennedy's letter to his father, but also the one written to his mother and quoted in Chapter 23. There are some inaccuracies in the work, however. Mrs. Kennedy said that Kennedy's appointment to West Point was endorsed by Colonel John M. Sandidge of the Fourth Congressional District, but Sandidge did not serve in Congress until 1855 (when he succeeded Roland M. Jones, the actual endorser). In addition, she places Kennedy's grave "on a beautiful sloping hill-side over-looking the Hudson," apparently a reference to Fort Hamilton (which actually overlooks the entrance to New York Harbor). She was evidently unaware that the cemetery there had been abandoned long before, and the bodies reinterred. Finally, Mrs. Kennedy quotes the "West Point Bulletin" as saying: "He was promoted to the rank of captain for gallantry upon the field. The vile wretch who gave the order for the death of this gentleman, patriot and scholar, a man all mind and soul, little knew the material he was destroying. The prayers of his

Christian mother will heap coals of fire upon the heads of the perpetrators of this atrocious deed." I could find no confirmation of this quote. Confirming the letter to his father is a short message on March 14 from Burke, who wrote the Department of the East headquarters that: "I have the honor to enclose herewith a letter from Robt. C. Kennedy, prisoner under sentence of death, to his father, which if approved by you please forward to its destination." The same, with Dix's signature, was sent to Major General E.R.S. Canby, whose headquarters were in New Orleans, with the request that he forward the letter across the lines (N.A., RG 109, CR, PMFPR, Lafayette Prison).

8. N.A., RG 153, JAG, MM-3729. Stoughton's letter, part of the papers attached to the trial proceedings, is not quoted in full because most of the legal argument is repetitious.

9. Papers of Abraham Lincoln, Vol. 192, 1865: March 11–22. Kennedy's letter to Lincoln was among the papers and documents held by Lincoln's son, Robert Todd Lincoln; they were not available for public inspection for more than ninety years after the war ended. With it is Dix's enclosure, in which the general says he believes Kennedy will confess.

CHAPTER 22

1. See New-York Times, March 17, 1865, for Howard's trip and interview. Background on Howard's career is from Sandburg, Lincoln, Vol. 1, p. 81, and Vol. 3, pp. 53–56, as well as the World, May 24 and 25, 1864, and Harper's Weekly, June 4, 1864. Inexplicably, no mention at all is made of Howard in Meyer Berger's history of the newspaper, The Story of The New York Times, 1851–1951.

2. Further descriptive material regarding Fort Lafayette is from inspection reports, N.A., RG 109, CR, Fort Lafayette Prison, N.Y.H. This is also the source of the number of bounty jumpers, other prisoners, and so forth.

3. New-York Times, May 26, 1864.

4. As is later noted, Colonel Burke and Chaplain Burke were not related. The prison commander was a Catholic, the chaplain an Episcopalian. Curiously, a number of individuals with similar last names, but unrelated, appear in the text: Kennedy and the city police superintendent (whose first name was John, as was Robert Cobb Kennedy's father); French of French's Hotel and Captain French at the fort; John Yates Beall and General Beall; Jacob Thompson and Meriwether Jeff Thompson; Bennett Young and Detective Young; Frank Clark and Orlando Clark, not to mention Clarke the photographer—all coincidental.

5. New York Herald, March 29, 1865. Kennedy's appeals to Canada went unheeded, probably because the Confederate organization there was in disarray after its repeated failures and the certainty that the war was lost. A letter from Levi F. Bowen, provost marshal in Lockport, N.Y., to Dix's headquarters dated March 4, 1865 (N.A., RG 393, USACC, Department of the East, Letters Received 1865) reported that the collector of customs at the Suspension Bridge had learned that Jefferson Davis had ordered all Southerners back to their lines. Seward received a letter from D.

Thurston, Consul in Canada, dated Feb. 23, that noted a "marked" change in the attitude and sentiments of Canadians toward the Confederacy, and one on March 25 from the same agent reporting that the number of Southerners in Toronto had fallen off and that a trip to the usual Confederate hangouts in Hamilton disclosed fewer than ever. (Both, Public Archives of Canada, Foreign Office Papers.)

6. N.A., RG 153, JAG, MM-3729. Both Bolles's rebuttal and Dix's covering letter that follows are attached to the trial transcript. No mention is made of the reward offer made by the hotel owners themselves, and no word of it can be found in the newspapers. Presumably the proprietors withdrew the reward for the same reason as Dix—that the conviction was not by a civil court.

7. N.A., RG 153, JAG, MM-3729.

8. N.A., RG 109, CR, PMFPR, Lafayette Prison. No explanation is given why Saturday was chosen for the day of execution. According to the *Times*, March 14, 1865, it was customary to hold a hanging on a Friday as symbolic of the day Christ was crucified. The *Times* also speculated that Kennedy would be taken to Fort Columbus for the execution. Kennedy also believed he would be taken to Governors Island, as Beall had been. Burke wrote Dix's headquarters on March 17 to forward a request from Kennedy that he be allowed to see Allison and Mulrennon before such a transfer took place (N.A., RG 109, CR, PMFPR, Lafayette Prison). The letter was endorsed "Granted" on March 19. As early as March 12, however, Bolles, acting in his capacity as aide to Dix, wired Burke that Kennedy was to remain at Fort Lafayette "By command of Maj. Genl. Dix" (N.A., RG 109, CR, PMFPR, Lafayette Prison). No reason is given.

9. N.A., RG 109, CR, PMFPR, Lafayette Prison. Kennedy's escape attempt was reported in a letter to Dix from Burke dated March 21, 1865. Fuller details appeared in the *Times*, March 21, 1865.

CHAPTER 23

1. Headley, *Confederate Operations*, p. 331.

2. Fell, "Escape of Prisoners," p. 428.

3. Jackson, "Forgotten Hero," p. 330.

4. Kennedy's behavior during the last days of his life as well as on the day of his execution was reported in detail in local newspapers, from which the quotations in the text are taken. Fell also noted that Kennedy exhibited a "rage against enemies," which may explain some of his irrational outbursts.

5. N.A., RG 109, CR, PMFPR, Lafayette Prison. The findings of the military commission, when published on March 21, 1865, were dated March 20, though the verdict had been arrived at on February 27 (N.A., RG 153, JAG, MM-3729). For purposes of brevity, only the pertinent parts are quoted in the text. The findings were printed in pamphlet form for purposes of the execution ceremony.

6. N.A., RG 153, JAG, MM-3729. Holt's judgment, affixed to the trial transcript, is in the form of an endorsement of the verdict.

7. N.A., RG 109, CR, PMFPR, Lafayette Prison. Burke, in his letter dated March 19, 1865, said he had agreed to let Kennedy's photograph be taken and requested Dix's staff to arrange to send a photographer. Dix's office issued a pass on March 21 to Joseph Barron and an assistant, Frank Smith, to visit the fort to do so (N.A., RG 393, USACC, Department of the East, Letters Sent 1865). They were employees of Clarke's Union Photographic Gallery. (See also note 1, Chapter 4.) On the same day, Dix wrote Marshal Murray concerning Burke's request for a gallows and executioner, and asked Murray to be present at the hanging if his official duties permitted. (N.A., RG 393, USACC, Department of the East, Letters Sent 1865.)

8. Ibid. Murray went to the fort with A.B. Newcomb, an assistant marshal, who was also present on the day of the execution. Dix's letter to Burke, dated March 22, 1865, said the two would be coming that day to confer on the execution and also that Young had permission "to receive in the presence of an officer of your Post, the confession of *Robt. C. Kennedy*"—which, of course, he did not get.

9. Ibid.

10. Ibid. Chaplain Burke told Stoughton about Kennedy's request to see General Beall; Stoughton, in turn, wrote to Beall. Beall immediately wrote to Dix for permission. Beall's office was at 75 Murray Street, where he was directing the sale of cotton to aid Southern prisoners of war. He was put on parole as a prisoner himself on Dec. 6, 1864, and allowed to go to New York to handle the arrangements. When the Federal vessel that was supposed to carry the Confederate cotton north from Mobile failed to arrive, Beall was rearrested on Jan. 4, 1865, and sent to Fort Lafayette for detention. He was released on Jan. 24, when 830 bales of cotton arrived. The delay, he said, was caused by the "miscarriage" of orders and an "uncommonly tempestuous voyage" (OR, Series II, Vol. VIII, pp. 748–749).

11. A copy of Kennedy's letter to friends at Johnson's Island, dated March 24, 1865, is in the possession of the Erie County Historical Society Library, Sandusky. Shriver and Breen's *Ohio Military Prisons* (p. 42) gives the name of Kennedy's "protege" as "Jack." On close reading I interpreted the handwriting as "Turk" and have assumed—I believe correctly—that it refers to Amos C. Smith, who aided in Kennedy's escape.

12. Mrs. Hyder Kennedy, *Trial and Execution.* (See note 7, Chapter 21.)

13. N.A., RG 393, USACC, Department of the East, Letters Received 1865. Also, OR, Series II, Vol. VIII, pp. 428–429. The confession was reprinted in full by local newspapers. It reads in full:

"After my escape from Johnson's Island I went to Canada, where I met a number of Confederates. They asked me if I was willing to go on an expedition. I replied, 'Yes, if it's in the service of my country.' They said 'It's all right' but gave no intimation of its nature, nor did I ask for any. I was then sent to New York where I stayed sometime. There were eight men in our party, of whom two fled to Canada. After we had been in New York three weeks we were told that the object of the expedition was to retaliate on the North for the atrocities in the Shenandoah Valley. It was designed to set fire to the city on the night of the Presidential election, but the phosphorus was not ready & it was put off until the 25th of November. I was stopping at the Belmont House but moved into Prince Street. I set fire to four places: Barnum's Museum, Lovejoy's Hotel, Tammany Hotel & the New England House. The others only started fires in the house where each was lodging & then ran off. Had they all done as I did, we would have had thirty two fires & played a huge joke on the Fire Department. I know that I am to be hung for setting fire to Barnum's Museum, but that was only a joke. I had no idea of doing it. I had been drinking & went in there with a friend, & just to scare the people I emptied a bottle of phosphorus on the floor. We knew it wouldn't set fire to the wood for we had tried it before, & at one time concluded to give the whole thing up.

"There was no fiendishness about it. After setting fire to my four places, I walked the street all night & went to the Exchange Hotel early in the morning. We all met there that morning & the next night. My friend & I had rooms there but we sat in the office nearly all the time reading the papers while we were watched by the Detectives of whom the Hotel was full. I expected to die then & if I had it would have been all right, but now it seems rather hard. I escaped to Canada, & was glad enough when I crossed the bridge to safety.

"I desired however to return to my command, & started with my friend for the Confederacy via Detroit. Just before entering the city, he received an intimation that the Detectives were on the lookout for us, & giving me a signal he jumped from the cars. I didn't notice the signal but kept on, & was arrested in the depot.

"I wish to say that killing women & children was the last thing thought of. We wanted to let the people of the North understand that there are two sides to this war, & that they cant be rolling in wealth & comfort, while we at the South are bearing all the hardship & privations. In retaliation for Sheridan's atrocities in the Shenandoah Valley we desired to destroy property, not the lives of women & children although that would of course have followed in its train."

14. *New York Herald*, March 27, 1865. Burke wrote Dix that he went with Howard to see Kennedy and "After some conversation relative to the matter for which he has been sentenced, he made the following confession. He requested that I would make no use of his confession to his detriment, in case a respite or a reprieve should be received." Kennedy offered to make a deal with Dix to save his life, according to several newspaper accounts.

CHAPTER 24

1. *New-York Times*, March 26, 1865. Howard is the chief source of Kennedy's activities on the day of the execution, although other newspapers provided details and quotations as well. Edward N. Tailer (Diaries, Vol. 14, Manuscript Division, New-York Historical Society), a merchant who was a friend of an officer on Dix's staff, witnessed the hanging and concluded in his diary that the *Times* account of the execution was the best he had read.

In some cases, where the newspapers were not clear, accounts of Beall's execution were relied on to fill out such descriptive matter as what the gallows looked like. Most newspapers seized upon the proximity and similar nature of the crimes involved in their deaths to make comparisons in which Kennedy fared poorly. "But of all his acts," the *Tribune* asserted, "the manner in which he met his death was the most revolting." The *World* said that Beall had shown the "truest evidence of personal courage and moral heroism to meet his fate, as though it were the lightest ruffle of the summer breeze; while Kennedy, on the contrary, went into the presence of his Maker, his mouth still hot with cursing, and the words of a low song still fresh on his lips." The *Brooklyn Standard* declared, "It was necessary that Kennedy, the Rebel spy and incendiary, should suffer death, but was it necessary that he should be made drunk preparatory to the last awful scene of the tragedy?"

Rushmore G. Horton's Copperhead *Weekly Day-Book* made only brief mention of the fact that Kennedy had been sentenced to hang on March 25 for what it called "allegedly" setting fire to Barnum's. The *Richmond Whig* carried a brief notice of his death on March 28 taken from the "latest file of Yankee newspapers" and commented, "Since the Yankees murdered the gallant and noble Capt. Jno. Y. Beall, and our authorities have patiently acquiesced, they have proceeded to condemn Capt. Kennedy to undergo the same 'murder—absolutely brutal murder.' " On March 31, it carried the *Tribune* story of the execution (a "malevolent account") and "a statement that purports to be a confession" of the "hapless victim of Yankee hate."

2. From newspaper accounts.

3. *The Brooklyn Daily Eagle*, March 25, 1865, described Isaacs as "an artist in his profession." Other newspapers called him the "Veteran hangman of New York," and said that "He hates to see a man die in a mean spirited manner, and never tires of lauding those who show a brave or reckless spirit to the very last."

4. The legend persists that Kennedy turned to the south and died with words of patriotism on his lips. Mrs. Vail said that his Negro valet quoted Kennedy as saying, "Turn my face to my beloved South and let them know that I fought the Yankees here on earth and that I'll fight them after death til Hell freezes over." It sounds more like a mixture of Beall's patriotism and Kennedy's bravado. There is absolutely no foundation for this, although the poem by Mayes quoted in chapter 25 fostered the myth. Kennedy, according to family verbal accounts, asked for the "death of a soldier"—that is, by firing squad—but was refused.

Burke noted simply in a report to Dix on March 25 (N.A., RG 109, CR, PMFPR, Lafayette Prison) that Kennedy had been executed in compliance with orders. He also noted that a substitute broker, Patrick Kienan, had been discharged on orders from Baker of the "secret Service."

5. Sandburg, *Lincoln*, Vol. 4, p. 144.

6. Cunningham, " 'In Violation of the Laws of War,' " p. 189.

CHAPTER 25

1. N.A., RG 109, CR, depositions of Hugh Shaw (PMFPR) and Alfred Wheels (LPMC).

2. N.A., RG 109, CR, Union Provost Marshal's File, Letters Received 1865. Superintendent Kennedy informed the Provost Marshal's office in New York in November of 1865 that Martin and Headley could be identified "as having passed by the names of Robert Maxwell and John Williams while here." On Dec. 30, 1865, Major General Joseph Hooker reported that "The justice has directed the release of Robert Martin, Hotel Burner, from Military custody and committed him to the custody of Warden of New York City Prison. Have you any other evidence in his case except that already received here?" (N.A., RG 393, USACC, Department of the East, Letters Received 1865.)

3. New-York Times, Feb. 20, 1866.

4. Headley, Confederate Operations, is the chief source of the fate of many of the conspirators.

5. N.A., RG 94, AGO, Commission Branch 1864.

6. Public Archives of Canada, Colonial Office Papers.

7. Ibid.

8. Kennedy family papers. On Dec. 18, 1865, Dr. Kennedy sold 1,900 acres of bottomland to T. H. Brown for $2,000. Five days later he sold 800 acres to Jos. and Wm. Oliver for $3,200. The last recorded land transaction by the family was the sale of 10 acres to one-time neighbor Thomas Hightower on May 22, 1874.

9. RG 29, Census of 1870. The estate was then in the hands of Dr. Kennedy's wife, who had only $500 in personal property at the time. Dr. Hopkins, living nearby in Vermillionville with his second wife, Susan E. E. Kennedy, his two children by his marriage to Mary Kennedy, and his and Susanna's infant daughter, had $5,000 in property and $1,000 in personal effects. Moses Portlock was living with his wife Winnie and their six children, the eldest of whom, aged thirteen and eleven, were working with them as field hands. When they all settled in Vermillionville in 1866, there were only five or six Protestant families in the town.

10. The information is from Kennedy family papers. In all, Dr. Hopkins had two children by Mary Kennedy and nine by Susanna, two of whom died in infancy. Kate had five children. Hyder and Elizabeth Richardson had four children. A granddaughter of theirs, Evelyn Olliphant, became perhaps the most famous of the Kennedy descendants. A pilot herself, she married Alexander P. de Seversky, the aeronautical engineer and designer. She died July 28, 1967, at the age of sixty in Northport, Long Island, New York.

11. This information is drawn from the author's visits to Lafayette and Homer, La.

12. Jackson, "Forgotten Hero," p. 330.

13. War Department, Quartermaster General, letter dated Aug. 21, 1886, from First Lieut. Frank Thorp, Fort Wadsworth.

EPIGRAPHS

1. *Universal Irish Song Book: A Complete Collection of the Songs and Ballads of Ireland* (New York: P.J. Kenedy & Sons, 1884), p. 119. A similar version of "Trust to Luck" appears on p. 3319, Vol. V, of *Irish Literature* (Justin McCarthy, ed. Philadelphia: J.D. Morris & Co., 1904) with a note that states: "This has for years been a favorite with the street singers and the people, and its refrain has been sung by more than one notable criminal before his execution, as a sort of *Nunc dimittis*." The song is attributed to S. Lover (apparently Samuel Lover, 1797–1868), although not included in his "Poetical Works" in Lover's *Collected Writings*. Sean O'Sullivan, former archivist of the Irish Folklore Commission, University College, Dublin, wrote me that as a youth fifty years ago he heard a man from County Mayo recite the first stanza on several occasions as a "favourite quotation of his when things were not going well."

2. All the Negro hymns and spirituals preceding the prologue and parts 2–8 are from Vallie Tinsley White, "Some Negro Songs Heard on the Hills of North Louisiana," *Historic Claiborne*, the Claiborne Parish Historical Association, 1962, pp. 95–99.

bibliography

MANUSCRIPT SOURCES

Allison, John D. Diary, written "while a prisoner at Ft. Lafayette, N.Y. (New York Harbor), Nov. 14, 1864 to March 29, 1865." Louisville, Ky.: The Filson Club.

Claiborne Parish, Office of the Secretary of Police Jury, Homer, La. Minutes of Meetings of Police Jury (parish governing body), Vol. A, 1856–1866, and Vol. 1, 1862–1865.

Cooper, Charles. Diary, 1853. Manuscripts and Archives Division, New York Public Library.

Cypress Hills National Cemetery. Confederate dead (Prisoners of War), Brooklyn, N.Y., Office of the Commissioner for Marking Graves of Confederate Dead, War Department, 1912; list of Confederate Prisoners who died while in camps in the State of New York.

Daly, Charles P. "On the Origin and History of the New York Fire Department," 1871. Charles P. Daly Papers, Manuscripts and Archives Division, New York Public Library.

Davidson, J.J. Address at centennial celebration of dedication of Court House, Homer, La., Claiborne Parish, La. Minute Book "N." Parish Records, pp. 119–123, July 20, 1961.

Diary of a school girl in New York City. Manuscript Division, New-York Historical Society.

Journal of Chief Engineer John Decker. Russell V. Bleecker, Cleveland, Ohio.

Kennedy family papers:
  Genealogical records, books, family Bible, wills, photographs and letters, including "Pictures," letter written by Dr. Thomas B. Hopkins, brother-in-law of Robert C. Kennedy, dated Feb. 5, 1908. Also, *History of the Trial and Execution of Robert Cobb Kennedy*, published privately in

1915 by Mrs. Hyder A. Kennedy (nee Elizabeth Richardson), sister-in-law of Robert C. Kennedy. All, Mrs. W.A. LaFleur, Lafayette, La.

Kennedy, Robert C. Letters to prisoners at Johnson's Island, Sandusky, Ohio, dated March 24, 1865. Erie County Historical Society, Sandusky.

Library of Congress:
Papers of Abraham Lincoln, Vol. 192, 1865: March 11–22. "A Leaf from History," report of J. (Jacob) Thompson, dated Toronto, C.W., Dec. 3, 1864. Published by Union Republican Congressional Committee. Rare Books Division.

Minutes of the Board of Fire Commissioners, log book of meetings. Manuscript Division, New-York Historical Society.

Miscellaneous records—hotel bills, receipts, etc. Manuscript Division, New-York Historical Society.

National Archives:
Record Group 59, "Department of State," Letters Sent 1864.

Record Group 92, "Quartermaster General, Cemeterial File."

Record Group 94, "Adjutant General's Office." Military Academy Records, Commission Branch Records, Compiled Military Service Records, Turner-Baker Papers.

Record Group 109, "Confederate Records." Adjutant and Inspector General's Records, Command Records, Rolls and Papers of Companies D, G and K, 1st Louisiana Infantry, Union Provost Marshal's File, Secretary of War, Papers of Confederate Notables, Compiled Military Service Records.

Record Group 153, "Office of Judge Advocate General." Military Proceedings in the cases of Robert C. Kennedy (MM-3729) and John Yates Beall (MM-3513).

Record Group 393 (formerly 98), "(U.S. Army Continental Commands) Department of the East," Letters Received and Sent, 1865.

Record Group 29. U.S. Census books—1850, Claiborne Parish, La.; 1860, white and slave inhabitants, Claiborne Parish, La.; 1870, Claiborne and Lafayette Parishes, La.

Public Archives of Canada:
Colonial Office Papers, Original Correspondence—Secretary of State, and Despatches from U.S. Consuls in Toronto, 1864–1906.

Foreign Office Papers, General Correspondence, U.S., 1864.

U.S. Military Academy, West Point, N.Y.:
Record Group 404. Descriptive lists of new cadets, oaths of allegiance, registers of delinquencies, weekly class reports, conduct and merit rolls, progress reports, payment statements, special orders, superintendent's letter books. Archives.

War Department, Quartermaster General, Consolidated File. Letters relating to the transfer of remains from Fort Hamilton for reinterment.

PRIMARY SOURCES

Dorr, J.W. "A Tourist Description of Louisiana in 1860." From letters of J.W. Dorr of *The New Orleans Crescent*, edited by Walter Prichard. *Louisiana Historical Quarterly* 21, No. 8 (October 1938): 1183–86.

Fell, T.E. Communication to *The Newnan* (Ga.) *Herald* dated April 5, 1891, included in "Escape of Prisoners From Johnson's Island," *Southern Historical Society Papers* 18 (January–December 1890): 428–31. Although the publication is dated 1890, it contains several addresses and article reprints from publications in 1891 and was apparently compiled in the latter year.

"Fort-La-Fayette Life: 1863–1864." Extracts from *Right Flanker*, reprinted as Extra Number No. 13, *The Magazine of History with Notes and Queries* 1911: 201–46, by William Abbatt, New York.

Headley, John W. *Confederate Operations in Canada and New York*. New York and Washington: Neale Publishing Co., 1906.

Jackson, Edward A. "A Forgotten Hero—R. C. Kennedy." *Confederate Veteran* 16, No. 7 (July 1908): 330.

Nevins, Allan, and Milton Halsey Thomas, eds. *The Diary of George Templeton Strong*. Vol. 3. New York: Macmillan, 1952.

Papers Relating to Foreign Affairs Accompanying the Annual Message of the President to the First Session Thirty-Ninth Congress, Part 1. Washington: U.S. Government Printing Office, 1866.

Thompson, Brig. Gen. Meriwether Jeff. "Diary of Prisoner on Johnson's Island—1863." *United Daughters of the Confederacy Magazine* 17, No. 9 (September 1954): 30–32.

War of the Rebellion, a Compilation of Official Records of the Union and Confederate Armies. Washington: U.S. Government Printing Office, 1880–1901.

SECONDARY SOURCES

Abbott, Richard H. *Ohio's War Governors*. Columbus: Ohio State University Press for the Ohio Historical Society, 1962.

Angle, Paul M., and Earl Shenck Miers. *Tragic Years, 1860–1865*, Vol. 2. New York: Simon and Schuster, 1960.

Asbury, Herbert. *Ye Olde Fire Laddies*. New York and London: Knopf, 1930.

Baker, Gen. La Fayette Charles. *History of the United States Secret Service*. Philadelphia: King & Baird, 1868.

Baker, Alfred E. "Fire Marshal's Report to the Mayor/June 1–Nov. 30, 1864." New York: Holman, 1865.

Barnes, David M. *The Draft Riots in New York.* New York: Baker & Godwin, 1863.

Biographical Directory of the American Congress, 1774–1911. Washington: U.S. Government Printing Office, 1913.

Biographical Directory of the State of New York, 1900. New York: Biographical Directory Co., 1900.

Blay, John S. *The Civil War: A Pictorial Profile.* New York: Crowell, 1958.

Boatner, Lt. Col. Mark M. III. *The Civil War Dictionary.* New York: David McKay Co., 1959.

Booth, Andrew B., Commissioner (La.) Military Records, comp., *Records of Louisiana Confederate Soldiers and Louisiana Confederate Commands.* Vol. 3, Book I. New Orleans, 1920.

Booth, Mary L. *History of the City of New York.* New York: W.R.C. Clark & Meeker, 1859.

Botkin, Benjamin Albert, ed. *Civil War Treasure of Tales, Legends and Folklore.* New York: Random House, 1960.

Boynton, Capt. Edward C. *History of West Point.* New York: D. Van Nostrand, 1863.

Bradford, Ned, ed. *Battles and Leaders of the Civil War.* New York: Appleton-Century-Crofts, 1956.

Brooklyn City Directory. Brooklyn: J. Lain & Co., 1865.

Butler, Benjamin F. *Autobiography and Personal Reminiscences of Major-General Benj. F. Butler (Butler's Book).* Boston: A. M. Thayer & Co., 1892.

Butterfield, Roger. *The American Past.* New York: Simon and Schuster, 1947.

Catton, Bruce. *Mr. Lincoln's Army.* Garden City, N.Y.: Doubleday & Co., 1951.

————. *Glory Road.* Garden City, N.Y.: Doubleday & Co., 1952.

————. *This Hallowed Ground.* Garden City, N.Y.: Doubleday & Co., 1956.

————. *Grant Moves South.* Boston: Little, Brown and Co., 1960.

————. *Never Call Retreat.* Garden City, N.Y.: Doubleday & Co., 1965.

Claiborne Parish Sketches. Homer, La.: Claiborne Parish Historical Association, 1956.

Collins, Rev. Lewis. *Collins' Historical Sketches of Kentucky: History of Kentucky,* Vol. II. Frankfort, Ky.: Kentucky Historical Society, 1966.

Colton, G.W., and Colton, C.B. *Colton's Louisiana.* New York: G.W. and C.B. Colton, 1855.

Cook, Adrian. *The Armies of the Streets: The New York City Draft Riots of 1863.* Lexington, Ky.: The University Press of Kentucky, 1974.

Costello, Augustine E. *Our Firemen: A History of the New York Fire Departments, Volunteer and Paid.* New York: by the author, 1887.

————. *Our Police Protectors: A History of the New York Police from the Earliest Period to the Present Time.* New York: by the author, 1885.

Cullum, George W. *Biographical Register of the Officers and Graduates of the U.S. Military Academy at West Point.* New York: J. F. Trow, 1891.

Dana, Charles A. *Recollections of the Civil War.* New York: D. Appleton & Co., 1898.

Dodson, William Carey, ed. *Campaigns of Wheeler and His Cavalry 1862–1865, from Materials Furnished by Gen. Joseph Wheeler.* Atlanta, Ga.: Hudgins Publishing Co., 1899.

Dunshee, Kenneth Holcomb. *Enjine!—Enjine!* New York: H.V. Smith, 1939.

Ellis, Edward Robb. *The Epic of New York City.* New York: Coward-McCann, 1966.

Federal Writers' Project, W.P.A. *Louisiana: A Guide to the State.* New York: Hastings House, 1941.

Freeman, Douglas Southall. *R.E. Lee, A Biography.* Vol. 1. New York, London: C. Scribner's Sons, 1934.

Frohman, Charles E. *Rebels on Lake Erie.* Columbus: Ohio Historical Society, 1965.

Gray, Wood. *The Hidden Civil War: The Story of the Copperheads.* New York: Viking Press, 1942.

Haco, Dion. *Rob. Cobb Kennedy, the Incendiary Spy.* New York: Hurst & Co., 1866.

Harper, Robert S. *Ohio Handbook of the Civil War.* Columbus: Ohio Historical Society for the Ohio Civil War Centennial Commission, 1961.

Harris, D.W., and Hulse, B.M. *The History of Claiborne Parish.* New Orleans: W.B. Stansbury, 1886.

Heitman, Francis B. *Historical Register and Dictionary of the United States Army.* Washington: Government Printing Office, 1903.

Hesseltine, William B. *Civil War Prisons: A Study in War Psychology.* New York: F. Ungar, 1930.

Historic Claiborne. Homer, La.: Claiborne Parish Historical Association, 1962.

Historic Claiborne '65. Homer, La.: Claiborne Parish Historical Association, 1965.

Horan, James D. *Confederate Agent: A Discovery in History.* New York: Crown, 1954.

Kernan, J. Frank. *Reminiscences of the Old Fire Laddies.* New York: M. Crane, 1885.

Klement, Frank L. *Copperheads in the Middle West.* Chicago: University of Chicago Press, 1960.

La Bree, Ben, ed. *The Confederate Soldier in the Civil War.* Paterson, N.J.: Pageant Books, 1959.

Lamb, Martha J. *History of the City of New York: Its Origin, Rise and Progress.* 3 vols. New York: A.S. Barnes & Co., copyright 1877–1880.

Lee, Fitzhugh, calendar memorial with poems and songs of the Confederacy.

Des Moines, Iowa: Kenyon Co., 1910.

Lewis, Lloyd. "Shiloh, Bloody Shiloh." *Men at War.* Ernest Hemingway, ed. New York: Crown, 1942.

Limpus, Lowell M. *History of the New York Fire Department.* New York: E.P. Dutton & Co., 1940.

Lossing, Benson J. *History of New York City.* 2 vols. New York: G.E. Perine, 1884.

Manual of the Corporation of the City of New York. New York: D.T. Valentine, 1861, 1865.

McCarthy, Justin, editor in chief. *Irish Literature.* Vol. 9. Philadelphia: J.D. Morris & Co., 1904.

Milhollen, Hirst D., and Johnson, Maj. James R. *Best Photos of the Civil War.* New York: Arco, 1961.

Miller's New York As It Is. New York: J. Miller, 1864.

Miller's Stranger's Guide for the City of New York. New York: J. Miller, 1864, 1866.

Mitchell, Lt. Col. Joseph B. *Decisive Battles of the Civil War.* New York: Putnam, 1955.

Mitgang, Herbert, ed. and narrator. *Lincoln As They Saw Him.* New York: Rinehart, 1956.

Morris, John V. *Fires and Firefighters.* Boston: Little, Brown, 1955.

Morris, Lloyd. *Incredible New York: High Life and Low Life of the Last Hundred Years.* New York: Random House, 1951.

Nevins, Allan, comp. and ed. *American Social History, as recorded by British Travellers.* New York: Henry Holt & Co., 1923.

Nevins, Allan. *The War for the Union: The Organized War to Victory, 1864–1865* (Vol. IV). New York: Charles Scribner's Sons, 1971.

New York (City) Fire Department. *Annual Report of the Chief Engineer of the Fire Department of the City of New York.* New York: Edmund Jones & Co., 1865.

New York (State). *Annual Report of the Board of Commissioners of the Metropolitan Police.* Albany: C. Wendell, 1865.

New York (State) Secretary of State, *Census for the State of New York for 1865.* Albany: C. Van Benthuysen & Sons, 1867.

Nicholson, James W. *Stories of Dixie.* Revised edition. Baton Rouge: Claitor's Book Store, 1966.

Pratt, Edmund. *The Eagle's History of Poughkeepsie, 1683 to 1905.* Poughkeepsie, N.Y.: Platt & Platt, 1905.

Pratt, Fletcher. *Ordeal by Fire: An Informal History of the Civil War.* New York: H. Smith and R. Haas, 1935.

Quain, Dr. Richard, *A dictionary of Medicine.* 9th ed. New York: D. Appleton & Co., 1885.

*Register of Graduates and Former Cadets of the United States Military Academy,
1802–1960.* New York: West Point Alumni Foundation, 1960.

Regulations for the United States Military Academy at West Point, New-York.
New-York: John F. Trow, 1853.

Rhadamanthus (collective pseudonym of Ammi Brown and Goldthwaite Hig-
ginson Dorr). *A History of Tammany Hall.* New York: privately printed,
1955.

Rhodes, James Ford. *History of the United States.* Vol. V. Port Washington,
N.Y.: Kennikat Press, 1967 (c. 1892–1919).

Sandburg, Carl. *Abraham Lincoln: The War Years.* Vols. I–IV. New York: Harcourt, Brace & Co., 1936–39.

Schaff, Morris. *The Spirit of Old West Point: 1858–1862.* Boston: Houghton,
Mifflin & Co., 1907.

Sheldon, George W. *The Story of the Volunteer Fire Department of the City of
New York.* New York: Harper & Bros., 1882.

Shriver, Phillip R., and Breen, Donald J. *Ohio's Military Prisons in the Civil
War.* Ohio State University Press for the Ohio Historical Society, 1964.

Smith, George Winston, and Judah, Charles, eds. *Life in the North During the
Civil War.* Albuquerque: University of New Mexico Press, 1966.

Smith, Zachariah F. *The History of Kentucky.* Louisville, Ky.: Prentice Press,
1895.

Stern, Philip Van Doren. *Secret Missions of the Civil War.* Chicago: Rand
McNally, 1959.

Still, Bayrd. *Mirror for Gotham: New York as seen by Contemporaries from
Dutch days to the present.* Washington Square: New York University
Press, 1956.

Stokes, I.N. Phelps. *New York Past and Present, Its History and Landmarks,
1524–1939.* New York: 1939.

Stone, William L. *History of New York City.* New York: Virtue & Yorston,
1872.

Todd, Frederick P. *Cadet Gray.* New York: Sterling Publishing Co., 1955.

*Universal Irish Song Book: A Complete Collection of the Songs and Ballads of
Ireland.* New York: P.J. Kenedy & Sons, 1884.

Walling, George W. *Recollections of a New York Chief of Police.* New York:
Caxton Book Concern, 1887.

Williams, T. Harry. *The Civil War in Louisiana.* Baton Rouge: Louisiana Civil
War Centennial Commission, 1961.

Williamson, James J. *Mosby's Rangers.* New York: Sturgis & Walton, 1909.

Wilson, H., comp. *Trows New York City Directory, 1864–65.* New York: J.F.
Trow, 1865.

Wilson, James Grant, and Fiske, John, eds. *Appleton's Cyclopedia of American
Biography.* New York and London: D. Appleton, 1888.

Wilson, James Grant, ed. *The Memorial History of the City of New York.* 4 vols. New York: New-York History Co., 1892–93.

Wilson's Business Directory. New York: J.F. Trow, 1863, 1864–65, 1865–66.

Winks, Robin W. *Canada and the United States: The Civil War Years.* Baltimore: Johns Hopkins Press, 1960.

Winters, John D. *The Civil War in Louisiana.* Baton Rouge: Louisiana State University Press, 1963.

NEWSPAPERS AND PERIODICALS

The following newspapers and periodicals were employed extensively, chiefly to recreate the events surrounding Nov. 25, 1864, and March 25, 1865, but as otherwise noted in notes: *Brooklyn Daily Eagle, Brooklyn Standard, Claiborne Advocate, Frank Leslie's Illustrated Newspaper, Harper's Weekly* and *New Monthly Magazines, Montreal Gazette, New Orleans Daily Crescent, New Orleans Picayune, New York Daily News, New York Daily Tribune* and *Weekly Tribune, New York Evening Post, New York Freeman's Journal and Catholic Register, New York Herald, New York Journal of Commerce, New York Leader, New-York Times, New York Weekly Day-Book, New York World, Richmond Daily Examiner, Richmond Whig.*

Alexander, Jerome P. "A Deed of Deering: The Confederate Attempt to Burn New York City," *United Daughters of the Confederacy Magazine* (August, 1954): 7.

Andrews, Matthew Page. "Treatment of Prisoners in the Confederacy." *The Gray Book.* Sons of Confederate Veterans, 1920.

Bigelow, Martha Mitchell. " 'Piracy on Lake Erie,' or the Confederate Attempt to Capture Johnson's Island in Sandusky Bay." *Bulletin of the Detroit Historical Society* XIV, No. 1 (October 1957): 6–17.

Cunningham, O. Edward. " 'In Violation of the Laws of War': The Execution of Robert Cobb Kennedy." *Louisiana History.* Louisiana Historical Association 18, No. 2 (Spring, 1977): 189–201.

Goodwin, Katherine C. "A Hotel of Many Memories." *Daughters of the American Revolution Magazine* 61, No. 6 (June 1927): 409–418.

"Greek Fire, and Other Inflammables." *United States Service Magazine* 1, No. 1 (January 1864): 50–55.

Hoole, Wm. Stanley, ed. "Letters from Johnson's Island Prison." *Alabama Review* 12, No. 3 (July 1959).

Johnson, Ludwell H. "Beverly Tucker's Canadian Mission, 1864–1865." *Journal of Southern History* 29, No. 1 (February 1963).

Longacre, Edward G. "The Union Army Occupation of New York City, November 1864." *New York History*. New York State Historical Association 65, No. 2 (April 1984): 133–158.

Louisiana History, Louisiana Historical Association, in cooperation with Louisiana State University: Vol. 1, No. 4, Fall 1960; Vol. IV, No. 1, Winter 1963; Vol. IV, No. 4. Fall 1963.

Meek, Clarence E. "The Fire Zouaves." *WNYF* (With New York Firemen). New York Fire Department (Spring 1961): 12–13.

———. "Pride of the Village." *WNYF* (With New York Firemen). New York Fire Department (April 1959): 4–5.

Richardson, James F. "Mayor Fernando Wood and the New York Police Force, 1855–1857." *New-York Historical Society Quarterly* 50, No. 1 (January 1966): 5–40.

Sass, Herbert Ravenal. "The Fire Raid on New York City." *Saturday Evening Post*. July 16, 1949: 34.

Shepard, Frederick J. "The Johnson's Island Plot." *Publications of the Buffalo Historical Society* 9, 1906.

"Some Facts About Johnson's Island." From *Museum Echoes*, Ohio Historical Society. Reprinted in *Flashback*, Washington County (Ark.) Historical Society 13, No. 4 (October 1963).

Weiss, David A. "The Plot to Burn Down New York." *Coronet* 43, No. 1 (November 1957): 92–95.

White, Vallie Tinsley. "Some Folklore From North Louisiana." *Southern Folklore Quarterly*. September 1956: 164–177.

———. "Some Negro Songs Heard on the Hills of North Louisiana." *Historic Claiborne*, Claiborne Parish Historical Association (1962): 95–99.

"Who May Kill in War, and Who May Not." *United States Service Magazine* 4, No. 5 (November 1865): 385–394.

index

THE MAN WHO TRIED TO BURN NEW YORK

was composed in 11-point Compugraphic Quadex 5000 Goudy Old Style and leaded 2 points
by BookMasters;
with display type in Chisel Expanded by Rochester Mono/Headliners;
and ornaments provided by Jōb Litho Services;
printed sheet-fed offset on 50-pound, acid-free Glatfelter Antique Cream,
Smyth sewn and bound over 70-point Binder's boards in Joanna Arrestox B
by Maple-Vail Book Manufacturing Group, Inc.;
with dust jackets printed in 3 colors by Frank A. West Company, Inc.;
designed by Shawn Lewis;
and published by

SYRACUSE UNIVERSITY PRESS
SYRACUSE, NEW YORK 13244-5160